Giovanni Maria de Agostini, Wonder of The Century

The Astonishing World Traveler
Who Was A Hermit

First Edition

David G. Thomas

To a fellow follower of the
Hermit, JMA. Dec 10, 2014

David Thomas

Contents

Mesilla Valley History Series

La Posta – From the Founding of Mesilla, to Corn Exchange Hotel, to Billy the Kid Museum, to Famous Landmark

Giovanni Maria de Agostini, Wonder of The Century – The Astonishing World Traveler Who Was A Hermit

Acknowledgements

This book would not be possible without the groundbreaking research of Dr. Alexandre de Oliveira Karsburg. Dr. Karsburg, while working on his doctorial dissertation for the Universidade Federal do Rio de Janeiro, put together two never before associated historical figures: the Brazilian Monge João Maria and the New Mexican Ermitaño Don Juan Agostini. Dr. Karsburg realized that these men were in fact the same person, and his Ph.D dissertation, *O Eremita do Novo Mundo: A Trajetória de um Peregrino Italiano na América do Século XIX (1838-1869),* "The Hermit of the New World: The Trajectory of an Italian Pilgrim in Nineteenth-Century America (1838-1869)," is the first source to disclose this.

Dr. Karsburg contacted me about four years ago on learning that I was researching our common subject. He informed me of his discovery, and in the following years, generously sharing his research, which this book fully reflects. Thank you Alexandre for your innovative and recondite research.

I would like to thank my good friend Daniel Aranda, who, among other contributions, shared his early research on Agostini, read the manuscript, and caught numerous errors.

I was dependent on documents in languages other than English for many aspects of this book; I thank the following for their work in providing accomplished translations: Harry Echeverria, Ana C Pires, Francesco Paolo Di Salvia, and Rachele Duke.

For providing photographs and giving me permission to use them, I thank: Father Kenneth, Monastery of Saint Anthony (Deir Mar Antonios), Mount Colzim, Egypt; Ronaldo Cesar da Silva Messias, Researcher History Araçoiaba Area, Pathfinder Villas Boas; Thomas Peter Geisendorf, Equipe Ecoturismo Brasil, ecoturismobrasil.com.br; Celso Martins da Silveira, Júnior; Pedro Hauck; Patrick Cushing; Marco Soscia; and adventuresofacouchsurfer.com. Photos unidentified are from the author's collection.

The following assisted my research in essential ways. I apologize for not having the space to detail their contributions individually: the Archivists at New Mexico State University's Special Collections; Daniel Kosharek, Photo Archives, Palace of the Governors; Tomas Jaehn, Fray Angélico Chávez History Library; Martha McCaffrey, Las Vegas Citizens' Committee for Historic Preservation; Rosemary M. Leyva, Saint Genevieve Catholic Church; Valerie Nye, Santa Fe University of Art and Design; Mary Bird, Gadsden Museum; Sally Kading; Joana Dias; Ken McCracken; Lanty Wylie; and Andy Winnegar.

A special thanks to my friend Omar Vicari, who put me in touch with Father Tarek of the Collegio Maronita della Beata Vergine Maria, in Rome; and to Father Tarek for his research in the Collegio archives.

The inevitable errors are my responsibility.

La Maravilla de Nuestro Siglo, "The Wonder of Our Century." Photo of Giovanni Maria de Agostini, taken in December, 1861, in Havana, Cuba. Agostini is wearing a blue cape. The Tau cross on his left shoulder is red. See Chapter 11 for a discussion of this photo. Courtesy Palace of the Governors Photo Archives (NMHM/DCA), Negative No. 110764a.

Introduction

In this book you will meet a remarkable man, Giovanni Maria de Agostini, born in Italy in 1801, who combined two seemingly contradictory aspirations: a fervent desire to devote his whole life to "perfect solitude" and an astonishing urge to travel incessantly.

As his decisions and actions emerge from the lightless silence – the time-covered past – a unifying purpose becomes evident.

Following extensive travel in Europe, Agostini takes vows revocable only by formal dispensation from the Pope. He immediately leaves forever his "beloved Italy" for South America. Twenty-one years he spends traversing that, at the time, greatly unexplored continent, visiting Venezuela, Colombia, Ecuador, Bolivia, Peru, Brazil, Argentina, Paraguay, and Chile – and so doing multiple times.

Seeking change and another continent, Agostini leaves South America for Mexico, passing through Panama and Guatemala, and then Mexico for North America, passing through Cuba. In Cuba, he is hailed as an extraordinary adventurer, his photograph is taken, and he is proclaimed "The Wonder of Our Century." After arrival in New York, he walks to Canada, where he spends almost a year, then "goes west," eventually reaching, in the midst of the American Civil War, the Territory of New Mexico, where he meets his merciless fate.

In 49 years of ceaseless travel, Agostini repeatedly achieves his goals. But he also faces beleaguering moral battles and life-threatening perils and humiliations, including death threats, unjust arrest, deportation, jail, and forced confinement in a mental asylum.

Agostini is remembered in many places, however his life story is encrusted with myth and false fact. As the veritable events of his life are unveiled, a man of fascinating originality, prodigious endurance, intelligence, self-discipline, and self-sufficiency, infused with an indomitable spirit of adventure, emerges.

Today in Argentina, as many as 15,000 people participate in a yearly festival initiated by Agostini at Cerro Monje, "Monk's Hill." In Brazil, at Cerro Campestre, "Campestre Hill," and Santo Cerro do Botucaraí, "Holy Hill of Botucaraí," over 10,000 people celebrate annual events founded by Agostini. In Lapa, Brazil, a national park protects the pilgrimage route to Gruta do Monge, "Monk's Grotto." At Araçoiaba Hill, near Sorocaba, Brazil, the Trilha da Pedra Santa, "Trail of the Holy Rock," is climbed annually by thousands of people desiring to pay respect to the memory of the Monge do Ipanema, the "Monk of Ipanema."

These are just a few examples of Agostini's cultural legacy, 145 years after his death.

As a quick glance at Appendix A indicates, this book documents Agostini's remarkable life, for many years almost month-to-month, beginning with his "call to travel" at age 17. During this time, Agostini covered astounding distances, often moving with bewildering speed. He made these travels without money of his own, having taken a vow of poverty, and without the formal support of the Catholic Church, as he was not a member of the clergy. How he was able to travel so extensively under these conditions is one of the mysteries of his life.

Much of this book is based on Agostini's own words, set down in his own hand, the sources of which are discussed in the first chapter. The second chapter examines the discoverable details of his childhood and his travels in Europe. The third chapter discusses the historical figure after which Agostini modeled himself, upon making the most important decision of his life. The dozen chapters that follow describe Agostini's time in South and North America. In these chapters the guiding purpose of Agostini's peripatetic and eremitic conduct becomes apparent. The fifteenth chapter discloses for the first time the particulars of his brutal death, as related by the person who discovered his body. The concluding chapters deal with Agostini's funeral and burial, the enduring puzzle of who murdered him, and his extant possessions.

Chapter 1 | Tragedy – Agostini's Missing Papers

Most Fascinating Human Documents Ever Compiled

"The diary, a thick volume bound in tanned sheepskin and cloth, primitively done, is one of the most fascinating human documents ever compiled. It is an assemblage of written meditations by the hermit, of letters from ecclesiastical authorities testifying to his holiness and residence for long periods in the wilderness, qualifying him to act as priest, elaborately engraved passports from Sardinia, Rome, Rio de Janeiro, and Spain, of letters from consuls, bishops and officials, friends and religious. Dates go back as far as 1829." [1]

So writes a dazzled E. Dana Johnson, editor of the Santa Fe *New Mexican* newspaper, in 1933, about the astounding collection of papers accumulated by Giovanni Maria de Agostini during his lifetime.

These documents trace Agostini's astonishing life journey, beginning with his travels in Italy, France, and Spain in Europe, to Venezuela, Columbia, Ecuador, Peru, Bolivia, Chile, Brazil, Argentina, and Uruguay in South America, to Panama and Guatemala in Central America, to Cuba in the Caribbean, and to Mexico, United States and Canada in North America.

Johnson continues:

"Letters in this diary trace his course all the way. Nearly all documents are in archaic Spanish, Italian or Portuguese. They relate almost entirely to religious and ecclesiastical subjects. There are printed and illustrated devotions in Latin from Italian and Spanish churches, elaborately illuminated religious credentials, clippings from religious journals." [2]

Agostini somehow manages to retain these documents in spite of the incredible hardships endured in wildernesses, deserts and mountains, across three continents, facing dangers from men, animals and nature, in a journey covering an estimated 27,000 miles, nearly the equivalent of the circumference of the Earth, which began in 1820 and ends with his mysterious, unsolved murder in 1869.

The owner of these documents in 1933 is Hipolito C. de Baca of Las Vegas, New Mexico. He inherited them in 1917 from Margarito Romero, who knew Agostini well. Romero had hunted down the documents following Agostini's murder in Mesilla, New Mexico, and purchased them for $200.[3] Most had Agostini's *"autograph on the fly leaf."* [4]

The first reference found by the author to Agostini's documents is in an 1863 Kansas newspaper, which states *"He has passports from nearly all the principal nations of Europe and North and South America, and Mexico."* [5]

In 1866, the Santa Fe *Nuevo Mexicano,* reports:

> *"This rare hermit left his country as a pilgrim and traversed almost every sanctuary and mountain in Europe and after many years of wanderlust, he embarked for the Americas, crossing oceans, conquering deserts, and penetrating mountains. Finally, he has arrived in our Territory, choosing the Serro del Tecolote as his abode, bringing only a sack containing his library."* [6]

In the same year, the *Times-Picayune* of New Orleans, Louisiana, notes:

> *"He possesses a great quantity of curious books and documents, many of the latter from crowned heads, showing that at one time he was a personage of considerable note, all of which he seems gratified to show those who visit him."* [7]

Katherine Stoes, who was born in Mesilla shortly after Agostini was murdered, relates that when he visited Mesilla, he would always carry *"his diary and a book of the saints under his arm."* [8]

Following his death, sources continue to write about his papers. For example, the 1890 *Kansas City Times* writes:

> *"The hermit priest had of earthly possessions so little that he could have almost vied with the lowly Nazarene in the 'splendor of his poverty.' Of crucifixes, devotional mementoes and other religious trinkets, sweetly suggestive of better and happier days, he had preserved a few. His greatest solace was in half a dozen well thumbed small volumes between whose covers none peered but himself."* [9]

The secrecy of Agostini suggested by the last sentence is an example of how Agostini's story was beginning to be embellished by myth.

Margarito Romero's ownership of the papers is noted in the 1908 *Montgomery Advertiser:*

> *"The monk's passport is still a treasured heirloom in the Romero family, prominent today in the affairs of Northern New Mexico."* [10]

In 1911, Eleanor Hinde Powell writes:

> *"Domingo Gonzales, the owner of many wagons, invited the hermit to accompany him to Las Vegas, New Mexico. Declining the luxury of a carriage, or even of the prairie schooners which made up the train, he, with a pack of forty pounds of books on his back, walked all the way to Las Vegas on the flank of the wagons."* [11]

Beginning in 1907, Dr. Giuseppe Cuneo, the Italian Consul in Denver, Colorado, begins collecting biographical information on Agostini. In 1922, he produces an unpublished manuscript entitled *"Vita, Viaggi E Tragica Fine Del Padre Giovanni Maria de Agostino Da Sizzano."* [12] In this document, he says Agostini's papers are in a book:

> *"fastened [with] a piece of coarse red-checkered cloth, which perhaps*

was once part of a pair of pants given him by some Indian." [13]

After viewing Agostini's papers, the anonymous writer "Fanchon," in a 1925 letter to the editor of the *Las Vegas Daily Optic*, observes that:

"Pictures on his passport reveal him as an old man with great masses of gray, bushy hair." [14]

Hipolito C. de Baca writes about the documents himself in a 1931 letter to the American Ambassador to Italy in Rome:

"In the data which constitutes an important feature of the historic events of his career is a 'Portfolio' (now in my possession) containing printed and written passports, certificates, memories, and testimonials, all bearing the official signatures and stamped seals of high Eclesiastical (sic) Dignitaries and Magistrates from the different countries he went through." [15]

In this letter, Baca asks the Ambassador, John W. Garrett,[16] if he can locate some of Agostini's kinfolk. Baca is evidently considering giving the documents to any relative who would *"cherich [sic] the idea to perpetuate the memory of their illustrious relative."* [17]

Baca relates that Agostini's:

"...luggage consisted only of a few books and papers which were found scattered around the place where he was killed. These were gathered together by members of the searching party who later turned them over to the proper authorities at La Mesilla." [18]

In 1937, Mesilla resident Elizabeth Fountain Armendariz is interviewed by Marie Carter [19] under the auspices of the Works Progress Administration (WPA) Federal Writers' Project. Armendariz is the granddaughter of Colonel Albert J. Fountain, Sr., a Mesilla pioneer who knew Agostini well. In the questioning, Armendariz is asked:

"'And these?' I inquired, pointing to some odd-looking books."

"'Were written by the Hermit,' she replied. 'The brown book is written in Spanish, and its cover is crude cowhide. The other book is written in Italian, and is covered with sheepskin.'" [20]

These are two of the books that Agostini had when murdered, but neither is the diary that contained his travel papers, even though many writers have so stated. The two books are currently in the Gadsden Museum, founded by Ms Armendariz's father. (See Chapter 17 for more details.)

In the early 1950s, Arthur L. Campa begins researching Agostini. He relates the following:

"Having learned that Senor Hipolito Baca, grandson of the original Romero, had the binder with the most important papers, I drove... to see him...." [21]

Campa asks about the papers.

"'You are certainly welcome to see them,' he [Baca] answered, 'but I don't have them in the house. I loaned them, or rather, put them up as

security with one of my former associates when I had to make a loan. Miss Belles, who lives not far from here, has them.'"

"...I contacted her [Miss Belles]. The lady was very surprised, however, to learn that Mr. Baca had forgotten that she had returned the Hermit's papers many years before." [22]

After more looking, Campa concludes:

"The ultimate source on the Hermit's life was apparently lost or misplaced." [23]

At some point in the 1950s, Agostini's papers and other documents are deposited in the Archives of the Archdiocese of Santa Fe, New Mexico. In 1961, however, the documents are removed. When the author visited the archives several years ago, following up numerous leads on the location of Agostini's papers, the following was found in Agostini's file:

"This is to certify that on October 3rd, 1961, the following documents were handed over to Mrs. _____ of _____, Santa Fe, New Mexico."

"A manuscript entitled 'L'Eremita' (103 pp)"
"Photos supporting documents"
"Photos of Hermit himself"
"Photos of Hermit's Peak area"
"Vita breve dal Dr. G. Cuneo (7 pp)"
"Correspondence on the subject"

"These said documents were extracted from the Archives of the Archdiocese of Santa Fe listed under the year 1869, Giovanni Maria d'Agostino." [24]

Also in the file was a document stating:

"Original copies sent to Mr._____, Santa Fe, NM."

"Consisted of various documents, passport photos of Hermit, etc, which I described in Archives of the Archdiocese of Santa Fe, p 134. Also a good photo of Padre José de Jesús Baca."

"If donors insisted that they had been merely lent to the Archives, then the Chancery priests should have made photo copies of everything before turning them over!" [25]

From these notes, it is sadly evident that Agostini's surviving documents were removed from the Archdiocese Archives with – tragically – no copy kept!

Prior to the documents being taken, Frederick G. Bohme reviews the documents in the Archdiocese Archives and writes of them:

"From this time forward [1829] there is practically point-to-point documentation of his amazing travels, for he not only obtained passports and letters of safe conduct, but also collected affidavits for the life he led." [26]

Ten years after the above described documents' removal from the Archives, in 1971, an Italian writer, Florio Santini, publishes two articles in which he quotes extensively from Agostini's papers. In the articles, written in Italian and published in Italy, he describes his source:

> *"The book is about 25 cm high and 52 cm long. It's wrapped with a piece of cloth, which maybe belonged to some Indian trousers, and it's covered with deerskin. It contains 152 items, – letters and documents, – sewn together; but there are some gaps. Some pages have faded because of the weather of two Americas."* [27]

Santini adds:

> *"...the manuscript belongs to the G____ family..."* and *"I would like to thank... Mrs. J___ G____ from Albuquerque, New Mexico, who sent me the material...."* [28]

Strenuous efforts by the author over the last four years have failed to locate the documents. The person who took the papers from the Archdiocese Archives is no longer living and descendents have not been located.

From the comments by Santini, it seems probable that he wrote from the originals, not a copy. My belief is that the documents are likely still in Italy. Otherwise, it is hard to believe that they wouldn't have surfaced in the 50 years since they were removed from the Santa Fe Archdiocese. Santini died in 2007. He was a prolific writer and poet, well-known in Italy. A search of the internet failed to turn up any sign of Agostini's papers in Italy or any archival depository of Santini's papers.

A Word on Sources

As the text of the book shows, the author in telling Agostini's story draws on many newspaper accounts of Agostini and his actions, including contemporaneous articles from the Brazilian and Mexican press.

But with Agostini's original documents missing, it is also necessary to rely on accounts of his life produced by those who saw his documents. Fortunately, two sources, Charles Wolfe [29] and Florio Santini,[30] quote extensively from his personal documents. In the case of Charles Wolfe, almost three-quarters of his article consists of direct quotes. For Santini, it is nearly 50 percent.

Of his fidelity in meticulously reporting on Agostini's papers, Wolfe writes:

> *"These papers have been examined thoroughly and classified by the author.... The work of the writer has been limited to arranging and translating these documents."* [31]

Besides Wolfe and Santini, several writers saw Agostini's documents and quoted from or paraphrased portions of them. In referring to these accounts, I note that the source viewed Agostini's documents.

The author found additional sources that recount personal or third party oral histories of Agostini. These references along with the many sources that have worked from prior accounts are listed in the Bibliography.

Photo

Two books owned by Agostini, Gadsden Museum. Photo courtesy Archives and Special Collections, New Mexico State University.

Chapter 2 | Europe

Initium Vitae

Giovanni Maria de Agostini's life story begins with no certain answer to the question, "When was he born?"

This dilemma seemed to have been answered definitively in 1955 when Father Ottavio A. Coggiola-Mower, Chancellor of the Archdiocese of Santa Fe, wrote Sizzano, Italy – Agostini's birthplace – requesting his baptismal record. Father Santino Tognacca replied with the following:

> "Sizzano, (Novara), Nov. 30, 1955"
>
> "Most Reverend Mister Professor,"
>
> "I have transcribed for you the Baptismal Act of GIOVANNI DE AGOSTINI."
>
> "'In the year of our Lord 1802 on the 25th of December Assistant Parish Priest De Ambrosio baptized an infant born today to Joseph De Agostini son of the late Vincent from Parone and to Francesca Comera daughter of the late Joannes Maria from Sizzano and of his wife Parezia, to which child the name of Joannes [John] was given. [His] godfather was Francis Comero, son of the late Victor from Sizzano.'"
>
> "I have transcribed word by word."
>
> "Yours faithfully,"
>
> "Father Santino Tognacca, Archpriest" [1]

But is this really Agostini's baptismal record? In 1933, E. Dana Johnson examined Agostini's extant papers, then in the possession of Hipolito C. de Baca. Johnson begins his article on the papers as follows:

> "'I was born in Lizzano, province of Nubara, Lombardo, Reyno de Piamonte, in 1801. My father was Matias de Agostini, my mother Dominica Mofrina de Funtaneto....'"
>
> "So reads the faded writing on yellowed, worn paper in the diary of Don Juan Maria Agostini de Augustiniani, known in New Mexico as the Hermit of Hermit's Peak near Las Vegas; 'el solitario' who lived in caves and deserts all over the world. This letter is dated 1841." [2]

The birth years in the two accounts do not match, but critically, neither do the names of the parents. Given that it is unlikely Agostini would not know his parents' names in 1841, it must be concluded that the quoted baptismal record is incorrect.

Which means his birth day is unknown.

The next puzzle in his biography is, "What is his real name?"

The most common first name used to identify him in documents from South America to Mexico to the United States is John Maria, or a translated or corrupted version of this. For example, in many Brazilian texts, he is called João Maria; in Spanish, Juan Maria, or often, Don Juan Maria, "Don" being a Spanish honorific meaning "man of distinction."

In the Sizzano baptismal record located by Father Tognacca, the child is named Joannes, Latin for John, which is probably why Tognacca considered the record to be Agostini's.

In Italian, John is Giovanni, which can be sourced as his name as early as 1844.[3] That is the name by which he will be referred to in this book.

His family name Agostini is often given as Agustini, Augustine, Agostine, Agostino, Agostinho, Agustino, Augustiniani, Augustini, Augustinian, Justianini – even – bizarrely – Boccalini.[4] Agostini is derived from the Latin name "Augustinus," a name which originates in Imperial Rome. The first emperor of Rome claimed the title Imperator Caesar Divi Filius Augustus, which can be translated as "Emperor Caesar Augustus, son of the deified one." The word "augustus," adopted by the first Caesar as his name, means "eminent, majestic, venerable, revered."

The Christian church father Aurelius Augustinus Hipponensis, better known as Saint Augustine of Hippo (354-430 AD), author of the work *City of God,* also carried a name derived from "augustus."

In the 13th century, an order of Christian monks known as Ordo Eremitarum Sancti Augustini ("Hermits of Saint Augustine") was founded based on the teachings of St. Augustine (hence the name). Members of this order are known as Augustinians.

The confusion of Agostini's name with its derivations and with the order of Augustinians has led many who wrote about him to assume his name was Augustiniani, as given in the 1933 Santa Fe *New Mexican* article quoted earlier. "Augustiniani" is Latin for Augustinian. He was not an Augustinian, as will be shown. (Note: the spelling of Agostini's name as it is given by quoted sources will be retained – the meaning is clear and scattering "sic" throughout the text is distracting.)

Sizzano – Kingdom of Piedmont-Sardinia

Agostini is born in Comune di Sizzano, the town of Sizzano. At the time of his birth, Sizzano is in the Kingdom of Piedmont-Sardinia, one of the two large states making up what is now Italy. The other large state in 1801 is the Republic of Venice. The remainder of Italy is divided into smaller states, including a group of Papal States controlled by the Catholic Church.[5]

Prior to 1713, for 150 years, Italy's monarchies are dominated by Spain. In that year, Hapsburg Austria gains control of most of the Italian states.[6] Then, in 1796, Napoleon Bonaparte begins his conquest of Italy, with the goal of taking it from the Austrians. On June 14, 1800, Napoleon wins the Battle of Marengo, breaking the Austrian army and giving him sovereignty of Piedmont-Sardinia. The king of

Piedmont-Sardinia, Charles Emmanuel IV, who had put his military forces in the service of the Austrians, is driven into exile.[7]

Thus, Agostini is born under Napoleonic conquest in a period of large-scale, extended, European wars. Some of Agostini's male family members, not excluding his father, likely served in these wars.

Sizzano is located in the Province of Novara in northwest Italy, 50 miles from Turin (Torino), the old capital of the Piedmont-Sardinia Kingdom and 12 miles from Novara, the provincial capitol. In 1801 it was a small town and remains so today, with web sites giving the population in 2005 as about 1,500 people.

The Agostini family name still exists in the town today and is a common name in the province of Novara, as an internet search shows.

Childhood

Discarding the (incorrect) baptismal record, Giovanni Agostini's father was Matias de Agostini and his mother was Dominica Mofrina de Funtaneto. Based on her name, his mother or her family probably came from Fontaneto D'agogna, a small town about six miles northeast of Sizzano.[8]

Many sources claim Agostini as a descendent of nobility, but is that true? The earliest source for this assertion is an unsigned Las Vegas *Daily Optic* article dated May 13, 1908, perhaps written by M. M. Padgett, the editor. [9] The *Daily Optic* article is based on information from Las Vegas residents.[10] Padgett would have had but an outsider's familiarity himself with Agostini's story, since he came to Las Vegas from Ohio only in 1907.[11]

The biography of Agostini by Manuel Romero, printed in Spanish in *El Nuevo Mexicano* in 1866, doesn't make this claim.[12] Manuel and his son Margarito Romero knew Agostini well and their early stewardship of Agostini's documents is discussed in Chapter 1. Their involvement in the Sociedad del Ermitaño ("Society of the Hermit") is discussed in Chapter 13.

Nor does a 1908 article by E. Dana Johnson, based on Agostini's papers, make this nobility claim.[13]

The claim, however, is picked in 1925 up by Charles Wolfe, one of the most important sources of primary information on Agostini. Wolfe says:

> "His father... was of noble descent, tracing his genealogy back to Emperor Justinian. His mother... was also of noble rank and both were held in high esteem in Italy, the family being known far and wide in the kingdom of Sardenia." [14]

Most of Wolfe's article consists of quotes from Agostini's papers. The statement above is from the portion of the document composed by Wolfe, source unspecified.

The earliest information on Agostini's family is a quote from the Chilean newspaper *Valparaiso Messenger,* which simply states that Agostini is *"of an honorable family."* [15]

Thus, with no primary source for the noble linage claim, it remains an open question.

The 1908 *Daily Optic* author also asserts that Agostini was the only son of wealthy parents.[16] This is the earliest appearance of this claim, and one not repeated by Wolfe. As Agostini was educated, it can be surmised that his family was of some financial means. Whether he was the only son is unknown, but by asserting family wealth, the author is emphasizing the sacrifice Agostini makes with his life choice.

Wolfe states that Agostini's mother died when he was eight months old.[17] This claim is not based on a direct quote from Agostini's papers, nor is it repeated by other sources known to have viewed the papers.

The sole thing Agostini says about his childhood is: *"At the age of five years, more or less, I began to incline toward a solitary life."* [18]

Here is Agostini offering an explanation, or a partial explanation, of what would become his lifelong obsession – living for months or years as a hermit. There may be another factor that contributed to his sense of social isolation, a badly crippled left hand (more on this later in this chapter).

At 17, Agostini has a vision in which the Virgin Mary appears to him. She lifts her hand and points into the distance with her finger. This experience is recounted in both the 1908 *Daily Optic* article and by Florio Santini.[19] Agostini interprets this mystical experience as a divine call.

Shortly thereafter, Agostini departs Sizzano, seeking education. The 1908 *Daily Optic* states he spent three years in study. The *Valparaiso Messenger* says he studied in *"various colleges and universities."* [20]

Some later writers claim his studies were in Rome, but Santini states it was only after completing these studies that he left for Rome.[21] This would make his visit to Rome about 1821.

Lazio

After his visit to Rome – where his sense of being divinely called was profoundly strengthened by worshipping in the city's spectacular, historic churches filled with relics of the Apostles and Martyrs – Agostini takes up a life of solitary devotion for seven years.[22] Santini says he spent these seven years living in the mountains of Lazio.[23]

Lazio is the region of Italy surrounding Rome. With the Tyrrhenian Sea bordering the west, it is an area of broad lowlands and mountain ranges, with the highest peak, Monte Gorzano, towering over 8,000 feet.

How he spent these years is pure speculation. Lazio is pervaded with Christian tradition and Christian places. Perhaps he spent part of this period in a monastery. If so, he had many to choose from. Monasteries then existing within a 100-mile radius of Rome include: Montecassino Abbey, Farfa Abbey, Casamari Abbey, Fossanova Abbey, Santa Maria di Grottaferrata Abbey, Argentella Abbey of Saint John, Valvisciolo Abbey, St. Scholastica Abbey, and San Benedetto Abbey in Subiaco.

San Benedetto Abbey in Subiaco is built against a rock cliff and enshrines the tiny cave – Sacro Speco – where Saint Benedict (480-547 AD) lived as a hermit before founding this monastery. Saint Benedict entered the cave at the age 20 and lived there for three years.[24] Agostini likewise is 20 when he begins his seven years of solitary devotion.

(The Abbey of St. Scholastica, also in Subiaco, is named after Saint Benedict's twin sister Scholastica.)

Devout Wanderer

In October, 1830, Agostini leaves Italy and travels across southern France to Spain.[25] This begins a period of his life as a pilgrim.

The *Catholic Encyclopedia* defines pilgrimage as a *"journey made to some place with the purpose of venerating it, or in order to ask there for supernatural aid, or to discharge some religious obligation."* [26]

It is interesting that this definition doesn't include the concept of visiting a place to gain knowledge. Origen Adamantius (184-254 AD), an early church theologian, made a pilgrimage from his home in Alexandria, Egypt, to Rome *"to see the very ancient Church of Rome."* [27] A prime part of the motivation for this trip is intellectual curiosity and it is hard to believe that curiosity and a search for knowledge doesn't play a part in many, perhaps most, pilgrimages.

Once in Spain, Agostini undertakes a series of pilgrimages. On March 1, 1831, Agostini is at the Abbey of Our Lady of Montserrat (Santa Maria de Montserrat), located on Montserrat Mountain, Catalonia,[28] 30 miles northwest of Barcelona.[29] The abbey is located near the top of 4,050-foot Montserrat Peak. Today the abbey can be reached by cable car, railroad, or road, but in Agostini's time it was a grueling climb.

Our Lady of Montserrat is famous for its sculpture of Mary, Mother of Jesus, known as La Moreneta ("The Dark One"), because of the statue's dark color. It is also famous as the place where St. Ignatius of Loyola (1491-1556 AD) threw away his arms and embraced the life of an ascetic, living in a nearby cave for ten months. Eventually, after various pilgrimages, prosecution by the Inquisition, and acceptance as a priest, Ignatius and his companions found the Society of Jesus (Jesuit Order).[30]

From Montserrat, Agostini travels to Zaragoza, Aragon, to visit Our Lady of the Pillar, arriving in April, 1831. Our Lady of the Pillar is a statue of Mary and Jesus as a baby in the cathedral of Zaragoza. Mary wears an intricate crown that contains 2,836 diamonds, 2725 roses, 145 pearls, 74 emeralds, 62 rubies, and 46 sapphires. The crown of Jesus is identical, except in size.[31]

In February, 1832, Agostini is at Santiago de Compostela, Galicia, visiting the shrine of the Blessed Apostle of Spain.[32] Galicia is positioned at Spain's northwest tip, bordering Portugal on the south and the Atlantic Ocean on the west.

The Blessed Apostle of Spain is James, son of Zebedee. James is the first of Jesus' Disciples to be martyred. The traditional belief is that his remains are at Santiago de Compostela, were they were taken following his beheading by King Herod in 44 AD.[33] *where*

The presence of James' remains in Santiago de Compostela makes it one of the top three destinations for Christian pilgrimages – Rome and Jerusalem are the other two. The pilgrimage to Santiago de Compostela is known as the "Way of Saint James" and it remains today as popular a pilgrimage as in Agostini's time.[34]

Return to Novara

A year later, in February, 1833, Agostini returns to Novara, where he obtains a passport to Naples, which notes that the fingers of his left hand are crippled.[35] His crippled fingers are mentioned again in a note made by an immigration clerk on December 24, 1844, in Sorocaba, Brazil.[36] It is also evident from examining a least one of Agostini's photos, as discussed in Chapter 17.

It is impossible to know if he was born crippled, but if so his handicap probably contributed to his sense of alienation. Being crippled, especially being born crippled, was viewed as a sign of personal impurity and was sufficient to disqualify one from serving in the priesthood, without a special ecclesiastical dispensation. This rule had been formalized by the Council of Trent (1545-1563 AD), which recognized 12 physical blemishes that would prevent a priest from performing church services. These were: blindness, lameness, a flat nose, anything superfluous, broken-footed, broken-handed, crook-backed, dwarfism, blemish in the eye, scurvy, scabbed, and broken stones (inability to reproduce).[37] (Broken stones meant a visible deformity.)

From Agostini's return to Novara until 1837, no source furnishes any indication of his actions, except Wolfe states that at some point during this period he was a novitiate in both the Carthusian and Trappist orders.[38] Based on this, he twice made the first step toward becoming a monk, and twice decided against it.

The Carthusian Order is an order of enclosed monastics. It was founded in 1084 by Saint Bruno of Cologne (1030-1101 AD). As an enclosed order, Carthusians live as hermits, in small cells. They spend most of their time within their cell, which they leave only for daily prayer services, twice weekly communal meals taken in silence, and occasional meetings or events. They are permitted one annual visit by family members. All the actions of living, such as preparing their food, they do themselves in their cells.[39]

The Trappist Order is a branch of the Order of Cistercians, founded in 1664 at the La Trappe Abbey by Armand Jean le Bouthillier de Rancé (1626-1700 AD). Trappists follow the Rule of Saint Benedict, taking vows of stability, fidelity to monastic life, and obedience. Speaking is discouraged, but not enforced by vow. Meals are taken in common. Work is required, so most Trappist monasteries produce goods which are sold to obtain money for the monastery. The order does not require abstinence from alcohol, so some Trappist monasteries produce and sell wine, beer, or other alcoholic drinks.[40]

The appeal of both of orders to Agostini is obvious, given his desire for an ascetic life. That he chooses not to become a monk probably reflects his rejection of even the very minimal social life of these orders.

New Life

In 1838, Agostini does take religious vows, but not that of an eremetic order. He accepts the vows of Saint Anthony the Abbot.[41] The life of Saint Anthony and its impact on Agostini are explored in the next chapter.

Becoming an Antonian is obviously a fateful decision in Agostini's life, perhaps the most significant since deciding to pursue an ascetic life. But he follows this decision with another momentous decision, one that will affect his life in ways beyond his imagination. He decides to go to the "New World," to South America.

He leaves Italy, crosses the Alps, and travels to Nantes, France.[42] There, in March or April of 1838, Agostini boards a sailing ship for Venezuela.[43] He knows he is facing 30 or more arduous and dangerous days at sea. He knows he must provide for most or all of his food. Since he probably travels by the least-expensive class, he will live packed with other passengers on the lowest deck. During the trip, he will be exposed to the varieties of weather – sun, wind, cold, storm. His exposure to the elements would have been a familiar circumstance; the exposure to cramped humanity less so.

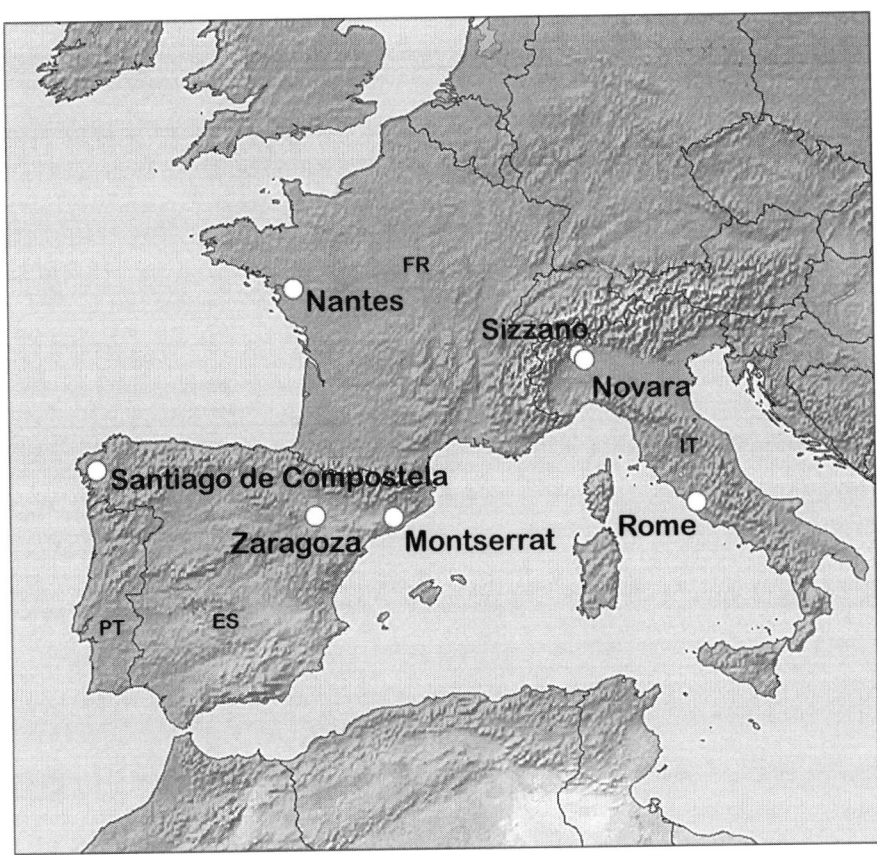

Agostini's travel in Europe 1821-1838: Sizzano, Rome, Lazio (Rome), Montserrat, Zaragoza, Santiago de Compostela, Novara, Nantes.

Photo

Agostini's parish church, San Vittore, built 1651-1653, Sizzano, Italy. Courtesy Alessandro Vecchi, released under GNU Free Documentation License.

Chapter 3 | Saint Anthony the Abbot

After 17 years of restless seeking, almost half of his life, Agostini commits himself to the vows of Saint Anthony. As we shall see, Agostini not only accepts the severe self discipline of the vows, but he actively models his life after Saint Anthony's.

"Father of Monks"

What is known about Saint Anthony's life is provided by Athanasius of Alexandria's (296-373 AD) *Life of Anthony*. This document, written about 360 AD, is accepted by most scholars as a reliable historical record.[1]

Anthony (family name unknown) was born about 250 AD in a small village west of the present town of Beni Suef, Egypt, which is about 95 miles south of Cairo.[2] In 250, Egypt is a province of the Roman Empire.

Although Anthony bears a Greco-Latin name, Athanasius states he is Egyptian of noble, wealthy parents. He is raised as a Christian even though this is a time of intense persecution of Christians by Roman authorities. Emperor Trajan Decius (210-251 AD) issues an edict shortly before Anthony's birth in which he orders all residents of the Empire to sacrifice to the "ancestral gods," eat of the sacrifice, and obtain a certificate of such actions from a magistrate.[3] Obviously, compliance would be intolerable to Christians.

The number of Christians in the Roman Empire in 250 AD is estimated to be about one million. This had grown from an estimated 7,500 in 100 AD.[4]

As a boy, Anthony *"could not endure to learn letters, not caring to associate with other boys."* At 18 or so, his parents die and Anthony is left with the care of a younger sister. Less than six months later, Anthony is reading Jesus' extortion to sell what you possess and give to the poor when he is overwhelmed by the feeling that without complying, he has no chance of attaining a Christian life.[5]

He quickly gives his inherited land to his fellow villagers, sells everything else, and distributes the money among the poor, except for a small sum he reserves for his sister. When he receives a second revelation that his actions are still insufficient, he gives away the funds saved for his sister and places her in a house of Christian women.[6]

His early life is spent seeking:

> *"And at first he began to abide in places outside the village: then if he heard of a good man anywhere, like the prudent bee, he went forth and sought him, nor turned back to his own place until he had seen him."* [7]

To meet his few needs, he works *"with his hands, having heard, 'he who is idle let him not eat.'"* [8]

For 15 years, Anthony lives thus, sleeping in a cave, probably a burial vault, in a cemetery.[9] During this time, he struggles to maintain his asceticism in face of intense, almost unbearable temptations to abandon it. Leaving the cemetery, finally, he makes his way toward a mountain where he finds an abandoned military outpost, in which he encases himself, as in a tomb, taking in as food only a six months' supply of bread. The post contains a source of water. There *"he employed a long time training himself, and received loaves, let down from above, twice in the year."* [10]

He spends 20 years within the post. During this time, the fame of his enigmatic life spreads, and many people are drawn to imitate him. One day, his followers break into the post, concerned by lack of any response from inside. Anthony is found to be alive and – hard to believe – healthy. When he learns of the impact of his seclusion on the gathered crowd, he agrees to help organize a "community." [11] Although not a monastery in the formal sense, this nascent community is considered to be the beginning of Christian monasticism.

Anthony now enters a period of active life. In 303 AD, the ruling Emperor Diocletian (245-311 AD) decides to eradicate Christianity.[12] He forbids Christian worship and orders churches throughout the Empire destroyed and Christian scriptures burned. He issues edicts that Christian clergy be arrested, tortured, and compelled to sacrifice to the traditional Roman gods. He then extends this order to all Christians.[13]

To protest this oppression, Anthony and many of his followers travel to Alexandria, the Egyptian capital. There, they devote themselves to helping and supporting those tortured and imprisoned for practicing Christianity. In response, the magistrate orders them out of the city, but while the others comply, Anthony stands outside the legal hall in provocative defiance. The magistrate chooses to ignore him and he is not prosecuted.[14]

When Christian mistreatment declines, Anthony returns to his old place and his community. After some years Anthony feels called to withdraw and live apart. He travels into the desert and after several days arrives at a mountain known today as Mount Colzim (Al-Qalzam), which is about 80 miles south of the Egyptian town of Suez and 15 miles inland from the Gulf of Suez. There he finds a new place to live, in a cave toward the top of the mountain. At the base of the mountain is a spring.[15]

To meet his self-discipline of working, he cultivates a garden near the spring and weaves baskets and makes other items.[16]

At Mount Colzim, he again accumulates followers. With these, he organizes a more formal community, which evolves into the first eremetic monastery. Anthony's role in creating monasticism is recognized by his traditional appellation, "Father of Monks." [17]

In 351 AD, at the age of 105, Anthony dies.[18] Such a long life is surprising in one who practiced such extreme self-denial.

Monastery of Saint Anthony

The Monastery of Saint Anthony (Deir Mar Antonios) exists still, at the base of Mount Colzim. Over 1,650 years old, the monastery almost disappeared in the eighteenth century when it was down to a small handful of monks.[19]

The monastery is surrounded by walls up to 60 feet high. The first walls were built in the fifth and sixth centuries, during a period of fierce anti-Christian attacks. Many repairs and additions were made over the centuries, and a new wall enclosing the entire complex was added recently.

> *"For security reasons, the Monastery was not accessible at ground level until the mid 20th century. Access into the Monastery was only by means of a windlass or rope lift 'fatuli'. It was operated by means of a large winch which as turned would haul a person up who was secured by means of a hoop rope."*

> *"Next to the 'fatuli' is a smaller rope lift 'matama'. This rope lift was used for receiving food deliveries from the Monastery's Dependency at Bush in the Nile Valley, as well as to lower food for Bedouin."* [20]

Within the monastery are 10 churches. The oldest is the Church of Saint Anthony the Great. It contains relics of Anthony and the *"most exquisite and uniquely complete wall paintings dating back to the 13th century."* The paintings are *"unique in that they are unusually complete and cover the entire length and breadth and height of the church."* [21]

Nine hundred feet above the monastery is the cave where Anthony lived, which

> *"...comprises 3 parts: the terrace, the tunnel, and the cave. The narrow tunnel connects the outer terrace – where one can imagine St Antony would sit and weave his palm leaf baskets – and the inner cave where he once dwelt is now converted into a small chapel in which liturgies are celebrated daily."* [22]

The spring that provided water for Anthony still provides water for the monastery. [23]

Life in the monastery *"consists of two important components: prayer and manual labour."* The prayer practice is both communal and private. The required labor consists of *"handicraft, work in the garden, the farm, the kitchen, the bake-house, the various workshops, construction, [and] researching in the library, amongst many other things."* [24]

Saint Anthony Abbot

Following Saint Anthony's death, *"the monasticism established under St. Anthony's direct influence became the norm in Northern Egypt."* [25] Later, and elsewhere, particularly in Europe after it is Christianized, there are numerous other monastic orders established, such as the Carthusian and Trappist orders that Agostini contemplated joining.

Since Agostini eventually rejected these two orders, what order did he join?

Wolfe states, *"he took the vow of living according to the rule of Saint Anthony Abbot."* [26] Santini states, *"back in Rome, he joins the Order of S. Antonio Abate [Saint Anthony Abbot]."* [27] In Quito, Ecuador, in 1839, the Vicar General of the Archdiocese of Ecuador examines his documents and reports that he is a *"follower of the Abbey of Saint Anthony."* [28]

The only order of Saint Anthony that existed in Rome in 1833 was the Maronite Monastery of Saint Anthony Abbot. The Maronite branch of Christianity was founded by Saint Maron, who was born about 350 AD near Antioch, then the capital of the Roman province of Syria (it is now in southern Turkey).[29] After being ordained a priest, Maron felt called to asceticism. He travelled into the uninhabited Antiochian countryside and began living on a hill, becoming the first "open-air" hermit.[30]

> *"Embracing the open-air life, he repaired to a hill-top formerly honored by the impious.... he lived there, pitching a small tent which he seldom used. He practiced not only the usual labors, but devised others as well, heaping up the wealth of philosophy."* [31]

Maron died in 410 AD. As with Saint Anthony, his behavior attracted followers who organized themselves into monasteries. Unique among the monastic movements of the Third and Fourth Centuries, Maronite monasteries accepted people for short periods of time and what today would be called lay brothers and sisters. These lay members formed churches which developed by the Sixth Century into the Maronite Church.[32] Today, there are about three million Maronite Christians in the world, most of them living in Syria and Lebanon.

The history of a Maronite monastic presence in Rome began in 1707 when Pope Clemente XI gave the Maronite Church the Convent of Saint Peter and Saint Marcellino on Via Labicana. That site was located on marshland, close to a cemetery that *"gave off a bad smell,"* and consequently was considered unhealthy. In 1753, Pope Benedetto XIV permitted the sale of the Via Labicana property so the order could purchase a new site on the Piazza San Pietro in Vincoli ("Saint Peter in Chains"). The old site was bought by the Carmelite Sisters of Saint Teresa for the sum of 12,000 scudi. The new site was a villa that had been owned by the Mattei family for generations. As benefited a noble family dating to the Middle Ages, the palazzo (residence) on the property was substantial and incorporated a stone tower for defensive purposes. The villa's extensive lands were planted in vines and fruit trees (see map on page 28). [33]

On moving to the new site, the order adopted a new name, Santo Antonio Abate, and adopted Saint Anthony as its patron saint. All privileges and obligations that had belonged to the prior order were transferred to the new order, which was renamed the Order of Saint Anthony the Abbot. *"Even the favors granted to them by the Pope Clemente XI and confirmed by Pope Innocenzo XIII were transferred to the new convent."* [34]

Augustus Hare, who visited the monastery in 1869, described it as:

> *"a convent of Maronite monks, in whose garden is a tall palm-tree, perhaps the finest in Rome. In the view from the portico of the church[35] it forms a conspicuous feature, and the combination of the old tower, the palm-tree, and the distant capitol, standing out against the golden sky of sunset, is one very familiar to Roman artists."* [36]

There, Agostini took the rule of the order, the vows of Saint Anthony Abbot. Wolfe says:

"He made this vow with the complete approbation of his Bishop and several other prelates, reserving its dispensation to the Pope himself, so that the Pope alone could free him from this solemn promise...." [37]

The vows accepted by Agostini were poverty, chastity, obedience, and humility.[38]

The vow of poverty required Agostini to forswear all monetary gain, possessions, and inheritance, owning only such things as were necessary for survival. The vow of chastity required that Agostini avoid sexual desires and abstain from sexual acts. The vow of obedience required that Agostini attempt always to live in accordance with God's will as he understood it as a Christian and to accept the authority of the leaders of his order. The vow of humility required Agostini serve the needs of others before attending to his own needs.[39]

It is obvious that the Maronite Abbey of Saint Anthony was an obscure order in 1833. What was its attraction to Agostini? Given his extreme reverence for Saint Anthony, obviously the order's name was a reason. Another was probably that the order in its origin was the oldest monastic order in Rome. A third reason, probably decisive, was the order's willingness to accept Agostini as a member and let him leave and travel to South America. If he had joined any other order, he would have been required to live in a monastery, and permitted only sanctioned and brief periods of living outside.

Santo Antonio Abate Today

About 70 years ago, the Abbey of Saint Anthony changed its name to Collegio Maronita della Beata Vergine Maria, the "Maronite College of the Blessed Virgin Mary." The old Mattei villa residence that stood in Agostini's time was replaced with the current structure at about the same time.

In 2003, in celebration of its founding 250 years earlier, the Collegio was extensively renovated.[40]

The author contacted the College to see if their records held any information on Agostini. The College archivist made a search of their historical documents, but found nothing on Agostini. The College even lacks evidence of his membership in the Abbey, as the earliest registration book the College still retains dates to only 1902.[41]

The College's historical records covering Agostini's time, which might have included letters, were lost when the Abbey was looted followed the capture of Rome on September 20, 1870, by Giuseppe Garibaldi. This was the second time the Abbey had suffered that iniquitous fate. It had also been looted in 1808 following the occupation of Rome by Napoleon's army.[42]

Photos

St. Anthony's Monastery, Egypt, 1930-1931. Courtesy Byzantine Institute and Dumbarton Oaks Fieldwork Records and Papers, Photographer Unknown, ICFA.BI_DO.RE DSEA.0019, Image Collections and Fieldwork Archives, Dumbarton Oaks, Trustees for Harvard University, Washington, D.C.

St. Anthony's Monastery, Egypt, 1930-1931. Courtesy Byzantine Institute and Dumbarton Oaks Fieldwork Records and Papers, Photographer Unknown, ICFA.BI_DO.RE DSEA.0023, Image Collections and Fieldwork Archives, Dumbarton Oaks, Trustees for Harvard University, Washington, D.C.

Interior of Church of St. Anthony, St. Anthony's Monastery, Egypt, 1930-1931.
Courtesy Byzantine Institute and Dumbarton Oaks Fieldwork Records and Papers, Photographer Unknown, ICFA.BI_DO.RE DSEA.0010, Image Collections
and Fieldwork Archives, Dumbarton Oaks, Trustees for Harvard University,
Washington, D.C.

St. Anthony's Monastery, Egypt, 2010. Courtesy St. Anthony's Monastery.

Entrance to St. Anthony's Cave, Egypt, 2010. Courtesy St. Anthony's Monastery.

Inside St. Anthony's Cave, Egypt, 2010. Courtesy St. Anthony's Monastery.

St. Anthony's Spring, Egypt, 2010. Courtesy St. Anthony's Monastery.

Reproduction of a painting of Santo Antonio Abate as it appeared circa 1800. Note tower and palm tree as described by Hare. Courtesy Collegio Maronita della Beata Vergine Maria, Piazza San Pietro in Vincoli, Rome, Italy.

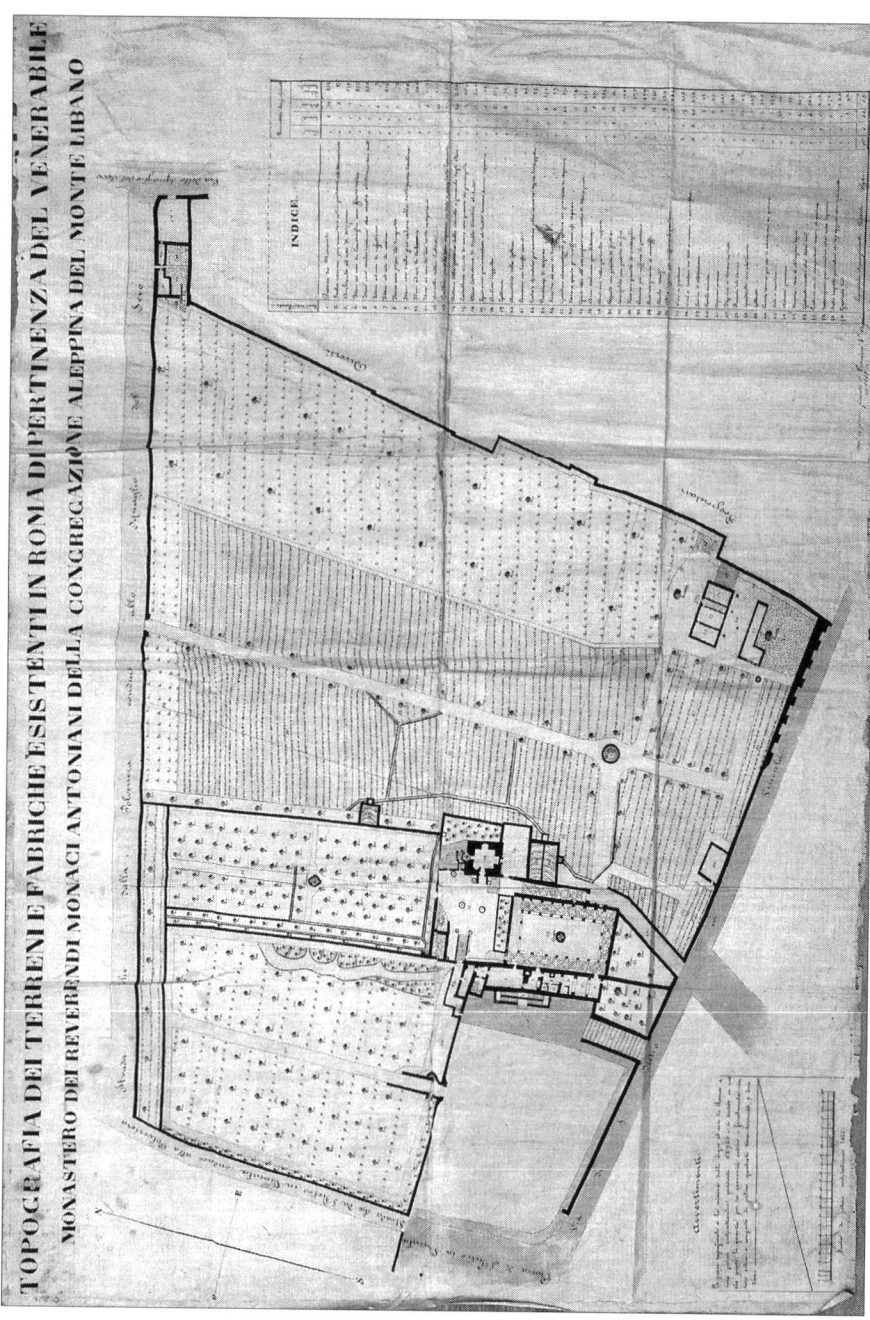

Map showing convent and lands of Santo Antonio Abate in 1863. Courtesy Collegio Maronita della Beata Vergine Maria.

Collegio Maronita della Beata Vergine Maria chapel. The altar is dedicated to Saint Anthony the Abbot. Courtesy Marco Soscia, 2014.

Fresco of Saint Maron, ceiling, chapel, Collegio Maronita della Beata Vergine Maria. Courtesy Marco Soscia, 2014.

Decorative ceiling, main entrance hall, Collegio Maronita della Beata Vergine Maria. Courtesy Marco Soscia, 2014.

Front entrance, Collegio Maronita della Beata Vergine Maria. Structure built in
the early 1930s. Courtesy Marco Soscia, 2014.

Chapter 4 | A New Life Begins

Venezuela

The ship Agostini boards in Nantes for his trip to South America is a sailing ship, as the first steamboat will not to cross the Atlantic until two years later.[1] If he travels in steerage, he has no private quarters, so he probably spends his daylight hours on deck.

What were his thoughts and feelings as he resolutely approaches landfall? Just a few months earlier, he had made the solemn decision to become an Antonian – a decision reversible only by the authority of the Pope – and to travel to the New World. He tells us something of his thinking in his own words:

> *"When I arrived at Caracas, the capital of the newly formed Republic of Venezuela, a new life began for me. In fact, I knew nothing of South America, except that it had high mountains and extensive deserts. This was what I was looking for in order to enter fully into a life of perfect solitude."* [2]

A new world for a new life.

Why pick Venezuela, a country with no particular connection to his home country? Perhaps it is the cheapest passage; or the only destination available the day he arrives in Nantes. As we shall see, moving quickly when travelling is one of his characteristics.

On arriving in Venezuela, he *"rested a few days,"* [3] then on June 5, 1838, he applies for a passport to travel to Bogotá, Colombia.

> *"I issue free and safe passage to Señor Juan Maria de Agustini so that he may have passage to the Bogotá province. The transit authorities may not delay him on his way, and should provide him all the protection [safe passage] for the proper behavior that he evidences."* [4]

The passport is signed by Martín Tovar, the governor of Caracas, one of Venezuela's most distinguished citizens. Martín Tovar y Ponte is a native-born Venezuelan, one of the signers of the country's Declaration of Independence in 1811, and one of the early leaders of the war against Spain that followed. Defeated in battle early in the War for Independence, he barely escapes capture and spends a year in exile in the West Indies and the United States. He returns to join Simón Bolivar in the final two years of the war. During the civil war that follows independence, he serves in the Venezuelan government, is exiled again, and then serves as ambassador to Holland.[5]

When Agostini arrives in Caracas, he undoubtedly has letters of introduction obtained in Europe, as that is his practice in subsequent travels. Demonstrating that he visits the local church authorities, he writes:

> *"In Caracas, Bogotá, and Papayan, the bishops wanted to raise me*

to the priesthood, and retain me in their diocese, but when I explained to them the vow I had made and the vocation I had received, they allowed me to proceed." [6]

The question arises here as it does many times later, how does he pay for his travel? We shall see that sometimes the state or its authorities pay for his travel, church officials often provide shelter, sometimes he does have a little money, and when he can, he simply walks or canoes. But for the rest, it remains a mystery. Perhaps the generous hospitality of those he meets is sufficient for what costs his travel requires.

Colombia

Leaving Caracas, Agostini is in the mountain village of Pamplona, Colombia, by July 13, 1838, where Máximo Valnera, Governor of the Department of Santander, stamps his passport.[7] To reach Pamplona, a distance of over 500 miles, he travels south from Caracas to the Orinoco River, then up the Orinoco by canoe to where the Apure River flows into it; then up the Apure to the Colombian border. From there, he walks over the Cordillera Oriental (East Andes) to Pamplona, which is situated on the eastern slope of the range.[8]

Although he is probably unaware of it, Colombia in 1838 is a troubled country on the verge of civil war. Under Spanish dominion, Venezuela, Colombia, and Ecuador formed one colony called the New Kingdom of Granada. Following Independence from Spain, the three countries remained united for about a decade under the name Gran Colombia, then separated into independent countries in 1830. In 1840, that civil war finally erupts, caused partly by the government's attempt to restrict the political power of the Catholic Church.[9]

A month after arriving in Pamplona, by August 17, Agostini is in Bogotá, the capital of Columbia.[10] This is a 300-mile journey south, through difficult, unpopulated, mountainous terrain. In Bogotá, Brother Cándido Torres, Superior of the Franciscans of the Department of Cundinamarca, provides him with a letter of recommendation to Brother Ramón Castro, of the Franciscan Convent of Cartago, Columbia, with instructions to host Agostini when he arrives. He cites as his reason for his letter:

"...the recommendation of the Governor of [this] Province and the letter [of introduction] presented [by Agostini] to the Guardian of this Convent [Torres]." [11]

Agostini has no intention of staying in Bogotá. He visits Pablo Hilata, Vicar General (Deputy) of the Bishop of Bogotá, and obtains information on how best to get to his next destination, Quito, the capital of Ecuador.[12]

Ecuador

By October 11, 1838, he is in Quito, a distance of about 750 miles.[13] There, he obtains the following letter of recommendation from the Vicar General of the Archdiocese of Ecuador:

"Because Christian charity interests itself in the good of its fellow

worshipers, I beseech those who cross paths with this religious man, Friar Juan María de Agostini, professed follower of the Abbey of Saint Anthony, to provide him with the assistance ensuing from this charity." [14]

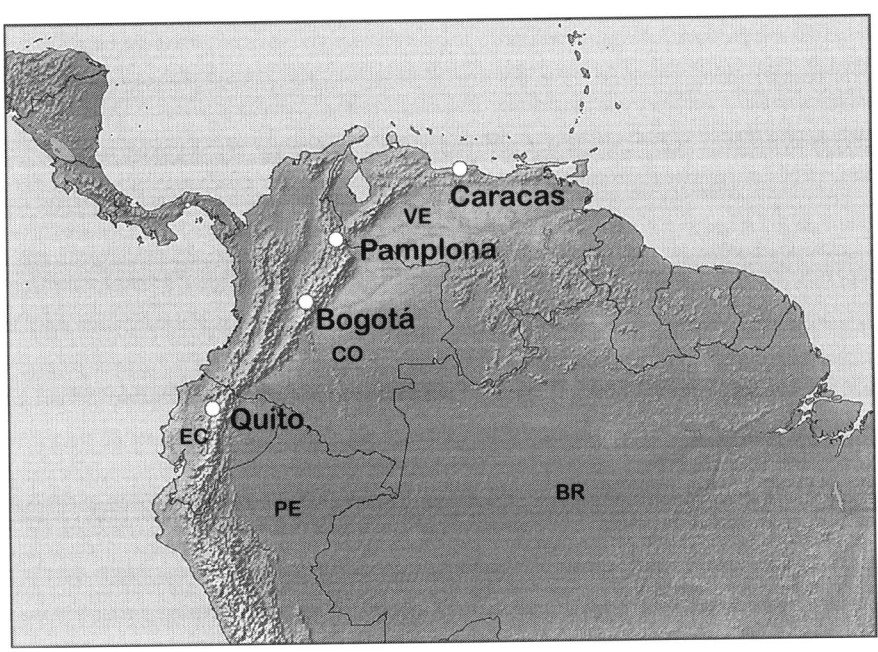

Agostini's travel June, 1838 to October 11, 1838: Caracas (Venezuela), Pamplona (Colombia), Bogotá (Colombia), Quito (Ecuador).

Through Peru to Bolivia

From Quito, he travels to La Paz, Bolivia, which he reaches on November 20, 1838. [15]

This is a huge trip, about 2,000 miles. The only information Agostini provides for how he makes it is that he travels on the Ucayali River. [16] The Ucayali is one of the major tributaries of the Amazon River and in places is not navigable by larger boats, due to lengthy sections of rapids. If we assume he moves as much as possible by river, he would have walked (probably) from Quito to the headwaters of the Napo River, then, crossing into Peru, down the Napo to where it joins the Ucayali.

At the junction of the Napo and the Ucayali, Agostini is in the midst of the upper Amazon rainforest. Explorers to this area in following years report the obvious dangers of disease (especially malaria), heat, rain, wild animals, and unfriendly natives, including many groups still practicing cannibalism. But what they complain most fervently about are the insects. Paul Marcoy, who visited this area 23 years after Agostini, writes of the agony of the *"territory of the mosquitoes."*

"A hundred pages filled with notes of exclamations and interjections, with all the ohs! ahs! ughs! alas's! and other expressions of disgust and horror borrowed from every language... would but give an imperfect idea

of the horrible torture and incessant rage in which we were kept by these wretched insects."

"During the day, [by] slaps and blows dealt by our fists upon every part of the body, we were able to keep the enemy in check.... But the night! Oh! the night!... Here we renounce the impossible task of depicting our sufferings." [17]

Agostini will return to this area in three years.

Once on the Ucayali, he can traverse all of Peru to within 150 miles of Lake Titicaca, which lies on the border between Peru and Bolivia. From the south end of Lake Titicaca, it is a 40 mile walk to La Paz. Both Lake Titicaca and La Paz are high in the Andes, above 11,000 feet.

When he arrives in La Paz, the superintendent of police, Juan Pérez, issues Agostini a passport to travel to Mount Illimani (Aymara).[18] Mount Illimani (21,120 feet) is the highest peak in the Cordillera Real, a sub-range of the Eastern Andes. The peak is about 60 miles south west of La Paz and is easily visible from La Paz. (He will return to Mount Illimani in 1857.)

Was this his destination when leaving Nantes? Evidently not, because after spending only two months on that mountain, he travels to Mount Illampu (20,890 feet), which is 130 miles northeast of Mount Illimani. There he is happier, spending at least 7 months living in a mountain cave, as attested by Father Eduardo Otaira. Otaira writes that on Sundays, Agostini walks down from the cave to attend church in the nearby villages of Amiso, Penachi, and Canchachula.[19]

Return to Peru

Sometime after December, 1839, Agostini leaves Mount Illampu and travels back to Peru.[20] His goal is Motupe in northern Peru, which is located in the Eastern Andes next to the Sechura Desert. About two-thirds of this 1,600-mile trip can be made by river, the remainder must be done overland.

"In Motupe, province of Lambayeque, I spent two years in a cave on the side of a high spur of the Andes. My dwelling was 12 miles distant from the village, but this did not prevent me from going to the parish Church every Sunday and feast day to assist at Mass. I was young then, and walking was a real pleasure."

"During the day I visited the sick and the poor, and did my best to bring joy to everyone. In the evening when the priest retired to his regular parish, I gathered the faithful in the House of God and we recited the Rosary, then I gave them short exhortations on the fear of God and other appropriate subjects. It was a delight to see with what eagerness these simple souls listened to the words and received the teaching of the Holy Church of which they had been deprived so long."

"One of the inhabitants of Motupe gave me a letter of recommendation saying, 'God has looked kindly upon us and has protected us from many evils as long as the reverend solitary has lived among us.'" [21]

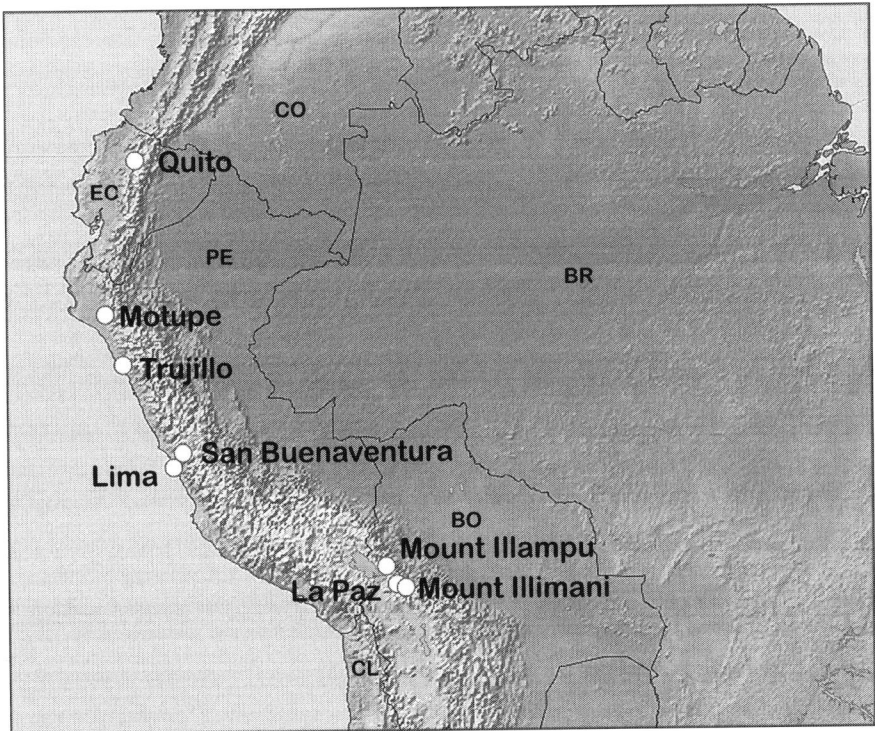

Agostini's travel October 11, 1838 to November 4, 1841: Quito, La Paz, Mount Illimani, Mount Illampu, Motupe, Trujillo, San Buenaventura, Lima.

Here we see Agostini organizing religious worship. This practice will evolve later into creating formal "communities" with appointed officers and written rules (see Chapters 8 and 13). This is also the first instance we see of Agostini leading worshippers in the reciting of the Rosary, a devotional that we will see is the foundation of Agostini's religious practice. Reciting the Rosary is a commemoration of Jesus and the events of his life that normally takes 10 to 30 minutes to compete.

The compulsion to move on must have descended on Agostini, because on October 15, 1840, he obtains documents to travel to Lima, Peru, from José María Lisarzaburu, Prefect of the Department of (La) Libertad.[22]

On his way to Lima, Agostini travels first to Trujillo, about 180 miles south.[23] From there, he goes to San Buenaventura (410 miles), where on January 3, 1841, Judge Francisco Badillo issues him a certificate stating that Agostini *"has been living for six months in a cave on the Vinjuatunne mountain, leading an exemplary life."* [24] The author was unable to identify "Vinjuatunne," but the context makes it clear this is the mountain at Motupe where Agostini was living. The six-month period must also be accurate, not the two-year period Agostini gives as his time in Motupe, as a two-year period does not fit the dates of his travel.

By November 4, 1841, Agostini is in Lima, the capital of Peru, 170 miles southeast of San Buenaventura. *"Here again the Archbishop insisted on my becoming a priest, but I could not consent; my vocation called me to solitude, not to the exalted ministry of the Priesthood."* [25] On December 4, 1841, Luigi Baratta, the Italian Consul General in Lima:

> *"...issues a certificate stating that Giovanni Maria De Agostini, Sardinian subject, native of Sizzano, province of Novara, is an honest person, belonging to the order of St. Antonio Abate."* [26]

After staying an unknown amount of time in Lima, Agostini heads north again, to *"the famous Cerro de Pasco where I spent several months at an altitude of 12,000 feet above sea level."* [27] Cerro de Pasco is located in the Central Andes and is Peru's highest-altitude city. To reach Cerro de Pasco from Lima, Agostini travels about 170 miles.

Continuing north from Cerro de Pasco, Agostini travels about 450 miles to Moyobamba.[28] Moyobamba is in the Amazon rainforest not far from where Agostini had been in 1838. To get there, he canoes down the Huallaga River, which rises just south of Cerro de Pasco, to a landing somewhere near today's Chazuta. From there, it is about 100 miles to Moyobamba, which Agostini probably walks.

His purpose in going to Moyobamba, the capital of the San Martín Region, is to obtain papers permitting him to leave Peru. In April, 1842, Gregorio del Camillo, Vice-Prefect of Moyobamba, issues him a passport with permission to cross into Brazil.[29] On August 4, 1842, Chaplain Juan Aguilar, *"on the behalf of the parish priest"* orders him *"to come to the Moyobamba church every Sunday and recite the Rosary."* [30]

Leaving Moyobamba, Agostini travels to Balsapuerto and Lagunas, small villages in the Loreto Region of Peru.[31] The Loreto Region is Peru's largest region, almost all of it rainforest. Even today, it is sparsely populated with virtually no roads in the portion that Agostini visited.

By March 6, 1843, Agostini is in Santa María (Santamaría), where Bruno de la Guardia, Vicar General, issues an order that Agostini be provided a canoe.[32] Santa María is on the Amazon River about half-way between Iquitos and the Brazilian border. It is named after a Jesuit mission founded there in the 1770s. Marcoy, who visited in 1866, says that all that remained of the village was:

> *"...a dozen habitable huts. The others, from which the people had taken the posts and rafters to use as firing, were fallen to ruins, and the thatch of their roofs was slowly rotting. The church, deprived in a like manner of its principal timbers, was only a heap of litter."* [33]

Agostini's next stop is Loreto, which Marcoy notes *"is the last Peruvian possession which the traveler finds in the eastern part of the [Amazon] river. It has existed thirty-three years."* [34] Here he comments again on the insects:

> *"If there is little to divert the residents there, at all events mosquitoes are very common, and the [chigoe flea] abounds; while the first feed on your blood, the second, like troglodytes, excavate little caverns and holes beneath the toes, where they increase and multiply, perfectly indifferent to the violent itching which you suffer from their filthy presence."* [35]

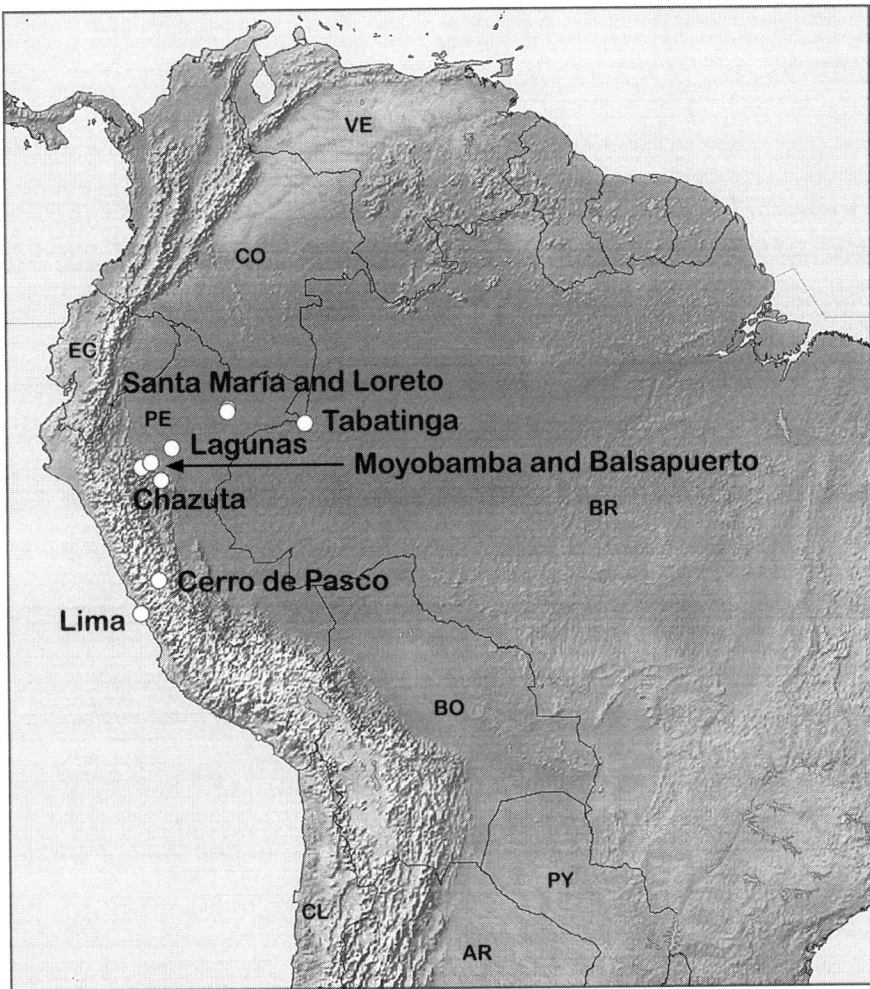

Agostini's travel November 4, 1841 to Mid-March, 1843: Lima, Cerro de Pasco, Chazuta, Moyobamba, Balsapuerto, Lagunas, Santa María, Loreto, Tabatinga.

To Brazil

From Loreto, Agostini canoes to Tabatinga, Brazil.[36]

As Agostini leaves Spanish South America, which now he knows well, to a country whose history, traditions, and language are unknown, what can we say about him?

He is 42 years old. He has been in South America almost 5 years. He is immensely confident, self-disciplined, and apparently fearless. He is wonderfully fit. He is committed to travel to an extraordinary degree. He knows how to travel without funds and how to deal with church and state authorities. He is evidently well-liked, and based on the numerous requests he has received to join the priesthood, sincerely respected as a religious man.

What we don't know is "Why the incessant travel?" His explanation is a *"call to solitude."* Solitude and travel – two pursuits in which it would seem that success in one would thwart success in the other.

Photo

Cerro de Pasco, Peru, 1854.

Chapter 5 | Brazil

Down the Amazon

Within a few days of departing Santa María, Peru, in March, 1843, Agostini is in Tabatinga, Brazil.

Tabatinga was founded in 1766 as a military outpost to protect the Western Brazilian border from Spanish intrusions. Marcoy's description of Tabatinga when he visits in 1861 gives a good idea of what Agostini saw:

> *"The military post, now a century old, is situated at an elevation of some thirty feet on a little hill which forms the termination of a vast naked plain. A rough staircase dug in the bank forms the means of approach on the river side...."*

> *"Behind the dwelling of the commandant, an abrupt descent led to a ravine, sheltered by clumps of figs, ricinea, and miritis. This dried-up ravine is the pathway which leads to the village; for at Tabatinga is a village of a dozen cabins, where dwell the brown partners of the defenders of the post, together with several Ticuna couples."* [1]

From there, Agostini travels the length of the Amazon to its outlet in the Atlantic Ocean, a distance of over 1,800 miles. About this trip, he says only *"I continued eastward and reached the mouth of the mighty river...."* [2] His transport is presumably the canoe issued to him by Bruno de la Guardia. He could not have gone by steamboat, because the first steamboat did not arrive in Tabatinga until 1853. [3]

Agostini gives no indication of how long it took to negotiate the Amazon, but six to ten weeks was not uncommon. After surmounting the dangers of what was universally then recognized as the most life-threatening river passage in South America, Agostini arrives at the port city of Belém (Santa Maria de Belém do Pará). Marcoy in making the same grueling journey describes Belém as follows:

> *"We cast anchor at that port of the bay called Arsenal Point, from which we could see at a glance the entire eastern face of the city... an interminable line of many-storied houses, square-built, and shining with white-wash; their summits standing out in bold relief against the clear blue of the sky...."*

> *"Along the whole extent of the town, at some twenty paces from the bank of the river, vessels and boats of the country – vigilingas, cobertas, égaritéas, montarias, uvas or canoes, were moored to stakes. Beyond the town... sloops and schooners were moored side by side.... Large ships of commerce, with their sails struck, lay sleeping at anchor, waiting for their lading."* [4]

Unable to refrain from commenting on the insects at Belém, Marcoy notes that not long after he enters the city, his *"socks were black with fleas."* [5]

Atlantic Coast

At Belém, Agostini presents the captain of the Brazilian corvette *Capibaribe* a letter of recommendation that gains him a free passage.[6] The ship heads south along the Brazilian coast, perhaps destined for Rio de Janeiro. Off the coast of the Brazilian state of Pernambuco, however, Agostini gets sick *"for the first time."* [7] He has severe malaria and is permitted to disembark, probably at Recife.

When Agostini recovers enough to travel, he heads north, to Natal, the capital of the state of Rio Grande do Norte.[8] Josiah Conder, in a visit a few years earlier, described Natal as follows:

> *"[The settlement] consists of a square, with houses on each side, having only a ground-flour, three churches, the governor's place, a town-hall, and a prison... No part of the city is paved, although the sand is deep."* [9]

What attracts Agostini is apparently the desert-like inland of the state, the *sertão,* to which he immediately retreats, living the life of an open-air hermit. After a first indeterminate stay, he travels to São José de Mipibu to obtain permission for

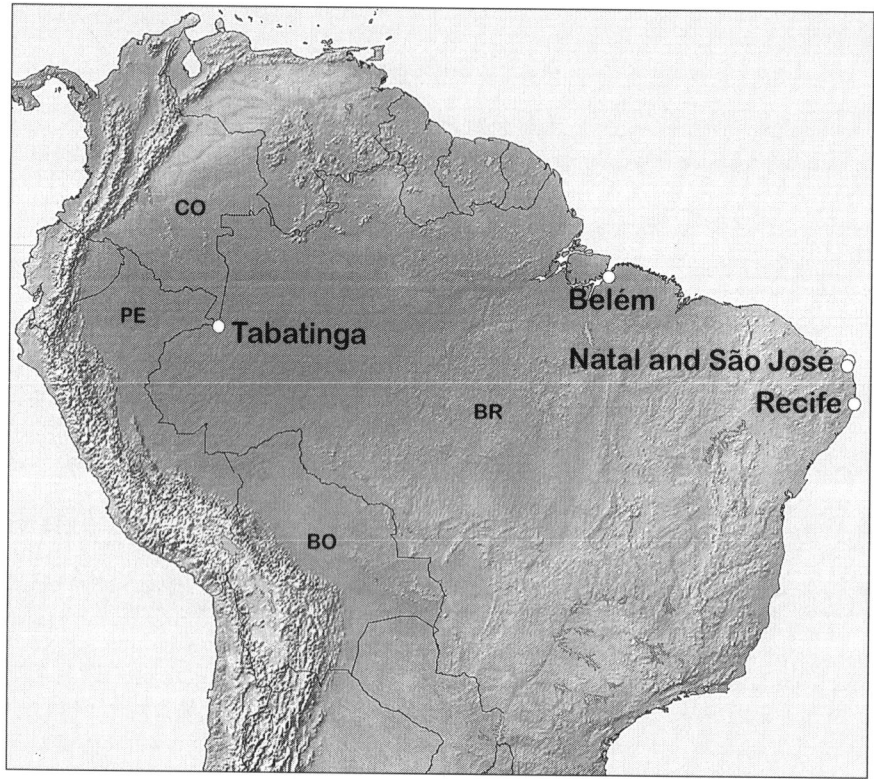

Agostini's travel Mid-March, 1843 to Early August, 1844: Tabatinga, Belém, Recife, Natal, São José.

a second stay. Francisco Ribeiro Susa, Municipal Judge for São José, grants this permission, letting Agotstini return to the desert for *"for 3 months and 22 days."* [10]

On June 20, 1844, Antônio de Almeida Zavier Garcia, General Vicar Forane of the state of Rio Grande do Norte certifies that Agostini has the right to preach in churches.[11] This establishes that Agostini has been in the coastal states of Pernambuco and Rio Grande do Norte (and maybe Paraíba and Bahia) for about a year since arriving at Belém.

Rio de Janeiro

The first independent verification of Agostini's activities appears in the August 19, 1844, newspaper *Diário do Rio de Janeiro.* The paper reports that on the prior day, the *"Italian Giovani Ma di Agostine"* arrived on the steamboat *Imperatriz,* commanded by Captain Lamego. The *Imperatriz* provided regular passenger service between Belém and Rio de Janeiro, with stops in between. The voyage from Belém to Rio de Janeiro took 23 days.[12]

The complete passenger list is:

> *"Francisco de Queiroz Coutinho Matoso Câmara, former President of the State of Rio Grande do Norte"*
> *"Commander José Pereira da Mota"*
> *"João da Costa Hayden"*
> *"Manoel Jerônimo Ferreira"*
> *"Antonio José de Brito"*
> *"Father Francisco Alves de Mendonça"*
> *"Bruno Antonio Meireles, Jr."*
> *"D. María Gonnet, and five children"*
> *"Portuguese Joaquim Ferreira da Cunha"*
> *"Portuguese Guilherme Augusto Rodrigues"*
> *"Frenchman José Hibbert"*
> *"Italian Giovanni Ma di Agostine"*
> *"3 Brazilian officers"*
> *"4 British soldiers"*
> *"4 Sergeants"*
> *"5 Recruits for the Army"*
> *"2 Marines"* [13]

Agostini probably did not get on the steamboat at Belém, but at one of the in-between stops. During his passage, he had plenty of time to become friendly with Ex-Governor Matoso Câmara, an important official whose brother would later become the Brazilian Minister of Justice.[14]

Perhaps it is these contacts that lead to Agostini getting an audience in Rio de Janeiro with the Emperor of Brazil:

> *"The Emperor Pedro II himself took me into his friendship and showered on me his kindness and favors as he could not have done for any other person. These honors, however, were not to my taste for solitude and hardships, therefore I left the Brazilian Capital, never to return."* [15]

Pedro II had become Emperor of Brazil at the age of five on April 7, 1831. Unlike the classic case often seen in royal history where a child becomes king or emperor because the prior ruler dies, Pedro II became emperor because his father, Pedro I, left Brazil to become Emperor of Portugal.

The history of Brazil is unique in colonial history – it is the only European colony that was for awhile the site of the government of the mother country. During the Peninsular War of 1807-1814 between Napoleon of France and the allied powers of Spain, Great Britain, and Portugal, the capital of Portugal was occupied on December 8, 1807, by French forces. The Portuguese government under Pedro I (then known as Pedro IV) fled to Rio de Janeiro, thus creating the only instance in colonial history where a colony becomes the ruler of its own mother country and its mother country's colonial empire. In 1813, when the French were driven out of Portugal, the government in Brazil considered staying and running Portugal and the empire from Rio de Janeiro. But rebellious domestic situations in both Portugal and Brazil resulted in Pedro I fleeing to Portugal to become the emperor there, abdicating power to his son in Brazil.[16]

This action resulted in Brazil gaining its independence from Portugal without enduring a war of independence. (If Brazil had remained in control of Portugal, would it have been Portugal that had a war of independence?)

As Emperor, Pedro II became known as "Pedro the Magnanimous," reflecting his tolerant and enlighten attitudes.

> *"He was a man of wide culture, and Brazil made great progress under his guidance. He travelled extensively, both in America and Europe, and devoted much of his time to studying systems of government and education."* [17]

It is not surprising that a man so engrossed in travel and culture would desire to meet someone as intriguing as Agostini.

On his arrival in Rio de Janeiro, Agostini undoubtedly visits the city's Convent of Saint Anthony, founded in 1608 and well-known throughout Brazil, but past its prime in 1844. When the convent was visited in 1843 by G. R. B. Horner, he described it as containing *"only thirty-four friars... but formerly it contained two hundred."* [18]

Seeking a solitary place to live, Agostini chooses Pedra da Gávea ("Rock of the Topsail"). Pedra da Gávea is the stunning 2,769-foot, granite-rock-topped mountain in the São Conrado neighborhood of Rio de Janeiro. It is the second largest monolith in the world that terminates directly in the sea. From the summit of Pedra da Gávea, the view:

> *"...is certainly the most picturesque in the world, with its surrounding verdure-covered mountains, and their easy slopes covered with the richest green. ...well-cultivated islands ornament and diversity the surface of the little inland sea of 105 miles circumference [of the bay of Rio de Janeiro]; and taken in all, there is not perhaps a sight elsewhere more imposing and agreeable."* [19]

Agostini's hermit life on Pedra da Gávea attracts the attention of José Francisco Ferreira, a plantation owner through whose property Agostini has to pass to climb the mountain. Ferreira notices slaves from his and other plantations taking food to Agostini. Suspecting there is more to Agostini's intentions than his stated reasons, Ferreira begins *"to spy on the monk when he went to the rock, and sometimes even when he descended."* [20] After watching Agostini, he concludes:

> *"...that during all the time that [the] Monk was living on the Gávea Rock, [I, Ferreira,] never saw or heard [anything suggesting] the Monk was a man of evil customs."* [21]

In exchange for the food he receives, Agostini gives away hand-made rosaries and small crosses.[22] This exchange of labor for food is undoubtedly Agostini's normal practice and is based on Saint Anthony's exhortation that those who would live like him work with their hands.

Santos and Sorocaba

On December 15, 1844, Agostini leaves Rio de Janeiro on the steamboat *Paquete do Sul* for Santos, State of São Paulo. He appears in the passenger list as *"Italian Friar João Maria Agustmi."* [23] His reason for leaving the gorgeous setting of Pedra da Gávea appears to be a desire to live in the hills of Sorocaba.

Moving fast as usual, Agostini is in Sorocaba by December 24, 1844 (Christmas Eve!). Sorocaba, São Paulo, is 120 miles inland from the port of Santos (Santos is 220 miles south of Rio de Janeiro).

On that day, Agostini registers as required by law in Sorocaba. His entry in the *Registration Book of Foreign Visitors of the Town Hall of the City of Sorocaba* reads:

> *"Friar João Maria D'Agostini, native of Piedmont, Province of Italy, aged 43, single, occupation Solitary Hermit, come to exercise his ministry."*

> *"Intends to reside while here in the forests of this city, very particularly on the hill of the Iron Factory of Ipanema, having arrived on December 24, 1844."*

> *"This document is filed, notarized for the record, by registrar Procópio Luis Leitão Freire, submitted and signed by him."*

> *"Procópio Luis Leitão Freire"* [24]

This document also gives the first physical description of Agostini, noting his crippled fingers:

> *"Stature: short"*
> *"[Skin]: light-color"*
> *"Hair: gray"*
> *"Eyes: brown"*
> *"Nose: normal"*
> *"Mouth: normal"*
> *"Beard: full"*
> *"Face: long"*
> *"Distinguishing features: crippled in three fingers of the left hand"* [25]

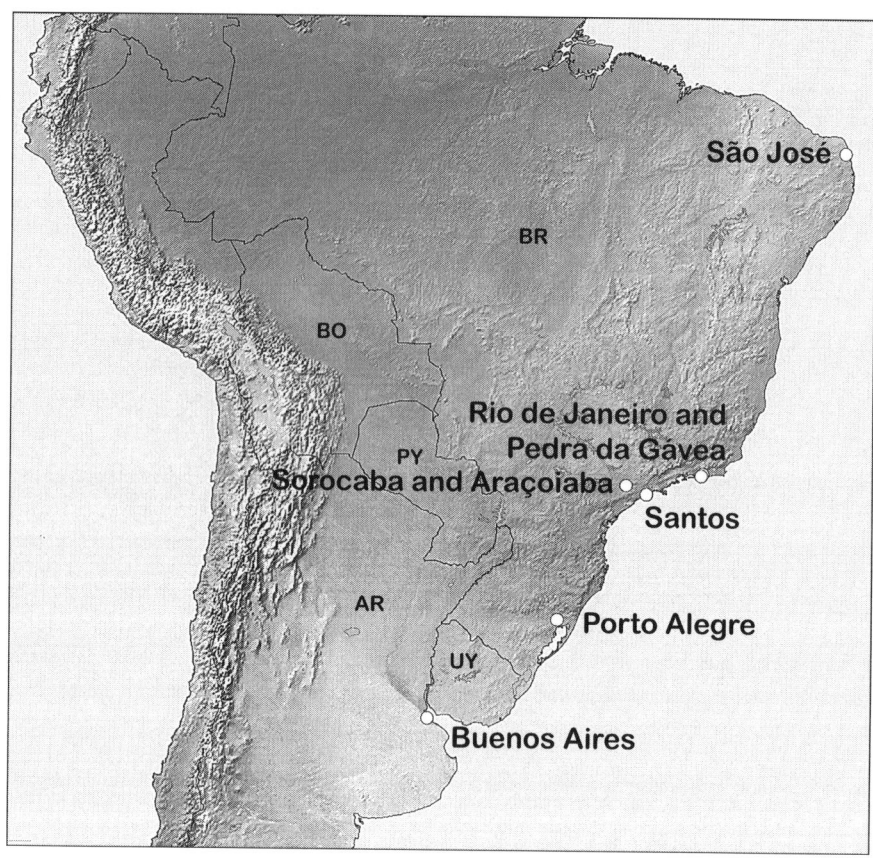

Agostini's travel August 18, 1844 to October-November, 1845: São José, Rio de Janeiro, Pedra da Gávea, Santos, Sorocaba, Araçoiaba Hill, Porto Alegre, Buenos Aires.

Ironworks at Ipanema

About 10 miles west of Sorocaba is Morro Araçoiaba, "Araçoiaba Hill." The discovery that the hill contained large veins of magnetite in the late 16th Century led to the development of an iron smelter at the hill's base, the only ironworks in Brazil until about 1890.[26] At the time of Agostini's arrival, the mine and smelter workers are predominantly state slaves and liberated slaves.[27]

Here is Daniel Parish Kidder's description of visiting the site just a few months before Agostini arrives:

> *"From Sorocaba I started early one morning to visit the celebrated iron foundry of Ypanema. About 11 o'clock I reached the Fabrica de Ferro, which is located in a beautiful valley at the foot of the mountain of Guaras-sajava [Araçoiaba]. This mountain contains vast quantities of magnetic iron ore."*

"The establishment belongs to the government, and consists of six or eight buildings, which subserve the usual requisites in smelting and casting iron."

"In order to have the benefit of a small stream of water, the works have been built at a considerable distance from the locality of the mineral. As a primary consequence, great labor is required to transport the ore in its rough state from the mountain. This fact will be understood when I mention that every particle of it is brought upon the backs of mules, and requires to be loaded and unloaded by hand." [28]

Araçoiaba Hill is evidently Agostini's destination from the time he leaves Rio de Janeiro. On the hill, he finds a shallow cavity in a rock outcropping in a crevice of which is a dripping spring. There Agostini chooses to live, sleeping on *"a hard board supported by two stones."* [29]

At night in his niche, Agostini spends long hours chanting psalms and saying prayers, which can be heard at the ironworks. This coupled with his ascetic life lead to his ridiculing by the non-Catholics at the ironworks, who are primarily German and Swedish technicians. The *"howler is snoring in the hills,"* was a common joke when his nightly devotions were overheard. [30]

To the Catholics, particularly the iron workers, Agostini is a holy man to be revered. He is asked to preach in the factory chapel, and hundreds gather to hear him. People from surrounding villages begin visiting him in his mountain retreat, and a popular feeling begins to develop that he has miraculous or healing powers. [31] This is the first evidence of an attitude by believers toward Agostini that will become a pattern and will lead in the future to serious trouble with government authorities.

Another practice of Agostini's reported at this time is walking *"the neighborhood to plant crosses."* He erects solitary crosses at high points, and at crossroads assembles groups of 14 crosses representing the Via Crucis, the stations of the cross. [32]

Monk of Ipanema

The river flowing beside Morro Araçoiaba is the Ipanema, which derives its name from a native word meaning "bad water." As the general excitement over Agostini's presence grows, he becomes known as Monge do Ipanema, the "Monk of Ipanema." The rock face where he is living was called Pedra Santa, the "Saint Rock," or Pedra do Monge, the "Monk's Rock."

On September 1, 1846, José Almeida da Graça visits Agostini's cave and finds him missing:

"Passing the Monk's Rock today, I no longer found him there. I noticed a few spots of old blood in the place where he lived, which may be a crime, I hereby notify the Senior Director of the Iron Factory of Ipanema.

"José Almeida da Graça, caretaker of the forest." [33]

This adds the belief that Agostini was murdered to the local accounts of the miraculous Monk of Ipanema.

Trilha da Pedra Santa

The Monk's Rock is revered after Agostini's presumed death as a sacred site, becoming a place of pilgrimage. Visitors today still follow the Trilha da Pedra Santa ("Trail of the Holy Rock"), a 3.5 mile trek that takes three to five hours to complete. The narrow slit where Agostini lived is known as the "Grotto of the Monk of Ipanema." The spring that provided him water still flows year-round and is considered salubrious.

Inside the Grotto is an iron cross cast at the Ipanema Ironworks dated 1818.

This is the first instance that can be documented of a place named after Agostini or his presence, but it will not be the last, as we shall see.

To Argentina

Agostini was not murdered, of course. Instead, he had left Araçoiaba Hill some time prior to October 16, 1845, for on that date he is in Porto Alegre, on his way to Argentina.[34] Porto Alegre is about 700 miles south of Araçoiaba Hill, which Agostini probably reaches by returning to Santos and taking a steamboat from there to Porto Alegre. From Porto Alegre it is another 500 miles by sea to Buenos Aires, his destination in Argentina.

Photos

Tabatinga, Brazil in 1861. Drawing by Elihu Rich, from *Travels in South America*, by Paul Marcoy.

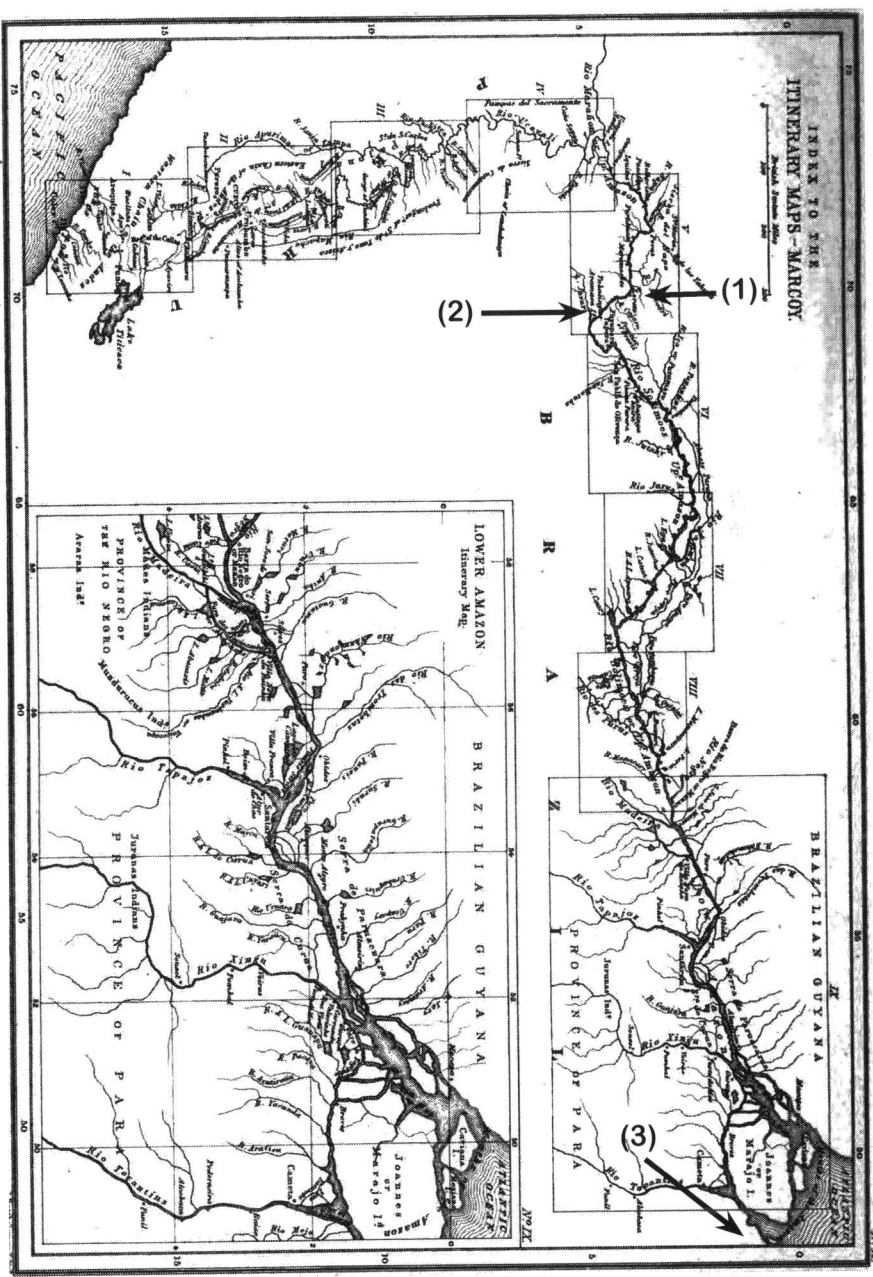

Amazon River and tributaries. From *Travels in South America*, by Paul Marcoy.
(1) Loreto, Peru, (2) Tabatinga, Brazil, (3) Santa Maria de Belém, Brazil (city is
just off the map).

Santa Maria de Belém , Brazil in 1861. Drawing by Elihu Rich, from *Travels in South America*, by Paul Marcoy.

Cathedral, Santa Maria de Belém , Brazil in 1861. Drawing by Elihu Rich, from *Travels in South America*, by Paul Marcoy.

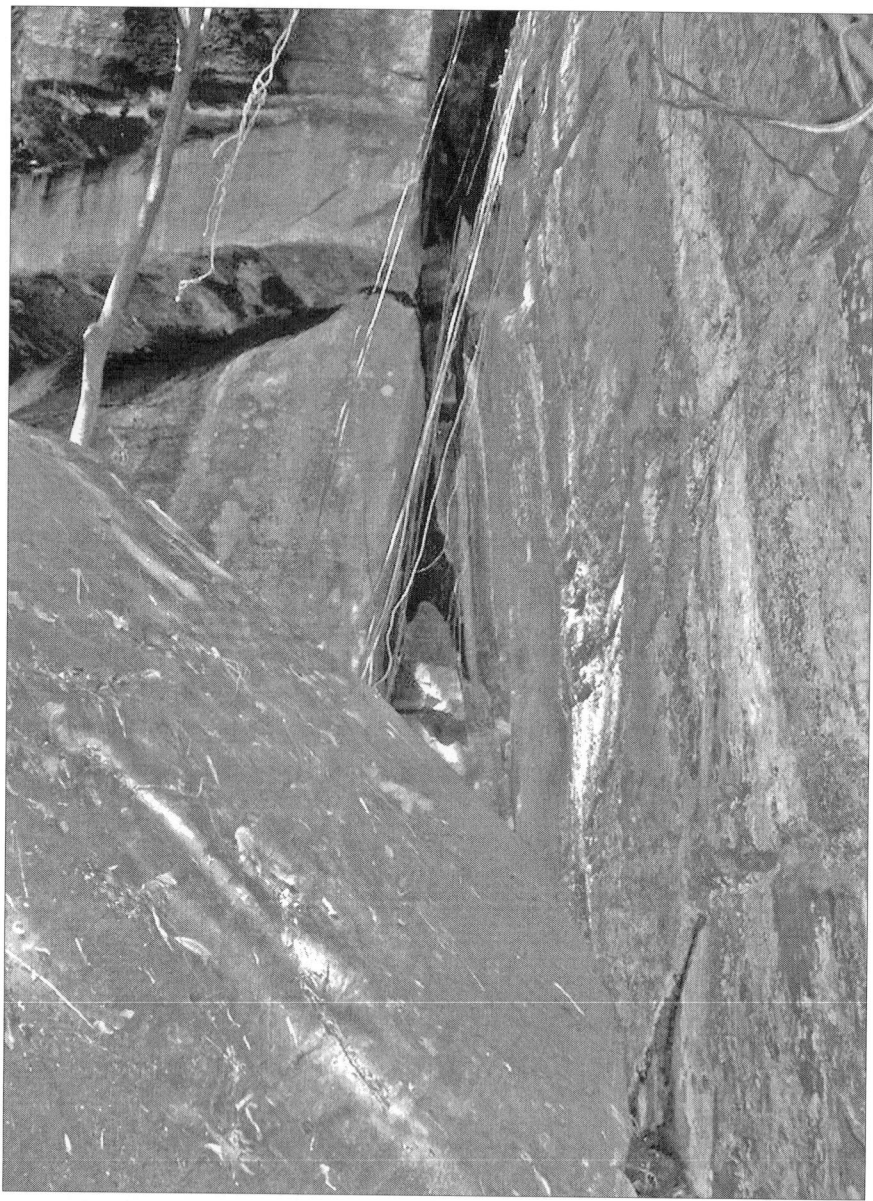

Entrance to the "Grotto of the Monk of Ipanema," Araçoiaba Hill, São Paulo, where Agostini lived from late December 1844 to early October 1845. Courtesy Ronaldo Cesar da Silva Messias, Researcher History Araçoiaba Area, Group of Researchers, Pathfinder Villas Boas.

Shrine outside Agostini's cave, Araçoiaba Hill. Courtesy Thomas Peter Geisendorf, Equipe Ecoturismo Brasil, ecoturismobrasil.com.br.

View from the top of Araçoiaba Hill. Courtesy Thomas Peter Geisendorf, Equipe Ecoturismo Brasil, ecoturismobrasil.com.br.

Chapter 6 | Argentina

Almost no information is available about Agostini's visit to Argentina in 1845-47, the first of his three visits to the country.

In 1849, Brazilian authorities investigate Agostini because of concerns about the political impact of his actions (discussed in the next chapter). In reports returned by various officials, one by the police chief of Porto Alegre states that he interviewed a Frenchman, John Coquet, about Agostini. Coquet tells the chief that he *"knew perfectly said Augustine."* He says further, that he had *"seen the monk mentioned in Buenos Aires, in the palace of Dictator João Manuel de Rosas, in company with whom he resided for some time."* [1]

This information prompts the Porto Alegre chief to travel to Pelotas, Brazil, seeking other informants. There he interviews Telemachus Bouliech, another Frenchman, who contradicts Coquet, saying Agostini had *"never resided in the palace of the Dictator Rosas in Buenos Aires."* Bouliech says that Dictator Rosas had sent Agostini into the little-explored northern territories to convert Indians to Christianity, and when he returned, having not been especially successful, Rosas imprisoned Agostini for a period. [2]

The "dictator" being referenced, Juan Manuel de Rosas, was born into an extremely wealthy family in colonial Argentina and participated in the war of independence against Spain. In the civil war that followed independence, Argentina split into several national states. Rosas, as governor of Buenos Aires, led the armies that unified Argentina in 1829. In return, he was granted "extraordinary powers" by the Buenos Aires legislature under the rationale that such powers were needed to deal with the challenging problems of the newly unified country. [3]

Although Rosas considered himself a benevolent ruler, he became more and more ruthless as he struggled to retain power, eventually becoming an unapologetic totalitarian, using secret police, torture, castration, tongue-cutting, imprisonment, murder, and mass executions to suppress political and economic opposition. [4] His rule lasted from 1829 to 1852, when he was forced to flee the country following his defeat by oppositional forces supported by Brazil. [5]

Agostini says that he visited the *"famous tyrant Rosas:"*

> *"He treated me with great honors, but as I could not refrain from reprehending his many misdeeds, I understood that the best thing for me was to keep on my way to the Pampas and the Comanche Indians."* [6]

Leaving Buenos Aires some time in mid-1846, Agostini travels north, up the Río Uruguay. Agostini's goal for this trip is to cross the South American continent into Chile, which suggests that if Rosas ordered this trip as Bouliech reported, then Agostini intended to proceed to Chile after fulfilling Rosas' task. [7]

The Río Uruguay serves as the border between Argentina and Uruguay for about 300 miles, then as the border between Argentina and Brazil for another 600 miles.

On November 22, 1846, Agostini reaches Uruguaiana, a town on the Brazilian side of the Río Uruguay about 350 miles upstream from Buenos Aires. (The town on the Argentinian side is Paso de los Libres.) There, Manuel Fernando de Silveira provides Agostini a letter asking Argentinian military and civil commanders to assist Agostini in his efforts to cross the Andes into Chile.[8]

From Uruguaiana, Agostini crosses the Río Uruguay into Argentina and travels 160 miles west to Goya. Goya is on the Paraná River, the second longest river in South America, after the Amazon. In Goya, Agostini apparently abandons his plan to cross the Andes and instead spends nearly a year in the area preaching to the Indians. Or, as the commander of Goya puts it a document, carrying on a *"pitiful mission among the savage tribes."* [9]

Some idea of how unsettled Goya and this part of Argentina are can be seen in Lauchian Bellingham MacKinnon's description of Goya, which he visits a year before Agostini.

> *"This day we took an excursion to the town of Goya, a miserable collection of huts, with here and there a good house. The streets cross each other at right angles, and are without drainage of any kind. The consequence is, that large ponds of feculant water are formed in hollows. ...canals in wet weather would be a fitter name than streets, and a small canoe after rains more applicable than a carriage."* [10]

The indigenous people of northern Argentina are the Guaraní, who are hunter-gatherers. MacKinnon writes about them:

> *"These Indians are a very warlike and brave race, although ferocious and cruel. They have never been conquered, and roam in a state of wild freedom from within a few leagues of the vicinity of Santa Fe to the Cordillera, or Andes."* [11]

Their villages consisted of communal houses in which as many as 120 people lived packed together. If Agostini's goal is to preach to them, he probably travels from village to village, and in doing so, doubtlessly risks his life. Living among them likely requires communal living in dreadfully unpleasant conditions.

Agostini's travel from October 16, 1845 to late 1847: Porto Alegre (Brazil), Buenos Aires (Argentina), Uruguaiana (Brazil), Goya (Argentina).

Chapter 7 | Return to Brazil – Success and Troubles

From Goya, Argentina, Agostini next shows up in Porto Alegre. How he gets there is unknown. Most likely, he returns to Buenos Aires by river, either the Paraná or the Río Uruguay, and then takes a boat. This is his second visit to the capital of Rio Grande do Sul, the southern-most Brazilian state; the first visit was in October, 1845, while on his way to Buenos Aires.

> "The monk João Maria Agostin, born in Rome, first showed up in this capital in the year of 1847. Small in stature, lively eyes, long grey beard, dressed in rough clothes, and with slippers over his naked feet. As he walked through the street, with his staff, he caught the eye of the public. He did not stay long here, soon moving on with his campaign." [1]

From Porto Alegre, Agostini goes to Cerro do Botucaraí ("Botucaraí Hill"). Botucaraí is about one mile south of the small village of Candelária, which is 120 miles inland from Porto Alegre. Seemingly, the hill is exactly what Agostini seeks. It erupts from a broad plain, stands 1,870 feet high, and is crowned by a granite cap-rock. And near the top of the hill is a spring.

But he is apparently unsatisfied with Botucaraí as he begins scouring neighboring mountain ridges, including those at Costa da Serra and Rio Pardo. Finally, he finds what he wants at Cerro Campestre ("Campestre Hill"), about 65 miles due west of Botucaraí. [2]

For the events that follow at Campestre, we have the most detailed description of Agostini's behavior to date, thanks to eye-witness accounts published by the Porto Alegre newspaper journalist Felicíssimo de Azevedo. As he writes:

> "I stayed there [Campestre] for thirty-five days (from September to October 1848), studying these mysteries." [3]

Miracle Water at Cerro Campestre

Campestre is about 15 miles from the town of Santa Maria da Boca do Monte ("Saint Mary of Mouth Hill"), a village of about 2,000 people when Agostini arrives in January, 1848. [4]

Campestre differs from Agostini's normal preference in that it is only 920 feet high, although it is unusually vertiginous. But what attracts Agostini is his discovery of "a stream of excellent water that makes its way through the wilderness, down the south side." [5]

At Campestre, Agostini quickly draws attention and soon followers:

> "His long beard and clothes attracted the peasants to him, who took him to be a new Messiah. He preached to the people every day. He said God inspired him; he drew crowds that loved him there." [6]

Convinced that the spring has healing properties of great benefit, Agostini enlists help to construct a pathway up the north side of the hill, to the spring:

"As the path was readied, he built 17 large crosses, always helped by his followers. They were afterwards erected along the path, evenly spaced. In the stream, they made a fountain, about a meter high, placing two or three tiles, so that people could get the water with the tin that was placed there." [7]

At the top of the hill, near the spring, Agostini and his followers build a small chapel to Saint Anthony.[8]

With these actions, Agostini suddenly achieves national attention. On May 17, 1848, the newspaper *O Porto Alegrense* reports a newly discovered *"fountain with water that has been producing some cures, which they call água milagros [miracle water]."* The paper reports further:

"...the sick are coming from all parts of the province, attracted by the many wonders that come from such water, which they say was discovered by a monk...." [9]

Skepticism by the medical establishment is immediate. Just three weeks later, Doctor Fidêncio Prates writes in the *O Porto-Alegrense:*

"How to persuade the two hundred souls at Campestre de Santa Maria that the waters have properties not different than the Ibicuí River...? How to convince them the waters contain no minerals?" [10]

Learning there is a carved, life-sized figure of Saint Anthony in an abandoned Jesuit Mission at Rio Pardo, Agostini travels to Porto Alegre to appeal to Rio Grande do Sul President General Francisco José de Souza Soares de Andréa for permission to move the image to the new chapel at Campestre:

"The monk went up the steps to the palace and asked the aide for help in talking to the General."

"He was taken to the presence of General Andréa, who asked him, in the abrupt way he was known for, what he wanted."

"'I've come to ask your Excellency for a saint, said the monk.'"

"'You want a saint? Go look for one up in heaven, where, according to our beliefs, there are many.'"

"But he explained himself. 'I beg your pardon. I come to ask for an image [statue] of Saint Anthony that is in one of the churches of the Missions,[11] so that I can build a chapel for him.'"

"'Then go see the priest Thomé, he's the one who rules the church; I don't have anything to do with that.'"

"The monk left, bowing first, and went to look for the late priest Thomé, who received him with kindness, offering him a place to stay, that he accepted."

"Praising his zeal for religious worship, priest Thomé ordered the Vicar to give him the saint." [12]

With the Vicar's permission in hand, Agostini travels to Rio Pardo:

"...where he stayed for a few days, being the object of curiosity for some, and of worship for others."

"He was so bold as to present himself in church, on a Sunday, in time for mass, which was led by the Vicar Vicente Zeferino Dias Lopes, where, after the Vicar left, he went up to the pulpit, to preach his sermon."

"The monk analyzed the ways of the families of Rio Pardo, saying that instead of looking for the house of God to pray, all they cared about was having fun and letting their children grow without any knowledge of religion."

"The then Lieutenant Colonel José Joaquim de Andrade Neves, later General and Baron of Triunfo, finding himself in the church with his family, waited until the unconventional preacher left the church, then offered him several hits with his cane, that [Agostini] accepted with all humility." [13]

The dismissive attitude that many, particularly the upper-class, have of Agostini is apparent.

Azevedo arrives at Campestre just after Agostini returns from his mission at Rio Pardo:

"...when I got to Campestre de Santa Maria, I found, on the top of the hill, the image of Saint Anthony, installed in some sort of hut covered with straw, in front of it a chest, closed with three keys, where the faithful placed the alms, most of it silver and even gold, as I could see for myself."

"At that time, Campestre was home to a large camp, with huts of all shapes and sizes, many of them closed with curtains and roofed with straw."

"There were about two hundred people installed there, coming from all over the province, looking for health." [14]

For those seeking healing by the "água milagros," Agostini establishes an elaborate ritual that begins at sundown:

"As there was no bell to call the faithful to the prayer, a gun was used for that purpose." [15]

"....after sundown, when the first shadows of the night came, the crowd, which was already about two hundred people, was called to prayer with the gunshot."

"With everyone kneeling before that symbol of the Christian religion, they prayed the rosary, after which, when the monk was present, he preached a sermon, counseling the people to practice all the Christian virtues and that they should faithfully ask God and His Holy Mother to end their suffering through the application of miraculous water of which they were making use."

"The sick person, after walking to the entrance of the path, took off his shoes and with bare feet and uncovered head, started his walk up a slope that can only be compared to the Antas Mountains. In the trees, there were ropes to help the elderly or the weak up the path."

"Next to each cross, the patient was supposed to kneel and pray."

"To walk the 17 crosses and pray at each one, you would spend about an hour, after which you would reach the top and find the saint in his little chapel, built with rough wood. It was common for people to sit on a crude bench there, where they would rest, and then hurry down to the place where the slope came out of the rock...."

"By the fountain, there was a stump where the patient would kneel to get the water that was poured by anyone, with a metal cup they had there, held in place by a chain."

"The water would be poured on the head of the kneeling patient, slowly, as many times as one wished, but always in odd numbers."

"After this, you would walk again to get your body moving."

"The clothes could only be changed after they dried naturally." [16]

Healings

Not surprisingly, given the desperation of the ill attracted to Campestre, many report successful – even miraculous – healings. Azevedo arrives with a skeptical attitude toward the cures, which he retains after his visit, but he does admit to seeing evidence of healing or at least improvement. He says:

"...curiosity led me to ask the people who walked the path about their health, so as to know how the treatment was improving it."

"I saw, for example, rheumatic people and patients with severe inflammations in the eyes being completely healed in a matter of days."

"Among all the patients, I was astonished by a leper, called José Rodrigues, who had often been found begging in [Porto Alegre], and was completely healed."

"I was so astonished with that healing of leprosy that I called the man to my hut to ask him about the miracle."

"This was his answer: 'It was a miracle of the holy monk that healed me, and also the holy water.' And, taking a paper out of his pocket, in which he had a prayer written, told me to read it."

"'And the medicine?' I asked."

"'The holy monk told me to go to the wilderness to look for a place where a certain tree grew and take out all the wax, with the respective honey. I was then supposed to put everything inside a new clay pot, add a bit of sweet olive oil and let it boil, blessing the pan with a crucifix, repeating the prayer until everything melted. Then I should rub my whole body with the ointment everyday.'"

"'And what was the medicine you drank?'"

"'The holy monk told me to take two baririçó purgatives, every week.'"

"'Nothing else?'"

"'I drank the holy water!!!'" [17]

Azevedo notes that it was not just the water that people believed could heal:

"There was also the holy clay, clay that was the mud around the stump, where the patients knelt to get the water poured on their head."

"That clay miraculously cured all kinds of wounds." [18]

The use of the clay sometimes reaches an extreme that leaves Azevedo shocked:

"I saw patients dissolve a bit of that clay in a glass of water and drink, the same clay that had previously been used by people with pustules."

"Pustules!" [19]

The exciting news of the água milagros continues to spread, both by word of mouth and in print. The *Diário do Rio Grande* writes:

"Such virtues have been told of the waters found in Santa Maria da Boca do Monte by a priest of the Society of Jesus that we must also talk about this subject. It is, after all, of the utmost transcendence to society."

"Such staggering effects were attributed to those waters since the beginning that we counted ourselves among the skeptics and believed it was nothing more than tales or superstition."

"Although we knew of how revered and worshiped the Monk was, and having been told that in Pelotas the people ran out to meet him and kiss his clothes and walking stick, we still thought that this was nothing more than an excess of religiosity."

"However, today, we have such testimonies of the miraculous virtues of the holy waters that we believe it to be a duty to proclaim with all our might its undisputed excellence and efficaciousness against all kinds of nervous, syphilis related, or any other sorts of ailments." [20]

The definitive report on the água milagros cures appears in the November 21, 1848, issue of *Jornal do Commércio*, which enumerates 40 *"incredibly real cases."* [21] The acclaimed healings include (see Appendix B for the complete list):

"Rofino Teixeira de Andrade, white, living in Santa Bárbara, age 22. Has been suffering from an internal problem on his right side. He arrived on May 13th, and by May 16th he was perfectly well."

"Nicolao José Manoel, half black/half white, age 26. Had been suffering for over 8 years of asthmatic flux and had a swollen leg that he had broken in three places. He went home completely healed."

"Rita, sister of Rodrigues de Moraes, age 35. Has been suffering from ear pain for 16 years. After six baths, she took some sort of skin shaped like

a funnel and with two little legs out of one ear, and from then on she did not feel anything more."

"Adriana Pompeo do Toledo, from Ramal de S. João. She had a severe wart for 18 years. She is completely well."

"Floriano José Rodrigues, age 55, living in Campestres. S[aint] Lazaro's disease. For 15 years, he could not move his legs and just two months ago, his body became an open wound. Today his health is fully restored."

"A person with almost 58 years of age, living near Arroio Grande, 4th district of Piratiny. A fistula in a dangerous place above his anus, since 1818. With three baths, he was healed." [22]

Government Investigates

Some of the cures reported by the newspapers are likely due to the "placebo effect," a phenomenon in which a person's belief in the curative value of a substance or treatment produces physically measurable beneficial results. Other cures might have resulted from the salutary value of cleaning a wound or from the medication effect of the plants that Agostini appears to have prescribed in some circumstances, such as the case of the leper José Rodrigues. In the ten years since arriving in South America, while interacting with different indigenous peoples, Agostini doubtless learned the medicinal properties of certain plants.

A reader today is likely to suspect that the majority of these "cures" are due to the suggestibility of mass hysteria, rather than out-right fraud. In Agostini's time, the explanations of placebo effect and mass hysteria were yet to be developed. Government officials and the scientific establishment were well-aware that leprosy could not be cured by spring water, and suspected fraud or – perhaps worse – just the ignorance and questionable intelligence of "simple" people. As a result, the Rio Grande do Sul government orders a scientific investigation of the water.

The person selected for this job is medical doctor Thomaz Antunes de Abreu, as he explains in the report of his investigation:

"I was nominated for this by the president of the province, in provincial degree number 141 of June 18th of 1848, to observe the so-called 'holy' waters of the fields of Santa Maria da Boca do Monte. Having been given my instructions by the president on December 30th of the same year, I left in January of this year to the mentioned fields, and, over the course of four months observing, what I say in this report will be the summary of what I observed and will be as close to the truth and as exact as I can be."

"I found between eight hundred and a thousand sick people in the fields, not counting the healthy people who followed them, and this number stayed like this until March. It decreased a lot in April, and it was then reduced to just a few people. By the expected and daily entrance and departure of new sick people, I think their numbers may have reached eight or nine thousand during the prior summer." [23]

Regarding the treatments, Abreu says:

"Just a quarter [of a cup] of water thrown on your head and half a quarter to drink was the dosage."

"The way of using the waters was totally irregular, some took them cold, some took them lukewarm, most of them would go up the Hill to get them when they were sweaty from the effort to go up there, and they would then use them cold, leaving right away, so that they would start sweating right away; others would let their bodies cool down so that they could use the water, leaving afterwards, and some who were not as shy, took them like that too, being restless and sweaty, and rested. This reckless use of the waters and the keeping of the wet clothes on their bodies until they were dry, made them stop sweating very suddenly, and caused acute inflammations of the more predisposed organs." [24]

Abreu's evaluation of the results of the treatments:

"I observed two hundred patients according to their illnesses.... Thirteen made a full recovery, fifty-one got better, many of them I consider to be obvious, one hundred and thirty-three, far from improving, stayed the same, many of them getting worse, and three of them died. With this data, you can see that the favorable results do not overweigh the sacrifices and hardships that the sick people go through." [25]

Here are Abreu's conclusions and recommendations:

"I find that the discovery of these waters are harmful to the province, not only because they are of no special use, but because they make way for all sorts of abuse, and taking into consideration the already critical state of the population, due to the civil war over nine years ago, and the general state of the commercial operations, and lately, the abandonment of the most vital interests of those who went looking for the waters... I am of the opinion that the government, far from protecting this discovery, should find the means to convince the people of their mistakes and stop them from doing this...."

"The doctors should be the ones to say which waters to use for certain illnesses, to prescribe how they should be used, choosing the best places that luckily are abundant in this province...." [26]

Return to Botucaraí

Based on the remarkable healings being reported at Campestre and the obvious veneration being accorded Agostini, it would not be unreasonable to presume that Agostini was beginning to see himself as the conduit of miracles, perhaps even a saint. Not true, however. Agostini writes:

"...I came to a retired solitude in Campestre, where I spent eleven months, moving there from Santa Maria de la Boca del Monte. In this last wilderness, I discovered a mineral spring with wonderful curative proper-

ties, and the place which had been a den for tigers and lions became a prosperous town."

"Ignorant people began to think that the cures produced by the water, and the natural remedies I gave them, were the efforts of my own personal holiness, and I had to leave the place to escape their constant visits and their too great honors." [27]

Agostini leaves Campestre and returns to his previous place at Botucaraí Hill in August, 1848. As Azevedo notes, Agostini was not at Campestre when he arrived in mid-September, and he *"took [his] leave without having seen the monk"* in October. [28]

Agostini left behind at Campestre an organized community which he intended and expected would continue to combine the religious rites he had started with the use of the água milagros. Based on what we know of his later actions in Argentina and New Mexico, he would have appointed officers with defined responsibilities.

A hint of his organization at Campestre is in the stewardship of the alms box:

"This chest was locked with three keys, one of which was kept by the monk and the other two by officers nominated and trusted by the monk. From time to time the chest would be opened, in the presence of the monk, which after taking what he needed for his cult, would distribute the rest to the poor." [29]

Arrest and Deportation

Abreu estimates the crowds drawn to Campestre in the summer of 1848 at eight to nine thousand. Other estimates are lower, but nevertheless sufficient to cause the authorities of Rio Grande do Sul to become gravely concerned about the political impact.

On October 17, 1848, Agostini is arrested at Botucaraí by order of Rio Grande do Sul President Andréa. José Martins da Cruz Jobim describes the arrest:

"General Andréa ...ordered a squad of cavalry to arrest him in order to deport him out of the province...when the Guard arrived, it was night... [they] forced the monk to descend, and in the morning, at dawn, the people, as was usual, flocked to the place. They gathered in a circle around the monk, more than 3,000 people.... [The crowd wanted to resist his arrest,] but he advised the people to let him leave for martyrdom [sake]...." [30]

The crowd of 3,000 probably came mostly from Candelária, only one mile away, upon learning of Agostini's impending arrest, perhaps from seeing the soldiers arrive the night before.

Jobin had a poor opinion of Agostini:

"...he was a fool... being Italian, [he] mixed that language with Spanish and Portuguese, so almost no one knew what he was saying." [31]

Azevedo reports after leaving Campestre, as he boarded the:

"...steamboat that was to take me back to Porto Alegre, the monk showed up with two orderlies, called by president Andréa." [32]

"As I got to Porto Alegre, the responsibility for the monk was passed to the Minister of Justice." [33]

Arriving in Porto Alegre four days after his arrest, Agostini is detained under guard at the state police barracks while authorities decide what to do with him.[34] On November 21, 1848, Agostini's arrest is reported to the public in the *Jornal do Commércio:*

"The Monk João Maria Agostinho, to whom we owe the discovery of the holy waters, was arrested on the hill of Botucaraí on the 17th of October as ordered by the deputy of that district and sent to the capital of the province."

"It seems that the police became aware of the fact that what the Monk was involved in was a threat to the public peace." [35]

After several weeks of indecision, it is decided to deport Agostini to the neighboring state of Santa Catarina. On November 26, 1848, President Andréa writes a private letter to Santa Catarina President Antero Ferreira de Brito explaining the reasons for Agostini's arrest and deportation:

"...the foreigner João Maria Agostinho, commonly known here as Monk, as a police measure [of safety], [is being] sent outside the province for having encouraged great fanaticism about [himself], and [because] he appointed employees and established certain regulations with good intentions, but which were not authorized, that could cause disturbances." [36]

On December 9, 1848, by order of *"his Excellency, the President of the Province [Andréa],"* the commander of the steamboat *Fluminense* is ordered to give *"the foreigner José Agostini, known as Monk, passage to the city of Rio Grande."* [37] And further, at Rio Grande, the *"agents of the Barges Steam Company"* are ordered to give Agostini *"one of the passenger seats to... Santa Catarina on the steamboat Imperador."* [38]

On December 15, Agostini gets off the boat at Desterro, the capital of Santa Catarina. He is received with great friendliness by President Brito, who offers Agostini the hospitality of his home, which Agostini accepts.[39] Agostini probably takes his arrest and deportation with equanimity, but nevertheless, Brito's surprising generosity must have reinforced his feelings of having done nothing criminal.

Grove Island, Santa Catarina

Desterro (now called Florianópolis), is on the southwest side of Santa Catarina island. The island is 33 miles long and 11 miles wide, and *"consists principally of pretty high land; the most lofty summits, however, rise only to a middling height, and are entirely clothed with trees; the ascents are steep, and they are much intersected with deep valleys."* [40] In Desterro, *"the houses are well built, have two or three*

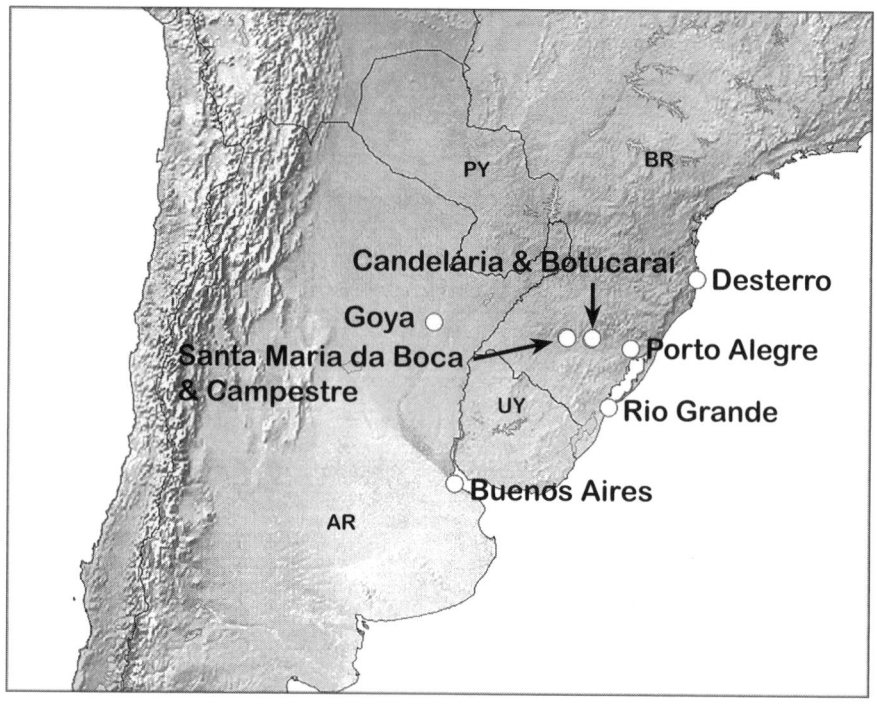

Agostini's travel from late 1847 to December 15, 1848: Goya, Buenos Aires, Porto Alegre, Candelária, Botucaraí, Santa Maria da Boca, Campestre, Botucaraí, Porto Alegre, Rio Grande, Desterro.

stories, with boarded floors.... Besides the church of Nossa Senhora do Desterro [Our Lady of Exile], which gives its name to the capital, it contains two chapels, a convent, a hospicio, and good barracks." [41]

After a few days at President Brito's home, Agostini seeks to leave. Jobim, in what is probably an invented quote, has him saying:

> *"Outside the bar... I see a very large island, that they tell me is called Ilha do Arvoredo [Grove Island]. I ask that you send me to this island, because I am already bored with men and want to live in a remote place, where one sees no one."* [42]

President Brito gives his authorization on or before December 27, 1848, and two fishermen are instructed to take Agostini to the uninhabited island – and to keep quiet about it.[43] Grove Island is about two miles long, heavily forested, and positioned five miles north of Santa Catarina island.

Word that the "Monk of Campestre" is at Grove Island quickly gets around, and Agostini begins to be visited by people seeking his blessings.[44] This causes the vice-president of Santa Catarina, Severo Amorim do Vale, to open a formal investigation of Agostini, worried that something similar to what occurred at Campestre could happen at Grove Island.[45] In the course of this investigation, Vale learns of Agostini's stay at Pedra da Gávea, in Rio de Janeiro, through obtaining the account by

José Francisco Ferreira of his period there (Chapter 5). He also learns of Agostini's meeting with Rosas of Argentina (Chapter 6). These reports make him thoroughly skeptical of Agostini's intentions.

While investigating Agostini's religious affiliations, Vale learns he is not a member of any monastic order represented in Brazil and concludes accordingly that he is not a monk.[46] Vale is well aware that there are many religious imposters who trade upon their presumed "holiness" to take advantage of believers.[47]

On February 10, 1849, Vale gives permission for Vicar Father Joaquim Gomes de Oliveira Paiva to visit Agostini on Grove Island. Oliveira is accompanied by two soldiers, Lieutenant José da Silva Ramos and Major Domingos José da Costa Sobrinho.[48] Oliveira produces a favorable report that successfully assuages Vale's suspicions:

> *"João Maria Agostinho is a true hermit, or anchorite, who, leaving the company [of people], became convinced that he could best serve God in seeking wilderness and solitude, and following the Institute of Santo Antão Abade, still lives in prayer, in complete abstinence, practicing vigils and mortifications. Possessing a background of no ordinary skill, knows Latin and French perfectly, and is well versed in theologies. The truth is that he has not taken holy orders, but in Rio Grande do Sul province, he obtained permission from the Vicar General [to preach].…"*

> *"Through our conversation [I learned] that he had been for some time in Cerro da Gávea in Rio de Janeiro and from there had retired to the South in Buenos Aires, [where he was] at first very welcomed by Rosas who invited him to exercise catechesis, but [became] displeased because his mission was purely evangelical, and the monk had to return to the Province of Rio Grande, where he took up his abode at Cerro Botucaraí and Santa Maria da Boca do Monte."* [49]

Oliveira asks Agostini about the miraculous waters he had discovered at Campestre:

> *"…they were very medicinal, healing for skin diseases, and he, moreover, [used] an ointment [to complete] the healing of wounds. I asked him then if [Grove Island] also had these waters, because I had heard [that] from many people…"* [50]

Agostini denies such waters exist at Grove Island, explaining:

> *"…this was a popular invention that afflicted him, causing public authorities to [consider him] an impostor and [put him under] continual suspicion.…"* [51]

Because people visiting Grove Island seeking his help are disturbing his solitude, Agostini desires:

> *"…to leave the Island, if allowed, and seek in the Andes a more suitable wilderness to live solitarily."* [52]

Oliveira then adds his opinion of Agostini:

"...I am convinced, Honorable Sir, he is not a hypocritical hermit, his austere and penitential life, his frank language, the purity of his morals, and the selflessness of all his earthly affairs [are] witness enough to his virtue. The people, however, coming to the island, full of wonderful ideas and prejudices wanting to drink the well water of [Grove Island], possessing the most ardent faith (which often alone is enough to cure serious diseases, as experience has shown)... cast suspicion on a dignified and admirable individual... [who] has adopted a lonely life, of which there are many examples from the early days of Christianity." [53]

Oliveira's whole-hearted endorsement of Agostini's honesty, austere life, fidelity to his vows, and intelligence contrasts with Azevedo and Jobim's dismissive opinions. His meeting allays Vice-President Vale's concerns about Agostini, which he relays to the investigating authorities in March, 1849, writing that Agostini is simply seeking a *"contemplative life... according to the rule of Santo Antônio Abade."* [54]

To Rio de Janeiro

Nevertheless, Agostini remains a concern of the Santa Catarina government and on May 19, 1849, he is awarded state-paid passage to Rio de Janeiro, as reported in the *O Conciliador Catarinense* newspaper in a section headed *"Report of the Police"* and signed by *"Augusto Galdino de Souza, Police Secretary."* [55] The reason given for the free passage is *"he had no means to pay."* [56]

Agostini is not leaving entirely on his own volition, evidently. The *O Conciliador Catarinense,* reporting on government orders issued by the Secretary of Santa Catarina, writes:

"Order – To the Illustrious President of the province of São Pedro do Sul, letting him know that he did the right thing with the letter of the Frenchman Telemaco Boulrech [Telemachus Bouliech], that was returned as a result of the order of April 27th, concerning the Monk João Maria Agostini." (Order dated May 15, 1849) [57]

This refers to the report on Agostini's activities in Argentina obtained during Vale's investigation.

The following orders are issued by Police Secretary Souza on May 20:

"Order – Praising the good way the Monk João Maria Agostini conducted himself, during his stay in this Province."

"Order – To the agent of the steam boats, it is ordered to grant passage, as a passenger of the state, to the mentioned above, Monk João Maria Agostini." [58]

Although leaving Santa Catarina at the request of the state, Agostini is praised for his good conduct, probably for the political purpose of not alienating his followers.

That same day the passage order is issued, Agostini boards the steamboat *Todos os Santos* commanded by Joaquim Salome Ramos de Asevedo for the three-day trip to Rio de Janeiro.[59]

The *Diário do Rio de Janeiro* reports Agostini's arrival in Rio de Janeiro on May 23, 1849. On the *Todos os Santos* with Agostini is Franciscan Father João Pedro Gay who will encounter and write about Agostini four years later (Chapter 8).[60] This is Agostini's second visit to the capital city; the first was five years earlier, in August, 1844.

Minas Gerais

From Rio de Janeiro, Agostini heads north to Mariana, Minas Gerais, arriving in June or July, 1849.[61] Minas Gerais ("General Mines") is the most mountainous state in Brazil and, as its name suggests, abundantly rich in minerals. Mariana is the state's oldest city, founded in 1696 when gold is discovered in the surrounding mountains. In the hundred years that follow, a massive amount of gold is removed from Minas Gerais mines, about half of the world's production. After that, gold output declines, but it remains a significant economic factor, with Minas da Passagem ("Passage of Mines"), the oldest gold mine in the state, yielding still today. The distance between Rio de Janeiro and Mariana is 250 miles.

In 1846, George Gardner, wrote that a journey:

"...through a hilly and thinly wooded country, brought me to the city of Mariana, the situation and appearance of which pleased me very much; it stands on the S. W. side of a broad level valley, on the gentle declivity of a rising ground which skirts the base of the range of the Serra de Itacolumi."[62]

Some years earlier, visitors Von Spix and Von Martius described the town as:

"...containing 4,800 inhabitants, consist[ing] of small cleanly houses, built in pretty regular and broad streets, and mak[ing] an agreeable impression on the traveler.... There are here a Carmelite and a Franciscan convent and a Theological seminary, at which most of the clergymen in Minas are educated."[63]

At Mariana, Agostini's purpose is to live on Mount Itacolumi, elevation 5,700 feet.[64] Von Spix and Von Martius, who climbed Itacolumi, write:

"When we arrived at the summit of this mountain, we saw some single chains joining the Itacolumi, irregularly crossing each other, and for the most part covered with woods, between which there are deep dark valleys; a gloomy picture, which was rendered still more melancholy by the loneliness of the surrounding scene, and the numerous crosses on the way, erected as monuments for those who have been murdered by fugitive negroes."[65]

From Mariana, Agostini travels to Ouro Preto ("Black Gold"), another mining town, founded in 1671. While there, he offered *"an admirable example of religion and holy life"* to the residents.[66]

Agostini's travel from December 15, 1848 to June 30, 1851: Desterro, Grove
Island, Rio de Janeiro, Mariana, Ouro Preto, Monte Alto, Lapa, Rio Negro.

Monte Alto, São Paulo

From Ouro Preto, Agostini heads 420 miles west, to Monte Alto, in the state of
São Paulo, arriving in July, 1850.[67] Monte Alto is about 220 miles north of Araçoiaba
Hill, at the Ironworks of Ipanema, where he had spent 10 months in 1845, becoming
known as the "Monk of Ipanema." (Chapter 5)

In Monte Alto, Agostini is expecting the delivery of some prayer and missal
books by a Pedro Amado from the city of São Paulo. These are not books for Agostini's illumination, but books he proposes to sell to avoid begging.[68] This is different
from exchanging his own handcrafts for food, as Agostini has done regularly, and
would appear to breach his vow of poverty, but perhaps he does not intend to sell
them, only to exchange them. In any case, Amado fails to show and Agostini retires
to the countryside around Monte Alto to live as a hermit.[69]

By October, 1850, however, Agostini is ready to move on.

Paraná

From Monte Alto, Agostini moves south, to the state of Paraná. Paraná borders
Paraguay and Argentina on the west, and the state of Santa Catarina on the south.
In Paraná, he is not far from Desterro, where he was held after being deported from
Campestre, suggesting that he is probably known in the state by church and govern-
ment authorities.

In Paraná, he appears at Lapa, probably in early 1851. Some Brazilian writers place him there earlier, but without definitive documentation – and an earlier date does not fit with the timing of his visit to Monte Alto.[70] (Lapa is 425 miles from Monte Alto.)

At Lapa, he finds a cave and a spring, just as so many times previously. The cave, known to this day as Gruta Do Monge ("Monk's Grotto"), was described in the 1882-1884 "Inventory Book" of the Parish of Santo Antônio da Lapa as *"just a cavity or cave on top of the hill opposite the town."* The spring is described as *"clear sparkling water that people rightly or wrongly connect with virtue."* [71]

In the "Inventory Book" for 1895, the following appears:

"Three-quarters of a league from the city, we can find a cave at the top of Lapa, with a cross and fountain. The cross and the [water] source are much venerated by the people. In the years 1840-1850 a monk lived there for a short time, who was probably a priest, because he had the permission of Vicar Father Luiz de Carvalho to preach in the main church – the place has never been blessed." [72]

It's unclear how long he stays at Lapa, but it is long enough to attract followers, as he had at Campestre. By June 30, 1851, he is in Rio Negro, also in the state of Paraná.[73]

The area is suffering from a smallpox epidemic when he arrives and the residents are in a panic. They *"implore the Lord to preserve them from the scourge."* In response, Agostini *"recommend[s] they build 19 crosses from the chapel door, straight to the river, ensuring they are [equidistant] from each other."* The crosses are built 30 feet tall, out of hardwood.[74]

Later, a Lieutenant Xavier de Assis:

"...judging [the crosses] to be a barrier to the passage of troops, ordered their removal... except one – the one beside the Chapel – which remained there and became the traditional cross [of the city]." [75]

From Rio Negro, Agostini decides to travel to the "Jesuit Missions" area of Brazil.

Festa do Campestre

The community Agostini formed at Campestre flourished after he left, as Abreu indicates, but for how long is unknown. For many decades it was apparently little more than a revered local tradition. Toward the end of the 19th Century it was revived as a broadly attended annual festival on January 17th, Saint Anthony's feast day.

On January 17, 1901, the newspaper *O Combatente* reported on the festival as follows:

"Today is held the most popular celebration of this county and maybe even of the whole Rio Grande do Sul."

> *"It is a religious celebration [based on] the story of the hermit, a monk who lived here decades ago, preaching under the invocation of the holy saint, today transformed into a festival."*
>
> *"Isolated, in a mysterious silence and prayer, the monk turned the few villagers of these barren lands into fanatics, transforming the hill, in just a few years, into a true Lourdes, where hundreds of sick people from all over the county would go to seek relief from their ailments...."*
>
> *"In a few years time, it was curious to see that on every January 17th, the steep mountain range that leads to the chapel would be filled with believers. Up the hill, counting the seven crosses that have been placed there, with the rosary in their hands, paralytics, crippled, deaf, lepers, blind, rheumatics, all fought for a bottle, a drop of water from the miraculous fountain! And on the small, dirty side of the mountain, without any clean conditions, many would wash themselves."*
>
> *"Up on the hill you can see the old little chapel, about 400 meters above sea level. The hermit – the miraculous monk lived there. There the believers made their requests, after the pain of going up the hill, after which it was mandatory to take a bit of the monk's water."*
>
> *"What some years ago made the population go to the pleasant place – the superstition – has ceased to exist; nowadays people gather there to have fun, to delight, abandoning the city and giving themselves completely up to the picnics, the dancing, to the country pleasure."*
>
> *"So, the 4, 5, or 6 thousand souls that go there on this day, although it is raining, go because everyone is there, to be part of the huge festival, to meet people from the neighboring counties."*
>
> *"Nevertheless, tradition is respected there."* [76]

The Campestre Festival continues today. On the Sunday before the Fiesta, the figure of Saint Anthony is removed from the chapel on the hill and taken to the base of the hill. This practice is said to have originated with Agostini so those too sick or weak to climb the hill can still view the image of the saint. The statue is returned to its place on the hilltop the following Friday.

What may have been the original statue collected by Agostini at Rio Pardo was destroyed in 1951 when the chapel burned (some assert it was the original, others dispute it). The image used today is a replacement.

Santo Cerro do Botucaraí

Botucaraí also has its annual tradition, derived from Agostini's presence. During Easter Week, many hundreds of pilgrims climb the "Holy Hill of Botucaraí." Their goal is to reach the spring located by Agostini, to celebrate his memory, seek solace, and make requests and vows. On Good Friday, 2010, over 7,000 people participated in events staged at the base of the hill.[77]

In February, 2008, Iuri Azeredo described the climb as follows:

"It was a grueling experience, but very rewarding...The trail is steep, slippery at many points, [and] the slope precipitous (calculated at some points to be more than 75 degrees).... But the sight of the trees, some gigantic, and the native vegetation, along with boulders and the flashes of light through the branches and leaves at the top of the forest, is extremely inspiring." [78]

He reports that besides the magnificent view, what impressed him was *"...the incessant wind.... The sound resembled a rough sea."* [79]

At the top of the hill are a shrine and an enclosed alcove to which Agostini's spring is piped. Both are built of handmade bricks that were transported to the hilltop by hand. The earliest report of a structure at the spring is 1863, which likely was built by Agostini or at his instigation. It was destroyed by vandals in the early years of the 20th Century. A bell removed from this structure is now in the Museum of Candelaria.[80]

Gruta do Monge (Lapa)

One mile east of the city of Lapa is the Parque do Monge ("Monk's Park"), which was established in 1962. It is named after the cave, which is little more than a cleft in a rock face, where Agostini lived (Gruta do Monge – "Monk's Grotto"). The grotto is approached through a slit between two high sandstone cliffs and then a steep climb up natural broken rock steps.[81]

The grotto has been a site of pilgrimages since Agostini's presence, traditionally during Easter Week.

In 2008, finding the park in terrible condition, the local government closed it to the public for restoration. As of mid-2013, it still had not been reopened.[82]

Photos

Spring at Campestre – Água Milagros – Discovered by Agostini, 2012.
Courtesy Dr. Alexandre de Oliveira Karsburg.

Opposite, Top: Chapel of Saint Anthony at Campestre, Rio Grande do Sul,
1902. From *Annuario da Provencia do Rio Grande do Sul.*
Opposite, Bottom: Chapel of Saint Anthony at Campestre, 2012. Courtesy Dr.
Alexandre de Oliveira Karsburg.

Santo Cerro do Botucaraí, "Holy Hill of Botucaraí," Rio Grande do Sul, 2008.
Courtesy Celso Martins da Silveira Júnior.

Spring at Botucaraí Hill, 2008. Courtesy Celso Martins da Silveira Júnior.

Chapel at Botucaraí Hill, 2008. Courtesy Celso Martins da Silveira Júnior.

Cerro do Monge, "Monk's Hill," Lapa, Paraná, 2008. Courtesy Pedro Hauck.

Gruta do Monge, "Monk's Grotto," Lapa. Courtesy Parque Monge João Maria.

Plaque of Agostini in Gruta do Monge, Lapa, 2008, photo detail. Courtesy Pedro Hauck.

Chapter 8 | Argentina Again

Agostini is 51. He has been in South America since 1838, 14 years. We have followed him from his arrival in Venezuela through the western countries of South America, down the Amazon River into Brazil, and then into and out of Argentina.

Do we know enough to understand him?

Agostini has created a method of devotional religious practice that is independent of church and clergy.

His modus operandi is to locate an imposing hill or mountain, live there as a hermit long enough to attract the attention of locals, then organize his followers into a "community" committed to supporting annual pilgrimages and devotional rituals. After the community is capable of sustaining itself, he moves on, to do the same elsewhere.

São Borja, Brazil

From Lapa, Agostini travels 550 miles southwest to São Borja.[1] São Borja is located on the Brazilian side of the Uruguay River and 110 miles upriver from Uruguaiana, which Agostini had visited in November, 1846.

São Borja was founded in 1682 as one of the "reductions" of the "Jesuit Missions." In 1608, King Phillip III of Spain granted the Society of Jesus political and economic control over a vast territory located along the upper Paraná and Uruguay rivers with the understanding they were to establish missions to the native Indians, the Guaraní. The plan was to create a utopian-like Christian Indian nation. The area, known as the "Jesuit Missions of Paraguay," encompassed parts of northern Argentina, western Brazil, and most of modern Paraguay.[2]

In pursuit of this goal, over an 80-year period, virtually the entire Guaraní population of the area, over 150,000 men, women, and children, were moved into the Jesuit-established villages.

> "The Indians in each village, or pueblo, or reduction, were subject to the authority of two resident Jesuits. One was called a cura.... He was the manager of all the property belonging to the reduction. The spiritual affairs were confided to the cura's associate, who was known as the vicario [vice-cura]....

> "The Jesuits exercised over their pueblos an authority that was practically absolute...."

> "Each reduction was a little theocracy, in which certain precepts and the will of the cura took the place of formal laws. There was no need of civil laws governing the relations of individual persons to property since the right of property was not one of the possessions of the Indian...."

> *"For violation of the precepts or the regulations established by the curas, punishments were frequently imposed on the offender by causing him to wear in a public place the garb of a penitent; and flogging in the plaza was resorted to for crimes of a more serious nature...."*

> *"The land belonging to the reduction was generally cultivated in common."* [3]

São Borja was the capital of the seven Misiones Orientales (Eastern Missions), located on the eastern side of the Uruguay River. This territory had been ceded by Spain to Brazil in 1750 when the Uruguay River was recognized as Brazil's formal border.[4]

In 1767, King Charles III of Spain expelled the Jesuits from the Missions and confiscated their properties. Within a few decades, almost all the Guaraní had left the reductions and returned to their prior ways of living.[5]

Agostini's presence in São Borja is established by Father João Pedro Gay who writes on January 7, 1852:

> *"Another day I will tell you how the monk José Maria Agostinho, so famous in S. Maria da Bocca do Monte, appeared in this village. He stated his strong desire to preach and my parishioners wanted so much to hear him that I granted the said monk a license in the name of the Vicar General for his prayers, if that's what I can call what he said. The listeners were so displeased by the trivial and unattractive things he said that he was sort of thrown out of the church and the village; some say he headed to the other side of the Uruguay [River], to a place called S. Xavier, on the other side of the ancient place of S. Nicolau, cursing the people for what they did to him."* [6]

This is Father Gay's second encounter with Agostini. When Agostini was deported from Desterro, Santa Catarina, on the steamboat *Todos os Santos,* as a result of the events at Campestre, Gay was a fellow passenger.[7] Gay has a poor opinion of Agostini, likely colored not just by his actions at São Borja, but also by what Gay knows and thinks about his past.

From Gay's letter, it appears that Agostini intends after leaving São Borja to visit the Jesuit Mission villages of San Javier (Argentina) and São Nicolau (Brazil). Both are north of São Borja.

At the time that Agostini is visiting São Borja, the rebellion against Rosas of Argentina is nearing its goal of forcing the Dictator from power. Brazilian forces are strongly supporting the Argentinean rebel army. On February 3, 1852, the opposition decisively defeats Rosas' army in the Battle of Caseros, leading to the Dictator's flight to England.[8]

In the midst of these dangerous events, Agostini must have decided it was prudent to obtain a new passport. As a foreigner in Brazil, he is probably worried about detention as an enemy agent or partisan.

Passport Request at Porto Alegre

On February 10, 1852, Agostini shows up at the police barracks at Porto Alegre seeking an interview with the chief of police. The office of chief is vacant and unfilled, so District Judge Ladislau de Figueiredo Rocha, the acting chief, meets with Agostini.[9]

Rocha is amazed to see Agostini, since he had been deported from Porto Alegre on November 21, 1848, with strict instructions not to return. When Rocha asks him what he wants, Agostini replies *"a passport."* Not knowing how to proceed, Rocha requests instructions from Porto Alegre Vice-President Luis Alves de Oliveira Bello.[10]

Bello replies:

> *"The vice president of the province declares to the Senior Law Judge Deputy Chief of Police in response to your letter n. 62 that you should give the Monk João Maria Agostine the passport he requests, with instructions that he is to leave the province within 30 days; and the same Chief of Police must order all delegates and sub-delegates to not permit the said Monk to linger any longer than required for his travel in their respective districts; if he should exceed the period of time of this passport, then he should be arrested and returned to this capital, and interned."* [11]

The next day Agostini is issued his passport (shown on page 92), which reads:

> *"PASSPORT No. 73."*
> *"Granted February 11, 1852 to João Mª Agostini"*
> *"native Italy"*
> *"subject Italian"*
> *"profession Monk"*
> *"to Paraguay"*
> *"and this has value only for 30 days extendable to exit out of the Province, shall be arrested and sent to this capital in case of exceeding the marked term"*
> *"Age 51 years"*
> *"Height regular"*
> *"Face long"*
> *"Hair short"*
> *"Eyes brown"*
> *"Nose regular"*
> *"Mouth regular"*
> *"Color white"*
> *"Beard lumber"* [12]

The travel restriction is harsh, as Agostini undoubtedly understands. There is no mention of his crippled fingers. This only difference in physical description between this passport and the one issued to Agostini in 1844 is the color of his beard: gray then and *"lumber"* (brownish) now.

Bello then writes to the police chiefs of Taquari, Rio Pardo, Encruzilhada, Cachoeira, Caçapava, São Gabriel, Alegrete, Uruguaiana, and São Borja (where Agostini had just been) – all Argentinean-Brazilian border towns – the following letter:

"On this date, in accordance with the orders that were sent to me by the Presidency, [I] granted a passport to Paraguay to the Monk João Maria de Agostine with the obligation that [he] leave this Province within thirty days; I recommend to the illustrious [authority] that if at the end of this term he is still found in any of the districts, hold [him] and refer to security at this Capital for an appropriate destination [to send him]." [13]

About a month after Agostini leaves Porto Alegre, Bello receives the letter from Father Gay quoted earlier complaining about Agostini's sermon in the church in São Borja.[14] Bello replies to Father Gay:

"As, however, to what you relate about the matter of the Monk, when [they] met, the Vicar was convinced to not be concerned about the sermon [Agostini] gave there; and when he was in this Capital last month, the Police ordered that he withdraw to Paraguay within thirty days." [15]

Monk's Hill – Argentina

Agostini's passport requires he leave for Paraguay. He is not being compelled to travel to the country of that name, however, but to the Jesuit Missions area of Argentina. Agostini doubtlessly meets his obligation to leave within the 30 day period – travelling fast is no difficulty for him.

Father Gay had noted Agostini's intention to travel to the Mission village of San Javier (San Xavier) and that is where Agostini appears next. San Javier is on the Argentinean side of the Uruguay River and is 390 miles from Porto Alegre.

Four miles northeast of San Javier is an isolated hill rising 1,000 feet from the surrounding river plain which draws Agostini's interest and is probably why he goes to San Javier. Today the hill is known as Cerro Monje, "Monk's Hill." After erecting a crude stone chapel at the summit of the hill, Agostini is digging a hole *"with the purpose of planting a cross,"* when he is surprised by flowing water: *"...the water came out of the rock at precisely the highest point of the hill..."* [16]

Looking for a sacred image for his chapel, Agostini finds a figure of the "Lord of the Desert" in the ruins of a neighboring Jesuit mission.[17] The Lord of the Desert is one of the traditional names for Jesus, based on the New Testament story of his temptation by the devil in the desert.

In 1917, the chapel is described thus:

"Inside.... is a crude and somewhat oversized altar, decorated with fabrics, etc., and some hanging ornaments; above the altar there is a wooden Saint of [2.3 feet] in height, even though it is kneeling, depicting the Lord of the Deserts; due to its style one can tell it once belonged to the Jesuit ruins of San Javier, as well as one of the Virgin Mary that is located very close." [18]

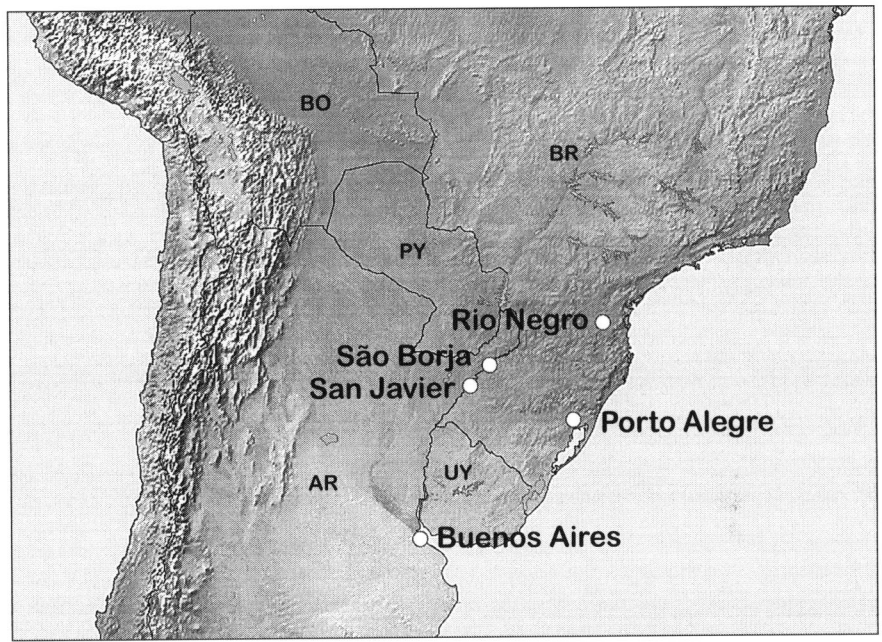

Agostini's travel from June 30, 1851 to August 31, 1853: Rio Negro, São Borja, Porto Alegre, San Javier (Monk's Hill), Buenos Aires.

But this certainly would have dismayed Agostini:

"On one side [of the altar], is a human skull covered with a cloth, and as they believe, it belonged to the primitive monk." [19]

As soon as Agostini begins to attract attention, he establishes a Via Crucis and promotes pilgrimages to the summit.

"...there are two periods during the year in which the arrival of pilgrims [to the hill] becomes considerable: during Holy Week and on the day of the Holy Cross, May 3." [20]

Because the spring is discovered in such an unexpected fashion, it is viewed as having beneficial properties.

"All sorts of sick people come to the Hill on a constant basis with the belief that drinking the holy water will heal them." [21]

In 1897, the spring is described as being:

"20 meters [65 feet] west of the chapel in the center of a large stone.... The hole is covered with a clay tile with two tin jars on top.... This is the miracle fountain from which the sick that wait to be cured... will take water." [22]

To benefit from the water, you must say, *"Give me some water, for the love of God."* [23]

"Further west of [the spring], there is a waterfall of four meters, with the shape of a stream, and that is where the sick can go to bathe... they say the water possesses great healing power for all diseases." [24]

Rules of the Community

On December 14, 1912, the Brazilian newspaper *A República* prints a "curious document." The newspaper notes it was obtained in 1895 by Colonel Telemaco Borba from D. João Queriel, who was given it in the San Javier area.[25] The handwritten document reads:

"I leave this place, and my eternal representative is Mr Antônio Valente, and afterwards his family, if that is not inconvenient, because the twelve protectors can nominate anyone else who is worthwhile, and as a sub-representative his son Januário."

"Each year there will have to be the following holy days: there are 2: the first is of Our Lord of the Desert and it should be held on the Thursday of the Holy Week; and the second one, on the third of May, is of the Santa Cruz."

"It seems to me that no one should be afraid of coming to this Holy Place and visiting the image of Our Lord of the Desert and Santa Cruz, because God will protect everyone; so you shouldn't be afraid of any mishaps, of the waters, the tigers, the snakes, the ill-intentioned men, nor the whole of hell combined, because God is bigger than all of that."

"If anyone is afraid, he shall do the sign of the cross and say with all its heart: 'My Lord of the Desert, help me in this travel, deliver me from sin and from the hell I deserve and from all the evil that can come my way as I travel to this place and everywhere else; Thy will be done and not my own.'"

"There are twelve protectors, all from S. Luiz:"

"1 Antonio da Silva, 2 José Leite, 3 Fidelis Antonio de Oliveira, 4 Joaquim Francisco, 5 Manuel Antunes, 6 Salvador Leite, 7 Urbano Marques, 8 José Antonio Calixto, 9 Antonio Daniel, 10 Antonio de Oliveira, 11 José Sarmento de Souza, 12 is Mr. Polycarpo, that will guide all for the greater good of this santuary."

"May God, in His Mercy, teach them by all the eternal glory of Heaven, as I have taught them here on earth for the benefit of all."

"Month of November of 1852, João Maria Agostinho, Solitary Hermit of Mount Palma Desert, located in the Corrientes province, Saint Xavier people." [26]

This document shows how systematically Agostini organizes his followers. He creates a formal structure with offices to which he names specific individuals, people he must have judged as reliable. He adds an additional layer of institutional longevity by recording it in writing.

The group structure is a leader, a sub-leader, and 12 protectors. The 12 protectors suggest the 12 disciples of Jesus. If a new leader is needed, it is the duty of the protectors to select one.

The document specifies the community support two annual events. Not surprisingly, these are the same as at Agostini's other high places, except Campestre Hill, where the annual festival is on Saint Anthony's day.

Three inferences can be drawn from the document: First, the office holders are expected to care for the chapel and its contents. Second, the annual events are to be supervised. And third, as at Campestre, the community officers are responsible for any alms given by visitors.

Two paragraphs of the document are devoted to addressing the evidently quite real fears of pilgrims. In Agostini's list of threats, he includes – dramatically – *"ill-intended men."*

A interesting detail is the way Agostini signs his name. He gives himself the title of *"Solitary Hermit,"* a title with no formal religious recognition. This clearly reflects his view of himself as someone with no official ties to the Catholic Church or its clergy.

Agostini's establishment of a community with officers was one of the charges made against him when he was arrested four years earlier for his actions at Campestre: *"he appointed employees and established certain regulations with good intentions, but which were not authorized...."* [27]

Consider how distinctive Agostini's method is. He is not founding a church or a mission, the standard evangelical practice of institutional Christianity; rather his devotional rituals are independent of clergy.

This is probably not the first time Agostini has written rules for his followers. Most likely he left similar documents behind at Campestre, Botucaraí, and Lapa.

Fiesta de Cerro Monje

By 1917, the hill at San Javier is widely known as Monk's Hill. The religious practices Agostini established 65 years earlier continue:

> *"The pilgrimages to the Monk's Hill are greatest mainly during the days of the Holy Week when hundreds of people from the villages of Brazil (San Luis, San Borja, San Nicolás, etc.) go there, full of faith in how effective these waters are, they deposit their poor offerings at the chapel, which receives a new coat of paint every year paid by them."*

> *"All of this is spontaneous because there is no priest to lead them in the practices...."* [28]

The stone chapel by this time had been replaced by *"one made of wood erected in its place"* (see page 94) [29]

Pilgrimage, prayer, and bathing in healing water are all practices that Agostini would embrace. But there are superstitious practices associated with the hill that he would not have approved of:

"...most curious is the practice of those getting married, who after going to the chapel and after they both pray, the woman must leave her wedding dress and the flower offerings which she places before the Lord of the Deserts; but because the figure is already dressed with prior dresses, they place the new one over the old one, in such a fashion that it has about ten overlapping."

"The workers and canoers of the Upper Uruguay, before traveling upstream, visit the chapel, drink water from the fountain and light candles to the saints, praying to them for quite a while. If they do not have any candles, they at least light a stub, by means of which they embark content; but if any of them does not, they are branded as a 'mason' and when the canoe suffers a mishap on the rocks, or there is a setback on the trip, the Brazilians above all, complain and with major discontent exclaim: 'This was bound to happen, my friend: you didn't honor the monk!'" [30]

The practice of ascending Monk's Hill during Easter Week continues to this day. On Good Friday, April 6, 2011, thousands showed up to ascend the hill, in spite of *"torrential rain, which hindered access to the site."* [31] In 2013, on Good Friday, an estimated 15,000 people gathered for a reenactment of the crucifixion of Jesus at the base of the hill with most afterwards climbing to the spring and chapel at the summit.[32]

Buenos Aires

The rules document shows that Agostini is at Monk's Hill in November, 1852. By February, he has left, as indicated by the following comments by Father Gay, in a letter dated February 6, 1853:

"But I should tell you that that part of my parish was recently visited by the Monk, who had established his home in a nearby Hill, called S. Xavier, in the western margin of the Uruguay, about half a mile from the river. There the famous Monk raised a Calvary, and sometimes more than a hundred Brazilian people surrounded him, and he occupied them with raising crosses, cleaning the Hill, excavations, etc."

"In those places and close by, they go searching to the people and tell them lies about the Monk that they call Saint, and they go unpunished." [33]

Father Gay remains displeased with Agostini, adding the serious charge of pretending to be a saint to his prior complaints.

By August 31, 1853, Agostini is in Buenos Aires.[34] His actions during the previous six months are unknown.

Photos

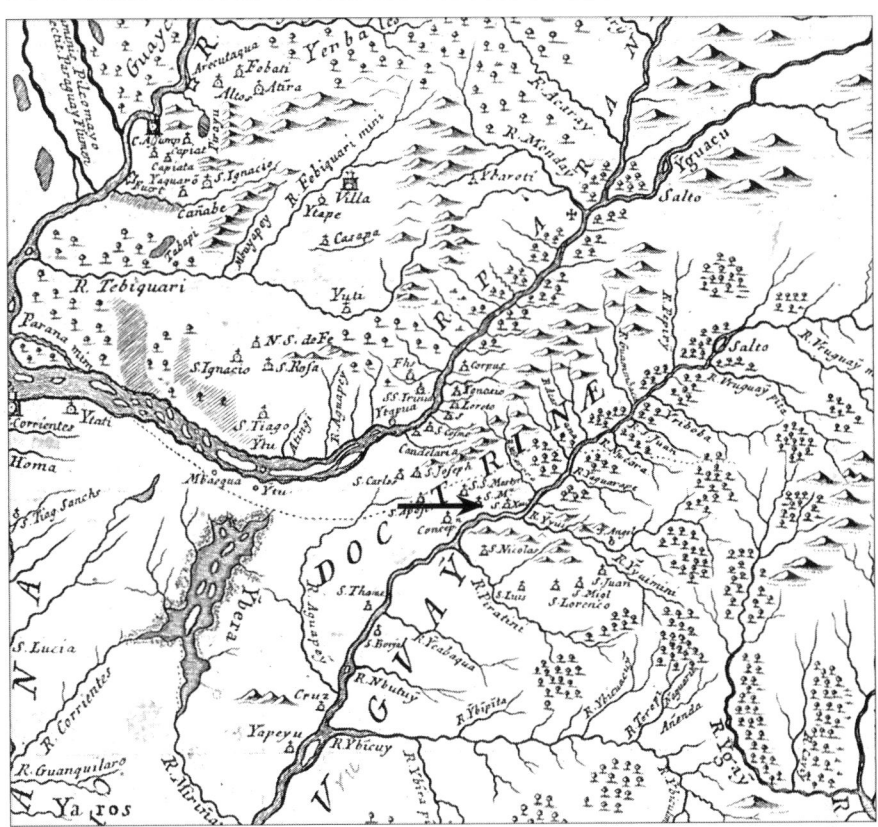

Detail from 1732 map of the Jesuit Missions showing the Reductions. Arrow marks location of San Javier.

Passport No. 73 Issued to Agostini February 11, 1852. Courtesy Dr. Alexandre de Oliveira Karsburg.

Followers of Agostini at Monk's Hill carrying the statues of the Virgin Mary (left) and the Lord of the Desert, 1897. The statues are *"decorated with fabrics."* From *Misiones* by Juan Queirel.

The wooden chapel at Monk's Hill, built to replace the stone chapel constructed by Agostini, 1917. From *Legends & Superstitions* by Juan B. Ambrosetti.

Cross and chapel, Monk's Hill, 2005. Courtesy Loco085, released under GNU
Free Documentation License.

| Chile and Bolivia – Crisis and
Trouble

Toward the Andes

From Monk's Hill, Agostini heads south, to Buenos Aires, a distance of 650 miles, arriving on August 31, 1853.[1] He would have made this trip by boat, down the Uruguay River. This is his second visit to Buenos Aires. Dictator Rosas is gone, but Argentina remains a divided country. Following Rosas' defeat, the winning rebels hold a constitutional convention and create a confederation; but Buenos Aires does not join – it remains independent until 1859.[2]

Agostini's purpose in visiting Buenos Aires is unknown. Probably he is seeking travel documents – or, as we shall see, travel funds. After a few months, Agostini is ready to leave:

> *"I took passage on a French boat sailing up the Paraná River to Rosario. The machinery broke and I landed, bought a horse, and proceeded on my way. Some days later while I had pitched my camp on a desert place by the road-side, and was taking my nightly rest, someone passed along and took my horse. I was thus left without means of continuing my journey."* [3]

This mention of purchasing a horse is the first documented instance of Agostini buying property or paying, however indirectly, for his travel. Presumably, his money comes from a source in Buenos Aires. His destination of Rosario is 180 miles. In September, 1853, Rosario has a population of 4,000. Just one year later, it explodes to over 15,000 residents, because following Buenos Aires' refusal to join the Argentine Confederacy, Rosario is made the Confederacy's official port of entry.[4] One of these huge inflow of immigrants is likely the "ill-intentioned" person who stole Agostini's horse.

> *"Travelling west [from Rosario] I reached the city of Mendoze [Mendoza]...."* [5]

Apparently this is a treacherous part of Argentina. Robert Elwes, who a year earlier made the same trip to Mendoza as Agostini, wrote:

> *"As we advanced, we obtained fine views of the Andes, particularly from one place, about six leagues from Mendoza, where the head of a murderer is stuck on the top of a high pole.... It was tolerably fresh, and appeared to be grinning at us in a ghastly way as we galloped past."* [6]

Mendoza, founded by Spaniards in 1559, is *"built on a flat plain... directly at the foot of the Andes...."* [7] (In 1861, seven years after Agostini leaves, Mendoza is hit by one of the worst earthquakes in South American history, destroying the city. Of the 16,000 or so people living in Mendoza at the time, as many as 10,000 are killed.[8])

From Mendoza, Agostini goes *"to live in a cave some 4 leagues to the west of the town."* [9] There he stays until May 1, 1854, when he returns to Mendoza and obtains the following statement from Father Daniel Báez, superior of the convent of Our Lady of St. Francis:

> *"Don Juan de Agostini chose to follow his vocation to the Solitary life and elected a rugged and shady place to the west of the city where he persevered in the most austere, humble, and penitent life, till he was driven out of his cave by the terrible weather of our winter season."* [10]

Being in the southern hemisphere, May is the beginning of winter in Mendoza. Agostini's purpose in collecting such personal testimonials is to ensure he has character references in any conflict with authorities.

When spring arrives (September, 1854), Agostini leaves for Santiago, Chile, on the opposite side of the Andes.[11] The only viable passage through the mountains is the 12,450-foot Pase de la Cumbre ("Summit Pass"). The pass is closed in the winter due to impenetrable snows. The distance from Mendoza to Santiago, through La Cumbre, is about 220 miles.

Elwes takes this same route to Santiago. On leaving Mendoza he notes:

> *"At dawn we were up and mounted, taking a northerly direction, and skirting the mountains for some distance. The country was parched and barren, only producing a few prickly bushes. We passed another pole with a man's hand and arm... nailed on it. He had been executed for robbery and murder."* [12]

It takes Elwes two days to reach the pass, which he describes as *"a large ridge, serrated at the top with a succession of rocky pinnacles."* [13] He writes:

> *"[The pass is] approached by a zig-zag path, around the foot of which were stretched the skeletons of forty or fifty horses and mules, and among them a few human bones...."* [14]

One of the members of his travel party, *"from a cleft in the rock pulled out part of the skeleton of a man, still retaining a portion of the jacket."* [15]

Chile

After reaching Santiago in October, 1854, Agostini spends three years travelling throughout Chile. Santini lists places Agostini visits, the only documentation available on this period of his life. Without giving dates, Santini notes Agostini's presence in the following Chilean towns: Nacugna, Curicó, Linares, Nacimiento, Melinka, Cartelera, Llevul, Caniular, Marijevi, La Ligua, Lo Oralle, Coquimbo, Copiapó, and La Serena.[16]

In late 1857, Agostini is in Talca, a town on the edge of the Atacama Desert north of Santiago:

> *"My confessor, [the] parish priest of Talca, ordered me to present myself to Don Justo Donoso, the celebrated Bishop of La Serena, to be ordained priest of La Serena, so that I might dedicate myself to preaching and converting the Indians. I felt, however, that I was not worthy of the Sacred*

Ministry; after seeing the Bishop and consulting with him, [I] went to live in the desert of Atacama." [17]

The Atacama Desert is a 600-mile strip of land along the Pacific Ocean. It is the driest desert in the world, experiencing virtually zero rainfall. In 1835, Charles Darwin visited the northern end of the Atacama Desert and described it as a *"barrier far worse than the most turbulent ocean."* [18]

Agostini spends eleven months living in the Atacama Desert.[19] With this action, Agostini avoids being pushed into becoming a priest, but his refusal to accede leads to the greatest moral crisis of his life since accepting the vows of Saint Anthony. He writes:

"In this desolate solitude I spent a great deal of my time within the Holy Scripture in Spanish, and exhorting those who came to visit me. I did not feel at ease about my refusal to be ordained when both my confessor and the Bishop advised me to do so, and this is what I wrote to the Most Reverend Justo Donoso of La Serena:"

"'I have made the vows of chastity and poverty as a religious of Saint Anthony Abbot, obedience I owe to my confessor provided he does not command anything contrary to my constitutions and rules of life. My conscience is ill at ease since I left La Serena. If you think me fit, you may ordain me, [and] I will go out of the desert every Sunday to preach and administer the Sacraments, and several times during the year I shall go and give missions to the people that need it most, and, as long as your Grace lives, shall reside in your diocese, remembering your Grace every day at the moment of the Mass.'"

"'Therefore I ask Your Grace to try me, to search my heart, and see if I am worthy of the ministry which is a terror to the very angels. If I become a priest, I will spend myself like a burning paper in the servitude of the Supreme Lord, our common Father, and our eternal Consoler in the labors of this world.'"

"'I am your humble servant,'"

"'Juan de Agostini'"

"This letter was hardly gone that I felt the weight of my misery more than before, and finally decided not to present myself to the Most Rev. Bishop Donoso, without further consulting with enlightened theologians. I had made vows and had to keep them, as no bishop could dispense me from their obligations. Besides, it did not seem to be the will of God that I should be a priest. I had never felt any inclination towards the priesthood, and on the contrary, dreaded its responsibilities more than anything else in the world. Again, I could not live with the indispensable obligations of the priest to preach and administer the sacraments."

"I wrote a second letter explaining that being unworthy to be a sacristan, I could not accept to be a priest."

"With this I departed for Bolivia."

"Up to this time I had worn the habit of the monastic life, but finally I had to part with it on account of some persons (may God forgive them), but having dropped the habit I was not ready to part with the solitary life, which has always been my vocation." [20]

Agostini's anguish as he wrestles with the demand that he join the priesthood is not made easier by the eminence of Bishop Justo Donoso Vivanco, probably the most dominant Christian intellectual in Chile at the time. Vivanco was born in 1800 and became a priest in 1822. Prior to becoming the Bishop of La Serena in 1852, he had been a lawyer, a rector of the Theological Seminary of Santiago, a member of the faculty of the University of Chile, and the founder of the newspaper *La Revista Católica*. In later years he would be the Chilean Minister of Justice, Worship and Public Instruction and a deputy senator of the Chilean legislature. Vivanco had strong connections with Talca, having been a priest there 1829.[21]

As the result of a complaint against him, Agostini forgoes dressing as a friar, the reason he is so often taken as a monk. This suggests he was threatened with prosecution as a monastic imposter, a serious ecclesiastic offense in a country where the Inquisition was still active.

Agostini, in discussing the pressure on him to become a priest, says: *"With this I departed for Bolivia."* [22]

Bolivia

In Bolivia, Agostini heads immediately for a familiar place, the cave at Mount Illimani where he lived for several months in 1838, just two years after disembarking in South America. He is still agonizing over whether to become a priest:

"In Bolivia, I fixed my abode in the Peak of Illimani and from my solitude wrote to the superior of the Franciscans of La Paz putting before him the case of my ordinations and asking him to decide if I should be ordained or not. I explained to this holy man the kind of life I had led up to the present, and what my sentiments were, without hiding anything from him, which would help him to decide."

"On May 2, 1858, Father José Maria Neva, the Guardian of the Angels in La Paz, answered me that I ought to be ordained for the glory of God and the good of the souls."

"This time it seemed that the will of God was manifest, but as I had still some doubts, I wrote again, and in the following year I received the following letter from Father José Nerva, the New Franciscan Guardian:"

"'Dear Friend,'"

"I tell you with all the sincerity of which I am capable what my conscience dictates to me. You must enter the priesthood to be useful first to the Catholic, Apostolic, and Roman Religion, second to the human society, and finally to the state.'"

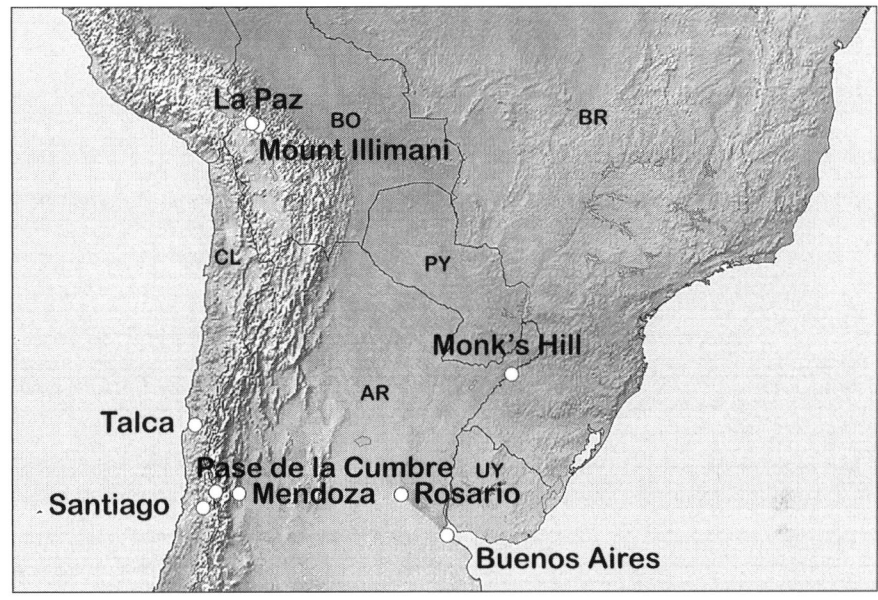

Agostini's travel August 31, 1853 to June, 1859: Buenos Aires, Rosario, Mendoza, Pase de la Cumbre, Santiago, Talca, Mount Illimani, La Paz.

> *"'Dear Sir, do this as soon as possible, there are so few workers in the American countries, that the Gospel is not known as it should be.'"*

> *"'I shall rejoice in my soul when I see you a priest of the Lord.'"*

> *"'José Nerva, O. F. M.'"*

> *"Several other priests had joined the good friar in this decision, among them Father Mariano Sanchez, Pastor of the Church of San Sebastian."* [23]

Despite such immense pressure, Agostini chooses not to become a priest, ignoring the unanimous recommendations – verging on commands – of the distinguished authorities he consults. Wolfe writes:

> *"The author has not been able to find why after so express advice, the good monk still refused to be ordained. There is no further mention of the priesthood in the existing documents."* [24]

Agostini describes his life at Mount Illimani as follows:

> *"My life on Mount Illimani was the same as I used to live wherever I stopped. I would spend the week in my cave, come down on Sunday for the mass, employing the day in doing whatever good I could."* [25]

On November 25, 1858, José María Delgado, magistrate in Cohoni, a small village about 4 miles from Mount Illimani, describes Agostini's cave as *"a place so narrow that he can barely sit in it."* [26]

After five months at Mount Illimani, Agostini decides to leave for Arequipa, Peru. He states as his reason for leaving: *"Some persons, however, did not like my presence, because it was so contrary to their vices...."* [27] His decision to reject the priesthood is also a likely consideration in choosing to leave.

Leaving Mount Illimani, he encounters:

"...official persecutors for the first time. Coming to a village I was arrested by the order of the 'Corregidor' [mayor] who was a drunkard and a man of loose morals. He looked at my passports and kept them, telling me to come for them on the next day."

"The following day, the petty tyrant could not be found. He had locked himself in some of house of debauchery, together with some of his satellites, and would receive no one. Meanwhile, they stole all my possessions: a traveling bag, some Chilean coins, religious pictures, and medals – As I complained and the good people of the village began to move [be upset], they gave me a bad horse with a saddle, and [I] escaped from that den of thieves." [28]

After fleeing from this unnamed village, Agostini reaches La Paz, Bolivia, where he obtains *"new passports"* [29] and spends 20 days resting at the Franciscan Convent of Our Lady of Angels. Agostini is committed to leaving Bolivia as swiftly as he can – and evidently – South America as well.

Chapter 10 | Leaving South America

With his characteristic speed, after reaching La Paz, Agostini moves fast. On June 30, 1859, in the El Alto district of La Paz, Agostini obtains a passport from Police Superintendant Ignazio Zapata stating his destination is Mexico. From El Alto, he reaches Peru by crossing Lake Titicaca.[1] This is his second trip across Lake Titicaca; the first, travelling in the opposite direction, was in 1838.

From the Peruvian side of Lake Titicaca, he travels west to Arequipa, and from there to the Pacific Ocean port of Mollendo.[2] In Agostini's time, Mollendo was the largest seaport in southern Peru.

Since his decision to leave his cave in Mount Illimani, Agostini has traversed more than 350 miles.

Agostini's purpose at Mollendo is to board a ship for Mexico. It is not likely he can obtain free passage, so how does he get the funds for his fare? What little money he had was stolen as he was leaving Bolivia, so he must have turned to monastic or church authorities for this help. It is surprising that either source would give him what would then have been a substantial sum. Yet evidently, Agostini was confident when he decided to leave South America for Mexico that he could get the necessary funds to do so.

Mollendo is without convents or a bishopry in 1859, so Agostini must have obtained the money for his travel at Arequipa. Arequipa was the seat of a diocese and had three monasteries and four convents.[3] Whatever the source, the person or persons were willing to provide him with what he required, trusting him sufficiently to advance the money for his boat fare and probably even some funds for his initial time in Mexico.

Agostini's only comment on leaving South America is:

> *"After several months in this latter city [Mollendo], I embarked for Panama and Guatemala. I had been twenty one years in South America."* [4]

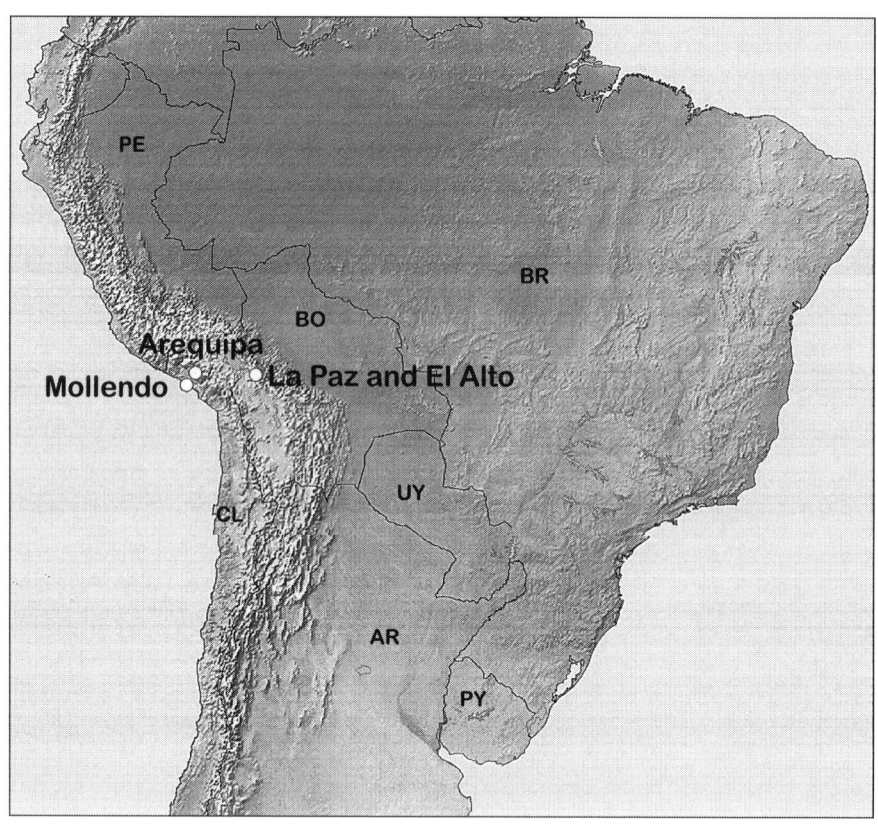

Agostini's travel June, 1859 to November-December, 1859: La Paz, El Alto,
Arequipa, Mollendo.

Mexico and Cuba

From Mollendo, Peru, Agostini embarks for Mexico. He supplies no details on his transit stops in Panama and Guatemala. He almost certainly travels by steamship as regular service between South America and Mexico by that method was established in the 1850s.[1] When he arrives in Mexico is uncertain. Based on dates for his time in Mexico, he probably leaves Peru in late 1859 and arrives in Mexico on or before January 1, 1860, spending only a few weeks or days in Panama and Guatemala.

In Mexico, Agostini lands *"on the coast of the state of Chiapas."* [2] The only port in Chiapas in 1860 is Soconusco (now San Benito).[3] Chiapas is Mexico's southern most state and is located on the Isthmus of Tehuantepec. It borders the Pacific Ocean on the south and Guatemala on the east.

On September 30, 1860, José Farrera y Gonzales, a judge in the village of Macuilapa, writes that *"the monk inhabited for 9 months a cave on the Jineta Mountain [Cerro de La Gineta], leaving the local people in pain when they learned that he was about to leave for the volcano of Orizaba."* [4] Again, Agostini attracts followers with his eremitic life.

La Gineta is a peak in the Sierra Madre de Chiapas mountain range that runs from the southern half of Chiapas through Guatemala and into El Salvador and Honduras. On a clear day, both the Pacific and Atlantic oceans can be seen from the 6,500-foot La Gineta summit.[5]

Pico de Orizaba

Leaving La Gineta, Agostini decides:

"...to go live on the highest peak in North America, the famous Volcano of Orizaba.... I reached El Cerro de las Estrellas ["Mountain of Stars"], or volcano, in November, 1860, and selected as my dwelling place a cave where the snow remained all the year round. It was just above the timber line and was very well suited to my purpose." [6]

The dormant volcano of Orizaba (Pico de Orizaba) at 18,490 feet is the highest peak in Mexico, but only the third highest in North America – geographers in 1860 mistakenly ranked it the highest.[7] The Native name for Mount Orizaba is Citlaltepetl, "Star Mountain."

Mount Orizaba is about 360 miles from La Gineta and located in the eastern state of Veracruz, which borders the Gulf of Mexico. Mount Orizaba is about 90 miles inland from the Gulf coast. The peak is visible from 50 miles out at sea [8] and from the upper slopes you can easily see the Gulf. [9]

In 1848, Brantz Mayer described climbing Orizaba. He found the snow line to be above 12,000 feet. At that point in the climb he noted:

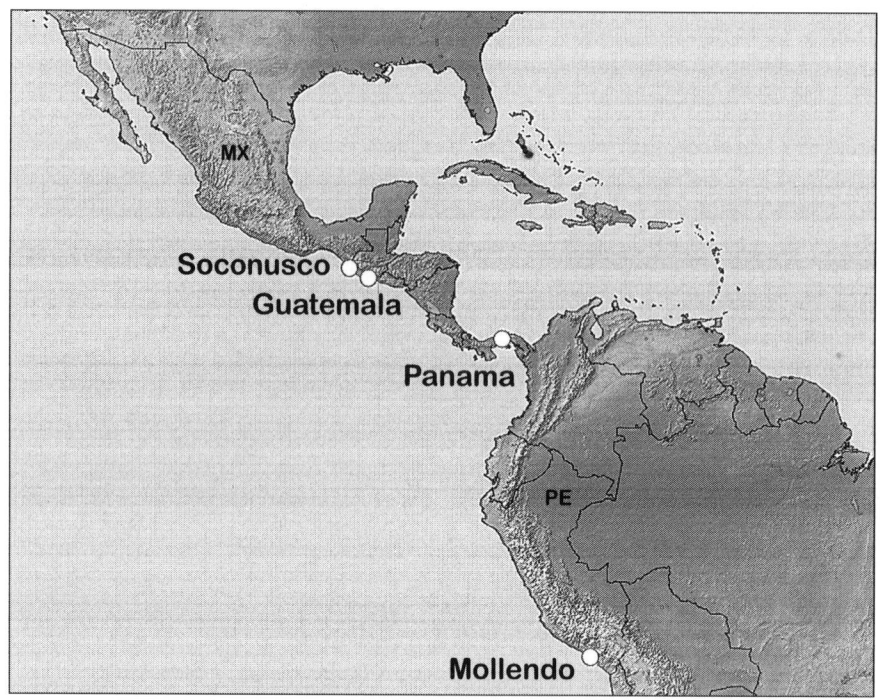

Agostini's travel November-December, 1859 to January, 1860: Mollendo (Peru), Panama, Guatemala, Soconusco (Mexico).

> *"On measuring the slope.... I found it to be 33 degrees. [This] was by far the most difficult portion of our ascent... we seemed to go back as far as we stepped forward, while the rarefied condition of the atmosphere made exertion painful in the extreme.... I can only compare the sensation to that felt by a person who, after running at the top of his speed, is ready to sink down from sheer exhaustion."* [10]

Agostini writes about his life on Orizaba:

> *"The Indians were the only ones that came to see me at first. They came in reduced number in the beginning, but little by little, the numbers increased, and at times as many as 4,000 visited me. Seeing their miseries, I decided to work for their spiritual welfare, and thanks to my long experience, and a certain knowledge of natural sciences, I was able to cure many of their diseases, both body and soul."*

> *"Soon the visits from these Indians and other people became so numerous that I resented them, not having sufficient time for my spiritual exercises. Besides, these good people brought me many things such as wax, fruits, sugar, rice. All this was contrary to my will, because I knew it would excite the jealousy of the clergy and of the civil authorities. In vain did I entreat these good people to refrain from coming to see me, because I foresaw the infamous arrest that they were preparing for me."* [11]

Denunciation and Arrest

By May 18, 1861, news of Agostini's presence on Orizaba is reported in the Mexican press. On that date, the newspaper *La Independencia* publishes a long, alarmist, accusatory letter by José Joaquín de Montes de Oca about Agostini:

> *"Messrs. Editors – I have seen that they have told you something about the hermit that is at the volcano in the jurisdiction of San Andrés; but I understand that it should be strongly brought to the attention of the government, so that they may investigate this issue in more detail, as the common folk are quite fanatical about the events being voiced."*

> *"It is told that four hundred or six hundred people from Orizaba, Córdoba, Coscomatepec and from here went to see this hermit during Easter week; that on Good Friday he fed all these people with two small pots of rice, and there was even some left over; that he preached quite a lot and summoned a reunion for the day of the Cross."*

> *"A person from Coscomatepec, which was here on the third of the current month, stated some two thousand souls from this location and some four thousand from Córdoba and Orizaba were on their way to the volcano on that day; that on the first visit he collected four arrobas of wax and around one thousand pesos of alms; that he spoke to him [the hermit] and heard from his mouth that he was Italian and that he was sixty years of age, that he had traveled through all of South America and had settled in that specific spot, that is to say, the volcano, because it was good there."*

> *"The same person told me that the hermit, of whom I am talking, lives in a cave, wears a bristle habit and treats the people with arrogance."* [12]

Joaquín by accusing Agostini of either perpetrating a con or of planning a civil revolt:

> *"It is also said that he possesses a beautiful garden among the rocks; that he gives everyone relics in exchange for the things they bring him; that he does not take the money from anyone directly, but asks them to deposit it in a basket that he has at the foot of a cross."*

> *"I believe that when that man is able to gather a regular sum, either he disappears or he undertakes a revolution with the fanatics. It is for this reason that I consider it essential to take strong providence with him. It is stated that they have tried to apprehend him and that those who tried to do so started shaking with fear, the moment they saw him."* [13]

Although he has no first-hand knowledge of Agostini, Joaquín fully intends to harm him. Just a month after Agostini had moved to Orizaba, forces led by president-to-be Benito Juárez defeated oppositional forces led by soon-to-be-ex-president Miguel Miramón y Tarelo, ending a four-year Mexican civil war known as the War of Reform. The two sides in the conflict are conservatives, who support a centralized government, and liberals, who support a federalized government. The conservative side is strongly pro-church and the liberal side even more strongly anti-church, to the extant of confiscating all church property in cities under their control.

Juárez's victory as leader of the liberals is made possible largely by financial support he obtains from the United States.[14]

Accusing Agostini of fomenting revolt is a match to gasoline in these circumstances. On May 19, 1861, *El Constitucional* publishes the following:

"The hermit of Orizaba volcano is an Italian friar."

"The authorities have instructed his apprehension because they confirm having reliable information that he is an agent of the revolution."

"The so-called hermit has a beautiful young girl in his cave and he demands contributions from the poor peasants in exchange for rescuing their souls from Purgatory."

"His holiness is such, that he does not touch money; but he demands they deposit it in an enormous basket he possesses." [15]

Of the charges made against him in this article, only the collection of alms is true. At Campestre, Agostini made the handling of donations public and did not take any for his personal use. There is no reason to suppose he behaved differently here.

By May 26, 1861, Agostini has been arrested and taken to Puebla, capital of the state of Puebla. On that date, *El Siglo Diez y Nueve* reports:

"Juan María Augustini has arrived in this capital with his corresponding custody detail....This rare entity, as he states, was used to living in the mountains for more than 35 years; he looks down on society, however he lives off all the poor people he can fool with lies and superstitions with a sense of extraordinary piety. He must be around 56 years old; he wears a blue cape with a red T on it and a hood: he lived at the Orizaba volcano, and presently he has been allowed live at the chapel of the ancient convent of Carmen, devoted today to housing the demented poor." [16]

Agostini describes his arrest as follows:

"One day eighteen policemen, 'Rurales' as they called them, armed like so many assassins, came up to my cave to arrest me. The poor fellows were much afraid and did not dare to come near me. Finally I went to meet them and gave them whatever things I had to eat, and invited them in, that they might take a rest."

"These policemen turned robbers, and took away from me all the things I owned, thus repaying my kindness by the blackest ingratitude. They stole more than 700 pesos worth of things from me, on the way from Orizaba to Puebla. In coin they took some 24 pesos and the rest in various articles such as: lamps, wax, shirts, and other clothing, and several tools for my personal use."

"From jail to jail we travelled till we reached the city of Puebla. It is incredible what I had to suffer among those wolves, lions, tigers, and snakes. Four pawed animals of like names never did me the least harm, but the two-legged ones have caused me too much suffering, but let the Almighty be praised for it all, to the end of time." [17]

In Puebla, he is taken before the governor of the state:

"The Governor of Puebla asked me if I were crazy, and I answered that I was, but that there were many more, crazier than myself."

"And who are they?"

"They are not very far, indeed. There was once a little boy who had a beautiful golden apple in his hand, and that same boy exchanged that golden apple for an ordinary one. For sure, that boy was crazy. And we ourselves, we are crazy, since we exchange God and his eternal glory for the infamous and nasty pleasures of the world."

"The Governor was in no mood to listen to sermons, and he sent me to the garden 'del Carmen,' a beautiful place with many flowers." [18]

Within a few days, the story of the "Hermit of Orizaba" and his arrest reach even the United States. The *San Francisco Bulletin* publishes a letter from a correspondent in Mexico dated May 29, 1861, which reports the events surrounding Agostini's arrest:

"Orizaba was in a fever of excitement. Knots of idlers were posted under the portals, gathered around the fan doors, grouped beside the fountains, swarming in the market place. 'What will they do next, I wonder?'"

"'It's shameful to treat the holy man as if he was a cut-throat.'"

"'Holy man, you say; I tell you it's San Antonio himself, as any one may see that has ever been to visit the blessed Saint.'"

"It seems that some three or four weeks ago a shepherd depasturing his flock in a wild desert region on the flanks of Orizaba happened by chance to enter one of the numerous caverns which dot the mountain side, and was struck dumb by the apparition of a venerable hermit, with long flowing locks and a fiery beard which descended to his girdle, evidently engaged in prayer."

"The news spread like wild-fire, and thousands, undeterred by the toils of the journey and the ruggedness of the road, came from afar with days of travel to see the wonder and receive his blessing...."

"Meanwhile, the rumor spread that the pious hermit was no mortal, but St. Anthony in person."

"The astute but impious prefect of San Andre's suddenly 'smelled a mice.' According to him, the pretended San Antonio was neither more nor less than an Italian monk, busily engaged in organizing a crusade against the Government. He dispatched a body of troops who bundled the hermit into a cart and trundled him off to Mexico, to the unspeakable horror and disgust of the faithful. At departing, he behaved in the most exemplary manner, beseeching the people to be untiring in their supplications to Our Lady of Dolores – and to await the result." [19]

Mental Asylum

The Carmelite Convent of Carmen to which Agostini is taken, had been confiscated by the Puebla government and converted into an insane asylum. The amount of church property confiscated in the state of Puebla was valued at the time at over 50 million dollars.[20] It might be presumed that incarcerating Agostini in an asylum instead of a jail was mere politically expediency, given his popular support; but apparently not totally so, for on June 2, 1861, *El Siglo Diez y Nueve* reports:

> *"A physician has examined Agustini, the hermit, indicating that he does not evidence any symptoms of mental loss."* [21]

Agostini writes of his time in the asylum:

> *"...I was left much to myself and often without the necessary food. When the good people of Puebla knew of my dwelling they came and provided me with every thing I needed; but this life in the middle of a big city, and exposed to the importune visits of friends and foes, was a regular martyrdom."* [22]

In spite of the certification of no mental impairment, Agostini remains confined in the asylum, while state and judicial authorities work out what to do with him. Liberal party control of the government is still tenuous, so authorities fear the effects of either of the options they face: punishing him harshly, which probably would be recognized as political persecution, or letting him go and thereby releasing someone useful to the opposition.

The political nature of Agostini's arrest is recognized by the *San Francisco Bulletin* correspondent, who writes:

> *"Here is a man who, whatever his private vices may have been, had done nothing to countenance or justify the suspicions of a stupid Prefect – living apart from society in the practice of devotional exercises – by military mandate, without form or process of law, seized, loaded with fetters, tumbled into a cart and hurried off to a prison some hundred of miles away."* [23]

The correspondent further states that Agostini's arrest is an example of *"the complete arbitrariness and disregard of civil rights"* of the new *"so-called constitutional government."* [24]

Deportation

After five months of incarceration with no apparent efforts at judicial resolution, Agostini writes *"to the editor of a local paper to ask him to bring the case before the people."* [25] Stimulated into action finally by the press and public opinion, the Mexican Ministry of the Interior, which holds jurisdiction over the country's legal system, issues a judgment based on the investigations of the magistrate assigned to the case. The ministry's legal ruling (not the judge's) is reported in *El Siglo Diez y Nueve*. Entitled *"on the conduct of the Italian, Juan María Agustini, called the 'Hermit,'"* the ruling, quoting six witnesses, alleges:

"Agustini is a lazy vagrant, a true vagabond, who has housed himself in two caves on Citlaltepetl: that his occupation has been to preach Christian morality; but in return he receives offerings from the farmers of the region, be it in the form of money, rice or carved wax." [26]

The ruling then states that seven other witnesses, after affirming the statements of the previous six, add that Agostini encouraged visitors to practice the Rosary and for that purpose erected a series of crosses – and *"at the foot of one… placed a small basket so devotees could deposit their coin offerings."* [27] (The "large" basket is now a "small" basket.)

Agostini's possessions are said to be *"of no real value: some books, worn out clothing, and some other insignificant items."* While he is found to have no money, *"witnesses unanimously declared he would procure a daily collection of anywhere from four to ten pesos, and two of the witnesses were sure that he had an important sum hidden somewhere."* [28]

Thus, *"Juan María Agustini's vagabond status is clearly proven."* And further, the ruling reports as proven that Agostini uses *"trickeries"* to take advantage of *"simple folk… with his own benefit in mind, harming the public morality."* Citing Article 33 of the Federal Constitution, Agostini is ordered expelled from Mexico as *"a dangerous foreigner."* [29]

About his deportation, Agostini says:

"They decided to send me out of the Republic, but fearing some mishap, some interference from the Italian Consul, they decided to take me out by night, and with a force of soldiers numbering fifteen hundred." [30]

On October 26, 1861, the editor of *La Orquesta* prints:

"…our friend Monsignor Antonini, has departed to Veracruz with his conduct escort, and his final destination is the United States: we wish him a good trip… maybe [he] will be happier there." [31]

Cuba

At Veracruz, Agostini is:

"…put on a boat which was steaming for Cuba, and landed in Havana in the month of October, 1861." [32]

Given his desire to go to Canada, Cuba is the most logical place to deport Agostini. The main steamship route between Mexico and New York is by way of Havana. From Veracruz, the passage to Havana takes three and a half days.[33] As a deportee, the Mexican government would pay for his passage, but probably only at the lowest class. In 1861, Cuba is still a possession of Spain.

About his time in Cuba, Agostini writes:

"Thanks to my many letters of recommendation, I was welcome in the Cuban capital, and everyone treated me with respect. In fact, some one having taken my picture sold plenty of them as each one was anxious to

Agostini's travel January, 1860 to October 26, 1861: Soconusco, La Gineta,
Mount Orizaba, Puebla, Veracruz, Havana (Cuba).

possess a souvenir of 'La Maravilla de Nuestro Siglo [The Wonder of Our Century].'"

> *"The flat surface and warm climate of the island did not appeal to a man who had spent 21 years on the highest peaks of the Andes or the Sierra Madre; therefore, I decided to go to Canada and find some place suited to my mode of life. I knew that Canada was a very Catholic country and I expected sympathy from the clergy and people. After the terrible moral sufferings I had endured in Mexico during the last six months, my heart yearned for the love of my fellow creatures."* [34]

"Wonder of Our Century"

The photo Agostini refers to is reproduced on page 114. The photo shows him in the clothes he was arrested in at Mount Orizaba. These clothes are described in *El Siglo Diez y Nueve:*

> *"...he wears a blue coat with a hood, and on his coat is a red T."* [35]

Without this description, one might think that the symbol on his left shoulder is a poorly executed cross – the symbol one would expect him to wear based on the reverence he has for it.

And yes – the "T" is a cross. It a form of the cross known as Saint Anthony's Cross, considered by many early Christian writers to be the original way of representing the cross. For example, the second century author Quintus Septimius Florens Tertullianus (160-225 AD) writes:

"The Greek letter T and our Latin letter T are the true form of the cross, which….will be imprinted on our foreheads in the true Jerusalem." [36]

It is named after Saint Anthony because of the long-held tradition that *"St. Anthony bore a cross in the form of tau on his cloak…."* [37] Virtually all early icons representing Saint Anthony show this T.

In this picture, it is not clear that his left hand is crippled. For a discussion of the other extant picture of Agostini and the iconic imagery of the photo, see Chapter 17.

The title "Wonder of Our Century" suggests he is a public sensation in Havana. All attempts by the author to research Agostini's time in Cuba failed, due to the non-response to written and emailed inquiries by Cuban historical institutions.

Photos

Mount Orizaba, Mexico, 2012. Courtesy Patrick Cushing.

"La Maravilla de Nuestro Siglo." Photo of Agostini, taken in December, 1861, in Havana, Cuba. Agostini is wearing a blue cape. The Tau cross on his left shoulder is red. The photo is clearly taken in a studio setting. Courtesy Palace of the Governors Photo Archives (NMHM/DCA), Negative No. 110764a.

North America

After a just few weeks stay, Agostini departs Havana by steamship, arriving in New York in late November, 1861.[1]

In the United States, the American Civil War is in its beginning stages, started by the attack on April 12, 1861, by secessionist militia on United States forces at Fort Sumter in Charleston, South Carolina. Prior to that date, seven states had announced their secession from the United States, forming the Confederate States of America. In the next month, they are joined by four additional states. President Abraham Lincoln's speech to the U. S. Congress on July 4, 1861, is generally considered as the United States' declaration of war against the Confederacy, no formal war declaration being passed by Congress.[2]

Prior to the Civil War, there is regular direct passage by steamship between Havana and New York, which takes seven to eight days. After the war, only that route is available, as stops at the in-between ports of Charleston and Savannah are no longer possible, due to Union blockade. The ticket price for steerage between Havana and New York is $15-$20, first class is $55-$70.[3] Agostini has no difficulty paying his fee, evidently; it is unlikely that the Mexican government paid his passage through to New York.

Canada

After only a few days in New York, Agostini leaves for Montreal, Canada.[4] His goal is *"to penetrate [the] Canadian forests, in order to preach to the Red Men."* [5] The distance between New York and Montreal is 370 miles – which he traverses by foot.[6]

About his time in Canada, Agostini says:

"But God had decided to try his servant. The cold climate of New France seemed to have congealed the heart of its inhabitants. My ragged clothes and mean appearance did not appeal to the Canadians, and I soon found that my ignorance of the French which I understood but could not speak, would work against me. I could not address the people and explain my attitude toward life, and my particular vocation; they distrusted me and ran away from me."

"It was the saddest period of my life. What was I to do? Return to my beloved Italy? The thought came to my mind as a temptation to relax in the resolution I had made of never again setting foot on my native land; to stay in Canada seemed impossible as I could hardly get enough to keep soul and body together." [7]

His decision, finally, is *"to go West."* [8]

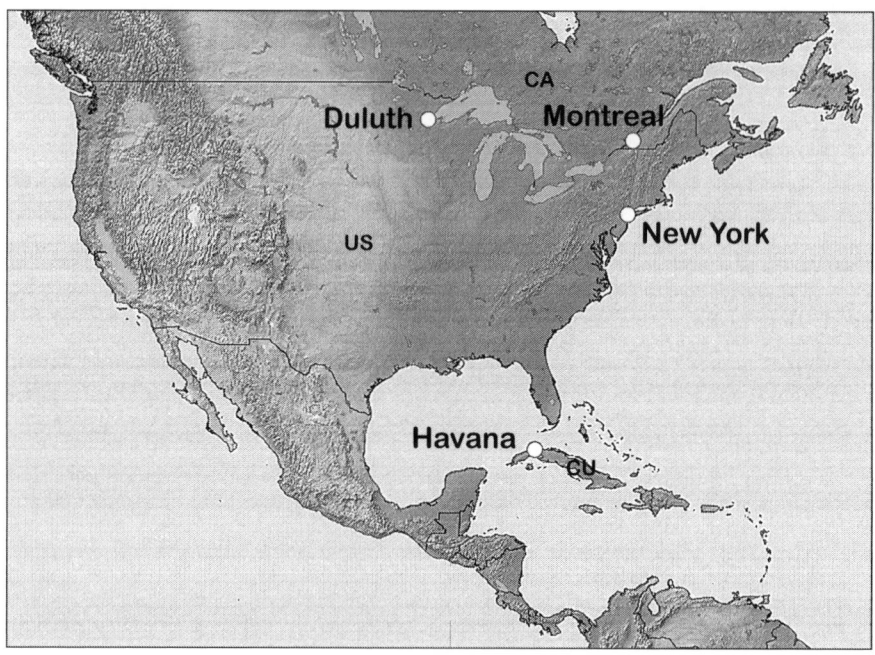

Agostini's travel mid-November, 1861 to July-August 1862: Havana, New York, Montreal, Duluth.

St. Louis, Missouri

By the time he decides to leave Canada, Agostini has been there eight months. He has crossed the states of Quebec and Ontario, a 1,200-mile trek through harsh, mostly unsettled territory.[9] His likely entry point into the United States is the Lake Superior port city of Duluth, Minnesota, which has regular steamboat connections with Canadian cities. From Duluth, he travels west toward the Mississippi River. After striking the Mississippi, probably at Minneapolis, he boats down it by canoe, to St. Louis, Missouri, a distance of roughly 780 miles.[10]

At St. Louis, on September 24, 1862, Agostini obtains a passport from the Italian Vice Consul. The passport states:

"Personally appeared before me, Louis Paris, Vice Consul for Italy at St. Louis, Mo., Rev. Giovanni Maria de Agustiniani, a monk of the Order of St. Anthony, a native of Italy, residing in the deserts of America, subject of His Majesty Victor Emanuel, King of Italy, who has been duly identified and who declares that he never renounced allegiance to his native land. Therefore do I politely request all civil and military authorities of the United States to let him circulate freely and protect him if necessary." [11]

Agostini also receives a military transit pass:

"This man's age is so evident that he needs no Certificate of exemption and the Guard should not molest him. By order of Jno. M. Keane, colonel commanding." [12]

Although, during the Civil War, St. Louis remained under Union control, there are battles and guerrilla actions between the two sides virtually everywhere else within the state, making Missouri a notably dangerous place to travel in 1862. The transit pass by Keane asks the "Guard" to permit Agostini free and untrammeled passage. Possibly, this refers to the Missouri State Guard, a Confederate militia created in 1861. If so, then Agostini has paperwork to protect him in any encounter with Confederate forces. The pass also confirms that Agostini is not subject to military draft, due to his age, and needs no formal certificate of that status. (The author was unable to identify Col. Keane.)

Westport, Missouri

From St. Louis, Agostini walks to Westport, Missouri, 250 miles, arriving in the fall of 1862.[13] Westport is the primary outfitting point for freight caravans traveling down the Santa Fe Trail, the traditional trading route into New Mexico Territory.[14] James F. Meline, who rode the Santa Fe Trail by horseback in 1866, describes passing:

"...numbers of the ox trains used in freighting merchandise to New Mexico."

"They are remarkable, each wagon team consisting of ten yokes of fine oxen, selected and arranged not only for drawing but for pictorial effect, in sets of twenty, either all black or white, all spotted, or otherwise marked uniformly."

"Each set of twenty oxen draws from 6,500 to 8,000 pounds, and makes the journey... at the contract rate of seven miles per day." [15]

During the Civil War, Westport is the focus of intense military activity. The city remains throughout in Union hands, but Confederates try several times to capture the city.

Agostini spends eight months at Westport. While there, he is interviewed by the *Kansas City Journal.* Noting that he had *"the pleasure of a sight of a real genuine live hermit, Don Juan Maria de Augustinian, a man of world wide notoriety,"* the interviewer writes:

"For the past thirty years he has dwelt in rocks and caves, and hollow trees, having the wild animals for his fellows, never during that time having entered a house unless especially invited to do so by its proprietor. His diet is very plain, being nothing more than a little meal or flour mixed up and baked on a bit of bark or stone, or in the ashes." [16]

The article reports the following about his travel:

"He came to Kansas City last fall on his way to Santa Fe, but as he would walk the entire distance (he was tendered a free ride, but declined, as he did not like to mingle with the world), put it off on account of the approaching cold weather, and for the past winter has had his headquarters in a hollow tree some distance from Westport. He is now en route for New Mexico at this time, where he proposes to live with the savages." [17]

Commenting on Agostini's character, the interviewer writes:

"Notwithstanding his age and the hardships he has undergone, he seems to evince powers of great endurance, as all his movements and speech are quick and energetic.... He seems to be a man of more than ordinary kindly feeling for his race, yet dislikes their society and influence." [18]

In preparation for trip down the Santa Fe Trail, Agostini obtains a letter of introduction from three prominent Westport citizens. The letter, dated April 9, 1863, reads in part:

"John Mary Augustiniani, the bearer of this, is a Catholic Indian priest about 62 years of age.... He has certificates from most prominent persons in every part of the globe."

"He is Italian by birth and speaks several languages. He has traveled in various countries and never asks for charity. He has some Spanish books and lives on a little flour, or meal, and water.... When invited, he will sometimes eat with a person, but never asks." [19]

The document is signed by Thomas J. Goforth, J. Bernard, and Fred Chouteau.

Goforth, who had arrived in Westport in 1850, has an outfitting business and a law practice. He is the first mayor of Westport, is mayor in 1863, and serves many times as the town's Justice of the Peace.[20] Joab Mitchell Bernard also comes to Westport in 1854. He is the first postmaster of the town, and like Goforth, runs an outfitting and freighting business.[21] Frederick Chouteau is born in St. Louis, Louisiana in 1820, before the Louisiana Purchase makes Missouri part of the United States. He owns a trading post and is a past Indian Agent.[22]

Council Grove, Kansas

Leaving Westport in early April, 1863, Agostini walks to Council Grove, Kansas (120 miles), the next stop on the Santa Fe Trail, a trip that normally takes ox wagons 12 days.[23] Council Grove is the last place to obtain provisions before the long trek to New Mexico – as suggested by its most famous outfitting post, the "Last Chance Store." [24]

Council Grove is located on the Neosho River, with bluffs on both sides rising *"almost perpendicularly to heights of one hundred, one hundred and fifty, and even two hundred feet."* [25] Agostini seeks his shelter there:

"High on the eastern face of the great bluffs, the stranger had made himself a shelter. This he had done by laying up a rude wall of loose stones until it met the brow of the overhanging ledge at the summit of the hill. This cave-like hovel faced south, and, seated in its entrance, one obtained a wonderful panoramic view of that portion of the valley, and of the old trail winding in from the east." [26]

In 1890, Henry Inman interviewed an old-time resident who recalled the following about Agostini's appearance at Council Grove:

"There came into Council Grove one morning at that time a strange, mysterious character...."

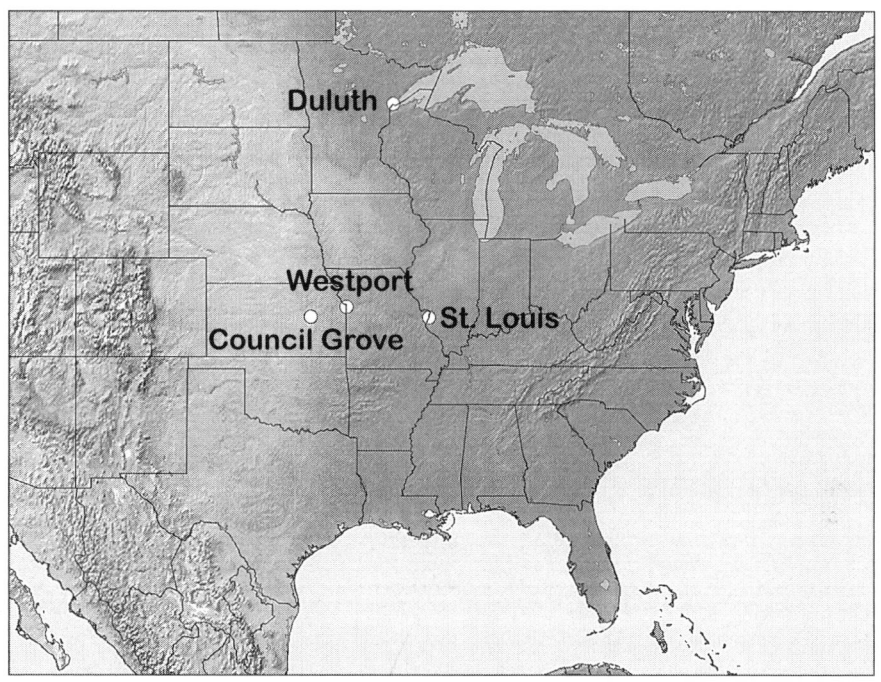

Agostini's travel July-August 1862 to May 1863: Duluth, St. Louis, Westport, Council Grove.

"[He] came as the 'tramp' has since come, unheralded and uninvited; but not to demand bread at the doors of its residents, as the later now does. Nor did he come to tell off his beads in the presence of the vulgar-curious, but he went upon the hillside beyond the town to seek the solitude and retirement of a natural cave he discovered in the limestone rock of the region, troubling no one, but an enigma to the world and a subject for the 'idle gossip.'" [27]

A few days after his arrival, the town newspaper briefly notes his presence:

"The Italian Hermit, Maria Gustianina, a Catholic Priest, is camped in a cave just west of town. He appears rather an intelligent man, speaks nine different languages. He has lived a Hermit some thirty five years; thirty of which he spent in Mexico, sleeping with Tigers and other wild beasts, in caves. Five years he spent in a cave in Indiana. Last winter he lived five months in a hollow tree near Westport Mo. He refuses to eat bread or meat; his food consists of corn meal mixed with water or milk without cooking." [28]

Although full of incorrect facts, this article does confirm that Agostini refrains from eating meat.

On May 28, 1863, Agostini locates an ox caravan willing to lead him to New Mexico.[29] Before leaving Council Grove, Agostini obtains a letter of good conduct and recommendation from *"two doctors and a third person."* The later states that: *"Don Marie Agustini, a Recluse, spent 40 days in a small cave and he is now en route to New Mexico, as a missionary to Indians...."* [30]

The freight caravans loading supplies in Council Grove in 1863 and returning to New Mexico are hauling primarily for the U. S. Army.[31] Southern New Mexico had been invaded by Confederates from Texas in July, 1861. Pursuing the conquest of all of New Mexico, they advanced northward on Santa Fe, occupying it on March 10, 1862. A little over two weeks later, they are defeated by Union forces at the Battle of Glorieta Pass, forcing their retreat back to Southern New Mexico.[32] In early August, 1862, confronted with advancing Union forces from California, the Confederate army abandons Mesilla, their last holding in New Mexico, withdrawing to San Antonio, Texas.[33]

Thus, when Agostini leaves for New Mexico, he is leaving an area where the Civil War is still being fought for an area where the War is effectively over, as New Mexico in 1863 is free of Confederate forces and under U. S. military occupation and government.

Hermit's Cave

The cave in which Agostini lived at Council Grove has been restored and is maintained as a Historic Site by the National Park Service.

Opposite: Council Grove, Kansas, 1890s. Photo taken from the hill where Agostini's cave was located. Courtesy Kansas State Historical Society.

Photos

Hermit's Cave, Council Grove, Kansas. Courtesy
adventuresofacouchsurfer.com

Chapter 13 | Las Vegas, New Mexico

The wagon train that Agostini joins at Council Grove is captained by Dionicio González. It arrives in Las Vegas, New Mexico in August, 1863, after a 9 week, 550-mile journey.[1]

During the trip, Agostini:

> *"...would not ride, either in one of the wagons or on horseback, despite the earnest invitation extended by the master of the caravan every morning. But he trudged along uncomplainingly day after day during the sunny hours, beside the plodding oxen through the alkali dust of the desert and faltered not. Neither at night would he partake of the shelter of the tent offered; persistently refusing, would roll himself up in a single coarse wrap, and seeking a spot on the prairie removed from the coral, for an hour or two under the scintillating stars, he would tell off his beads...."* [2]

Several times during the laborious trek south, Agostini leaves the train, once for eight days. Fearing that he has either gotten lost or been killed, the freighters are surprised when he rejoins them after his long absence, explaining that he has been preaching at Indian villages.[3]

One of the wagon drivers with the caravan is González's bother-in-law, Manuel Romero. Manuel introduces Agostini to his uncle, Miguel Romero, a wealthy Las Vegas merchant. Encouraged by both men, who will become loyal friends and followers, Agostini decides to stay in Las Vegas, rather than continue on to Mexico, his original plan.[4]

Miguel offers Agostini the hospitality of his home, to which Agostini reluctantly acquiesces, but he refuses to *"sleep in a bed or accept any luxuries or comforts."* [5] After a few days, Agostini locates a suitable cave in a canyon several miles south of Las Vegas, on land owned by Miguel, where he adopts his normal routine of solitary devotions, except Sundays, when he walks into Las Vegas to attend Mass.[6]

It is not long before Agostini attracts attention:

> *"People for miles about were so impressed with the religious character of the newcomer that they commenced making pilgrimages in large numbers to his lonely dwelling."* [7]

Hermit's Peak

After many of his visitors begin attributing extraordinary powers to him, fueled by false stories of miraculous cures, Agostini decides to move.[8] With his attraction to high places, it is not surprising he seeks shelter on the nearby El serro del Tecolote, "Hill of the Owl." The "hill," located 20 miles northwest of Las Vegas, rises 3,700 feet above its base. It is topped by a large, flat granite summit, faced with precipitous 1,200-foot cliffs.

Agostini's travel May, 1863 to August, 1863: Council Grove, Las Vegas, Hermit's Peak.

The cave Agostini chooses for his shelter is on a narrow ledge on the southeast side of the mountain a hundred feet below the summit rim, *"under an overhanging lip of granite,"* which can only be reached by descending from above. The cave roof is *"too low to allow [Agostini] to stand erect."* [9] To help shut out the elements and to protect himself from the sheer drop below, Agostini builds a rock wall around the mouth of the cave.[10]

Agostini's initial source of water is a slow drip at the back of the cave.[11] In searching for a better source, Agostini finds a patch of land on the western side of the mountain, which when scooped out, fills with *"pure and crystalline waters."* [12] A later visitor to the spring notes:

> *"Only a low, circular depression in the ground indicated its presence, for on top of the water floated a thick mat of brown and yellow leaves and pine needles. This thick mat had to be scraped away before the clear water of the small pool was revealed."* [13]

The unexpectedness of its location leads in later years to the myth that Agostini finds the spring by striking *"the earth with his staff."* [14]

On the eastern side of the summit, at the brink of the cliff, Agostini erects three wooden crosses, representing the crosses of the Crucifixion, the center cross being the tallest. They are set in piles of rocks and rise 12 to 15 feet. On the path leading to the summit, he erects 14 crosses, each 90 yards apart, for the Stations of the Cross.[15]

After spending one winter in his cave, his followers – which, of course, he attracts at El serro del Tecolote too – insist on building him a better shelter. Three *"roughly constructed wooden huts"* are built in *"a large crevice on the southeast side of the peak... close to three hundred yards below its cliffs."* [16] The shelter intended for living is *"without any doors or windows"* except for a tiny *"opening barely large enough for [Agostini] to squeeze through."* [17] It is *"not more than four feet wide and eight feet long, and of so scant a height that a man of customary stature cannot stand upright in it."* [18] The two other structures are for his possessions, including his books, which consist of *"about eighty volumes."* [19]

In the dwelling hut, Agostini drives large spikes, points inward, around the opening, *"making both ingress and egress a tedious and painful performance."* [20] This leads to the oft-repeated story that the purpose of the spikes is *"to tear at his flesh as he entered,"* as a penance. [21] This is certainly false – they are there to help keep wild animals out, as the opening has no door. [22]

For food, Agostini cooks corn meal *"into a sort of hard mush,"* which he keeps *"in a covered can, slicing it off with a string as he needed it."* [23] To buy the corn meal, he sells hand-made wooden crucifixes or religious emblems on his visits to nearby villages.[24]

In his shelter, even in bitter winter, when there is often four or more feet of snow on the ground, Agostini does not build a fire or use blankets. Margarito Romero, the son of Miguel Romero, reports that when he visited Agostini one February 26th, Agostini was wearing *"no heavy clothing, save an overcoat and a long cape, and there was no sign of a fire"* in his hut.[25]

At this time, Agostini is apparently still wearing his cape with Saint Anthony's Cross, as he is described as having *"formed an order which he called by a Mexican name signifying The Third."* [26] This is a clear misunderstanding of the "T" on the cloak.

As the news that El serro del Tecolote is home to a laudable hermit spreads, locals and visitors begin referring to the mountain as Monte Solitario, "Solitary's Mountain." Over the years, this has become in English "Hermit's Peak," its official name today.

Saved by a Monk

In 1896, Captain Benfrey publishes an account of how he and Mrs. Trethvyn and her 17-year-old daughter are saved from almost certain death by Agostini. The account could be fictional – but it contains enough accurate details to suggest it is based on a true event. Published first in the *Boston Daily Advertiser,* it is picked up and reprinted in other newspapers.[27]

Benfrey states he is in Las Vegas on a leave of absence, recovering from malaria, when he and the two women decide to ride to the summit of "Mount Solitario." It is November in what would be either 1864 or 1865.

The guide they used in prior horseback excursions is unavailable, so they hire a guide they know nothing about, El Lobo ("The Wolf"). They reach the base of the mountain about noon. When they reach the summit three hours later, they notice they have been abandoned by El Lobo. He had earlier tied his horse to a tree, saying he preferred from that point to continue by foot.

Retracing his steps down the mountain to look for El Lobo, Benfrey observes that their tracks are being followed by three Indians. They fail to see him, so he silently climbs back toward the waiting women; on the return, he is shot at by El Lobo and in response he fires twice.

When he gets to the summit, the weather has turned bad and it is beginning to snow. Uncertain as to whether it is safe to descend, they wait. They are not dressed for such cold weather and are getting desperate when they hear *"a surprising sound – the sound of a man's voice chanting a litany."*

Picking their way through the blowing snow toward the sound, they suddenly see a man standing *"beside a little hut of logs, bare-headed, with long hair and beard."* He is *"clad in a monk's frock, bound to his waist with cord... [it is] the hermit, John Augustinian."*

Noting that his tiny hut is too small to shelter them – and that there are enemies *"in their path"* – Agostini says he will guide them down the mountain to safety. He pulls the *"hood of his gown over his head"* and leads the way; they follow in single file on their horses.

Part way down, in a mound of snow, they find El Lobo on his back with an arrow in his chest. Agostini kneels and prays over the body, then fashions a cross out of sticks and plants it at El Lobo's head.

On reaching the base of the mountain, they continue to a small village (probably Gallinas, see page 134). Agostini leads them to the largest house, where he wakes the owner, who welcomes them. The owner sees that their horses are cared for, provides them food, and gives them a place to sleep. He also informs them that two men from the village were killed that day by Indians, probably the same Indians who had been tracking them on the mountain and had killed El Lobo.

Agostini eats only a single tortilla and a small bowl of soup. Expecting to thank him for saving their lives, Benfrey and his companions are surprised to find Agostini gone when they wake in the morning.[28]

Sociedad del Ermitaño

As Agostini expects – and intends – he accumulates followers at El serro del Tecolote. And, as before, he gathers them into a devotional community: the Sociedad del Ermitaño, "Society of the Hermit."

In 1898, the Society prints its rules in a 5-page pamphlet. In 1852, at Monk's Hill at San Javier, for the community he founded there, Agostini created an explicit set of rules – and signed them himself as the "Solitary Hermit of Mount Palma Desert." At Hermit's Peak, he takes a less formal approach. The Society pamphlet, under the heading "Regulations of the Society," states:

> *"[The rules] are same as the Hermit told the first members, when asked to give to them rules and statutes. He said: 'I have the rules that our Holy Mother the Church gives us; scrupulously keep these five precepts and you will be holy without other rules.' Besides, added the Hermit, we do not form a congregation, or brotherhood itself, which needs rules and statutes;*

just a meeting of devout people of the Passion of the Lord, and the Holy Rosary of the Virgin Mary. The Hermit concluded, if you have the willingness to persevere in these devotions, which are easy and profitable, the resulting good will supplant every rule and statute." [29]

Agostini's less duteous approach at Hermit's Peak is probably due to his recognition that an organization with more formal rules inevitably risks conflict with the authority of the church.

Without some rules, no matter how minimal, it is difficult for an organization to survive, which the authors of the pamphlet recognize, for they add:

"Here, then, is the only regulation which we the undersigned offer to our members, namely, a willingness to persevere in the two devotions of the Passion of the Lord and the Holy Rosary. The good volunteers agree to:"

"1. Attend prayer at the two indicated times, which are May 3rd and the first Friday in September;"

"2. Lend themselves willingly to help prepare the Mountain top before the two indicated times;"

"3. Do not lag behind the other faithful in communion and confession, as the ecclesiastical authority has granted us the privilege and joy to have Mass on this admirable Mountain favored with the appearance of the Mother of God and our Mother too." [30]

The sacramental days are Good Friday and Via Crucis (Holy Cross Day), as Agostini had established at Botucaraí, Lapa, and Monk's Hill.

The Society pamphlet specifies three officers:

"The Society of the Hermit, like any society, cannot make progress without a leader. So there will be a president, a vice president, and a secretary; all offices are perpetual with the right to name their successors on the member's death. The current president is Don J. B. [Juan Bautista] Córdova, who was a close friend of the Hermit and has always been loyal to the two devotions. The current vice president is Don Margarito Romero, who lives close to the Mountain, erected the new chapel, and has begun preparing the first, solemn and unforgettable celebration of first Friday, September 2, 1898." [31]

Membership in the Society is open to anyone who has received communion, including women, *"providing they conform to the two devotions without adding or removing anything."* [32]

Finally, in stating the origins and purpose of the Society, the pamphlet says:

"The aim of this society is to perpetuate the two devotions that the Hermit Juan Maria Agostiniani created and left in trust in 1863...."

"His recommendations have been scrupulously followed to date; and some of the first members of the Society of the Hermit, who are still living,

have had the joy of seeing his initial small numbers increase to 62 members...." [33]

The signers of the pamphlet are Benigno Romero, Porfirio González, and Plácido Sandoval. All are from wealthy, influential area families which are early supporters of Agostini. Benigno Romero is the brother of Margarito Romero, and like him, a rancher and Las Vegas merchant.[34] Porfirio González is the nephew of Dionicio González, who guided the freight caravan that brought Agostini to Las Vegas.[35] Plácido Sandoval fights for the Union during the Civil War under the command of General Kit Carson, participating in most of the major battles in New Mexico, is a wealthy merchant, and, at the time this document is signed, is a member of the New Mexico legislature and the Territorial Superintendent of Public Instruction.[36] Both Romero brothers and Plácido have large ranches near Hermit's Peak.

El Porvenir

In 1893, Margarito Romero builds a vacation lodge on his 480-acre ranch at the foot of Hermit's Peak, which he calls El Porvenir, "The Future." The two-story guesthouse has a large, surrounding balcony and sleeping facilities for up to 50 guests.[37]

"Within twenty yards of the hotel flows the beautiful Gallinas [River]." [38]

"Excellent hunting and fishing can be had near the hotel, while the deep, unruffled blue of the sky, the dry invigorating air, the primeval pine forests, with their balsamic odors and ceaseless sounds, conspire to make an ideal resort." [39]

One of the major attractions of El Porvenir is access to Hermit's Peak, for which the resort supplies burros at no additional cost.[40] By burro, the summit *"is only two hours climb from the hotel, at a point 11,000 feet above the sea from the top of which a panorama of great beauty, hundreds of miles in extent, unfolds itself to the visitor's eye."* [41]

For the festivals of the Society, El Porvenir is closed except for those joining in the rituals. On those days, the devotion begins a few hours before dark and consisted of climbing to the summit, pausing to kneel and recite the Rosary at each of the 14 Stations of the Cross, and then praying at the three crosses representing the Calvary.[42] The trail the Society follows:

"...leads through a steep cleft that cuts into the cliffs. Without doubt it is as arduous and wearying as any trail in the mountain range. The last two miles are a snarl of switchbacks with the end never in sight...." [43]

After the Calvary devotion, the penitents light large bonfires on the eastern edge of the summit. These fires are *"visible for dozens of miles and are plainly discernable from [Las Vegas]."* In the morning they return to El Porvenir, where food is served (the first since the morning of the previous day) and *"vesper services are held in the El Porvenir chapel...."* [44]

By 1908, Margarito has succeeded Córdova as president of the Society, probably due to Cordova's death:

> *"Mr. Romero, as head of the Brotherhood of the Hermit, is said to have received the mantle of the prophet, seer and saintly man who for so long a time made his home at the top of the cliffs and proved himself to be a friend of all who then inhabited this region."* [45]

With Margarito's financial backing and the grand facilities at El Porvenir, the Society flourishes. Several hundred devotes participate in the Society's 1908 Via Crucis ritual.[46] A similar number participate in the Society's 1908 Good Friday festival:

> *"Watch Hermit's Peak tonight!"*

> *"Don Margarito Romero... led a party of priests and others to the summit of the towering mountain today and tonight the crest will be lighted by fires, beacons shining as tokens to the faithful."* [47]

The next day the paper reports:

> *"Hundreds in Las Vegas last night saw the beacons at the summit of Hermit's Peak. The great distance made the great fires resemble the glow of a lighted match, but the shadows and reflections were cast until it took but a slight stretch of the imagination to conjure dreams of a volcano."* [48]

On March 15, 1917, Margarito dies after a brief illness.[49] The double blows of Margarito's death and the sale of El Porvenir that follows lead to the Society's gradual breakup. Men and women still show up to perform the devotions on festival days, but as individuals, not as members of the Sociedad del Ermitaño. Within a few years, the annual participants are almost all followers of an unsanctioned religious sect known as Los Hermanos Penitentes, "The Brotherhood of Penitents."

Los Hermanos Penitentes

The Penitentes' self-designation as a "brotherhood" is the reason why many sources, such as the newspaper article quoted above, mistakenly call the Sociedad del Ermitaño the "Brotherhood of the Hermit." The correct name for community founded by Agostini at Hermit's Peak is (in English), the Society of the Hermit.

The Hermanos Penitentes, as defined by the *Catholic Encyclopedia,* are:

> *"...a society of individuals, who, to atone for their sins, practice penances which consist principally of flagellation, carrying heavy crosses, binding the body to a cross, and tying the limbs to hinder the circulation of the blood. These practices have prevailed in Colorado and New Mexico since the beginning of the nineteenth century.... The society has no general organization or supreme authority. Each fraternity is local and independent with its own officers."* [50]

Various sources have suggested that Agostini was a Penitente. There is no evidence of this in Agostini's documents, as recorded by Wolfe and Santini. Milton W.

Callon asked Leo C. de Baca, a descendent of an original member of the Society of Hermits, about this contention. He replied:

> *"The Sociedad del Ermitaño... was founded by a group of citizens who lived around Hermit Peak and it was founded in veneration of the cross. Because it was in veneration of the Cross, on the day of La Invencion de la Santa Cruz (The Finding of the Cross), they would make a pilgrimage up the mountain to Hermit Peak. On the way up they would recite the stations of the cross – the way of the cross. The last station was at the peak which was marked by three crosses."*

> *"This was in direct contrast to the methods used by the Penitentes in their religious ceremonies of flagellation. It was, in a way, an educational program to instruct the people in the proper veneration of the cross without self-punishment. Also, in memory of the Hermit, they would light luminaries on top of the peak, and these lights could be seen as far as Watrous [about 21 miles]."* [51]

Photos

Hermit's cave, Hermit's Peak, c. 1900. Courtesy Milton W. Callon Papers, WH 904, Western History and Genealogy, The Denver Public Library.

Hermit's cave, Hermit's Peak, c. 1900. Courtesy Milton W. Callon Papers, WH 904, Western History and Genealogy, The Denver Public Library.

Hermit's cave, Hermit's Peak, c. 1900. The man standing on the roof of the cave is Margarito Romero. Courtesy Milton W. Callon Papers, WH 904, Western History and Genealogy, The Denver Public Library.

Hermit's Peak, viewed across the Gallinas River, 1911. Photo by Jesse Nusbaum, Palace of the Governors Photo Archives (NMHM/DCA), Negative #061276.

Hermit's Peak with Gallinas, the closest village to the Peak, in the foreground, 1938. Photo by Fritz Broeske, Palace of the Governors Photo Archives (NMHM/DCA), Negative #120600.

Opposite: Society of the Hermit at the summit of Hermit's Peak, 1908. The suited figure in the center holding a cross is Margarito Romero. Courtesy Milton W. Callon Papers, WH 904, Western History and Genealogy, The Denver Public Library.

Visitors on summit of Hermit's Peak, c. 1898. Photo by Rex Studio, Palace of the Governors Photo Archives (NMHM/DCA), Negative #077017.

Members of the Society of the Hermit on the summit of Hermit's Peak, c. 1900.
From The Overland Monthly, June, 1911.

El Porvenir, Margarito Romero's resort, 1908. Margarito is the figure on the front porch, far left. Hermit's Peak visible in background.

New Mexico, Texas, Mexico

On May 28, 1866, after spending three harsh winters on Hermit's Peak, during which he was sometimes confined inside his shelter by deep snow and sub-zero temperatures for 30 days or more, Agostini tells his followers he is *"going to leave them, as it [is] his mission to travel."* [1] On May 31, he obtains a letter of recommendation from his friend Manuel Romero, who writes:

> *"Giovanni Maria Augustine, during the three years he spent in the forests of the territory, exposed to the elements, especially on the Santa Fe mountains, from which Teocolote [Hermit's Peak] is formed, and that he had chosen as his home, even if it is infested by wild beasts and by Navajo and Ute Indians, has never molested any person, nor ever asked for assistance. On the contrary, his ardent spirit of charity urged him to educate all who asked, and to heal the sick."* [2]

From Las Vegas he travels to Mesilla, New Mexico, passing through Santa Fe and Albuquerque (290 miles). At some point on this journey, Agostini joins the wagon train of Ramón González, who is hauling freight from Kansas City.[3] Whether Ramón has any relationship with Dionicio González who had guided Agostini to Las Vegas is unknown.

Mesilla, New Mexico

In Mesilla, Agostini stays initially with Ramón González and his family. He then moves into the home of María Rafaela Barela, the divorced wife of Anastacio Barela.[4] Living with María Rafaela is her oldest son, Mariano, who is the county sheriff.[5] María Rafaela's ex-husband was one of the wealthiest men in Mesilla prior to the Civil War. He supported the succession of the Southern States from the Union, and when the Confederates occupied Mesilla on July 25, 1861, he welcomed them. After Union forces retook Mesilla, Anastacio fled to Texas to avoid arrest as a traitor. Prior to his flight, he divorced his wife and put the family home in her name. Anastacio's other property holdings were confiscated by the U. S. Government.[6]

Leaving Barela's home, Agostini moves to a cave about 12 miles away, called La Cueva, "The Cave." La Cueva is located in a yellowish-brown rock outcropping on the western slope of the Organ Mountains. A visitor in 1871 described it as:

> *"...a nicely arched cave about fifteen feet high and perhaps 60 feet in diameter. It had long been occupied by Indians and the wall and ceiling was covered all over with all kinds of figures made with the smoke of torches on the light colored limestone. The rock in which this cave was [located] seemed to be detached from the mountain and stood on end more than five hundred feet high. We all tried to fire over it with our revolvers but the balls would strike the rock about two thirds of the way up and fall back to the ground."* [7]

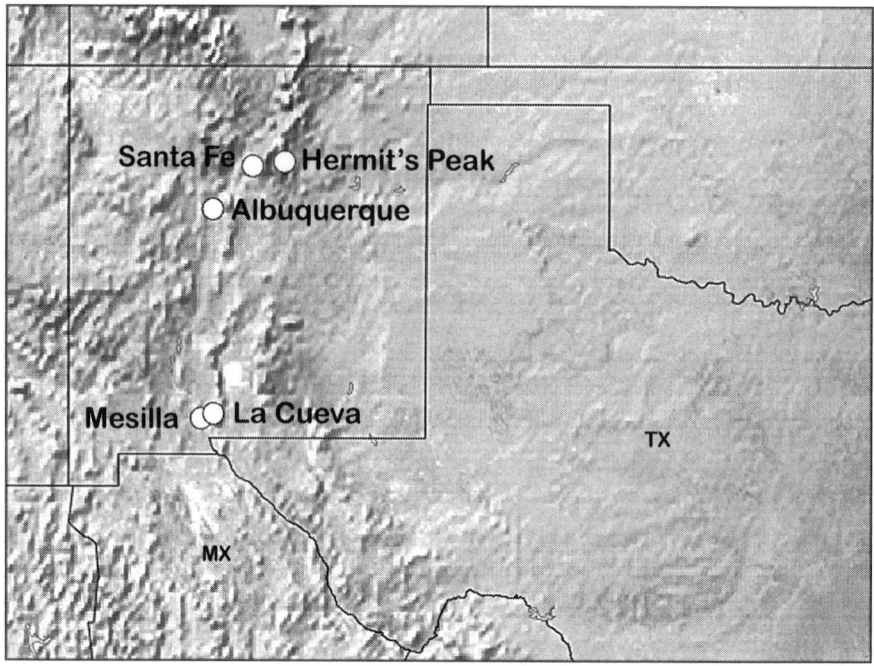

Agostini's travel May 31, 1866 to July-August, 1866: Hermit's Peak, Santa Fe, Albuquerque, Mesilla, La Cueva.

Near the mouth of the cave is "a spring of cold, pure water." [8]

On Sundays, Agostini attends mass in Mesilla. The parish priest, Father José de Jesús Baca, who has family in Las Vegas and is related to Miguel and Margarito Romero, warmly welcomes him:

> *"Father Baca advised the people to respect the Hermit and [to join in] the rosary which was given in the Barela home, where large crowds of people gathered to pray and to hear the Hermit preach."* [9]

On his trips into Mesilla, often pulling a small hand cart behind him with his possessions, he registers in the guest book in the county courthouse (since lost).[10] He dresses as he invariably has since being forced to give up his monk's habit, in a rough tunic tied with a rope, on which hangs a rosary. Over his tunic he wears a cloak tied at the neck with a hood for covering his head. He carries a cane with an attached bell. As has always been his practice, he sells small hand-made items to obtain money for food.[11]

Hueco Tanks, Texas

After a few months at La Cueva, Agostini leaves for Texas, where he finds his next shelter in the Hueco Tanks, a chain of massive granite outcroppings about 30 miles east of El Paso. The range gets its name Hueco, meaning "hollow," from its many naturally-created basins and craters, which collect rainwater.

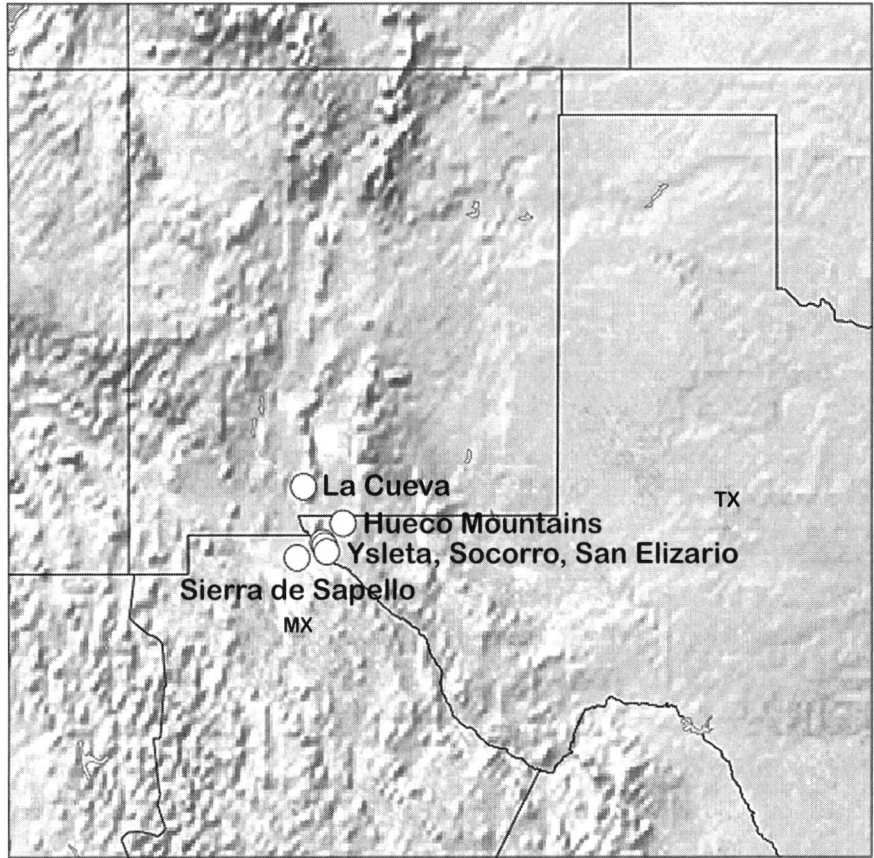

Agostini's travel July-August, 1866 to Winter, 1868: La Cueva, Hueco Mountains, Ysleta, Socorro, San Elizario, Sierra de Sapello, La Cueva.

His presence there is announced by the *Times-Picayune* on December 22, 1866:

> *"A hermit has taken up his abode in the Apache country, in the Hueco Mountains.... He is... believed by the simple Mexicans, who visit him by the hundreds, to be endowed with remarkable gifts, such as the working of miracles, etc."*

> *"He possesses a great quantity of curious books and documents... all of which he seems gratified to show those who visit him."* [12]

The cave in which Agostini decides to live has a narrow entrance: *"A fat man would have some difficulty in squeezing through."* [13]

Sierra de Sapello, Mexico

From Hueco Tanks, Agostini moves on, passing through Ysleta and Socorro, old Spanish mission towns, and San Elizario. He then crosses into Mexico and travels to Sierra de Sapello, "Scrub-Brush Mountain," an isolated range jutting out of the Chihuahuan Desert about 25 miles northeast of Juárez, Mexico.[14]

At Sierra de Sapello, Agostini has a frightening experience. Two men come to the cave where he is living with *"the intention to assassinate him."* He confronts them, saying *"Come on gentlemen I know you have been sent to kill me, I am ready for you."* The men back off, after admitting their murderous intentions.[15]

This story is relayed by Colonel Albert J. Fountain, Sr., a good friend of Agostini's at Mesilla. This is the first time a physical threat has been made against Agostini, as far as any documentation shows, in all of his travels. The declaration that one or more persons want to kill him, for unknown reasons, is certainly surprising.

Return to La Cueva

Fleeing Mexico after the threat on his life, Agostini returns to La Cueva. In a visit to Mesilla, he relates the account of his near murder.[16] To placate the concerns expressed by his friends, Agostini agrees to build a bonfire outside La Cueva every Friday evening. The appearance of this fire, which can be seen from Mesilla, will indicate he is well.[17] He tells them the absence of a fire will indicate that something has happened to him, that he is sick, or that he has gone somewhere. If the cause is that he has left for another place, he will *"leave a note in case you wish to come and see what has happened."* [18]

This is not the first time Agostini has used a signal bonfire to indicate he is alright. He used the same technique at Hermit's Peak, building the fire on the *"northeast brink of the peak,"* where it could be seen by the nearest ranches.[19]

Photos

La Cueva rock formation (foreground), east slope Organ Mountains, facing Mesilla.

La Cueva entrance.

La Cueva interior.

THE HERMIT

Born of noble parents in Italy, probably in 1800, Agostini-Justiniani may have studied for the priesthood but refused his vows and then spent many years walking through Europe, South America, Mexico, and Cuba. He had a photographic portrait made in New York City in 1859.

At age 62 he walked with the wagon train of Eugenio Romero from Kansas to Las Vegas, New Mexico, and lived for a while in Romeroville before settling on Cerro Tecolote northwest of Las Vegas. The hill has since become known as "Hermit's Peak". He had known Penitentes in Spain and got on well with them in New Mexico, for they were in awe of his healing powers and believed in his sanctity. A "Sociedad Del Ermitano" still makes rosaries of native plants to honor his memory at Easter time.

In 1867, he accompanied the wagon train of Don Ramon Gonzales to Mesilla to look up Colonel Albert J. Fountain on a legal matter, then walked to San Antonio, Texas, and then to a cave near Juarez, Mexico. In 1869, he visited often with the Barela family on the plaza in Mesilla, sometimes preaching in their home. He told the Barela family of his plans to live in La Cueva. When the Barelas warned him of the dangers of staying there alone he is supposed to have said, "I shall make a fire in front of my cave every Friday evening while I shall be alive. If the fire fails to appear it will be because I have been killed. I shall bless you daily in my prayers."

Among the many aware of El Ermitano's miraculous healing powers was Antonio Garcia who transported people with illnesses up to La Cueva for healing. The Hermit must have found abundant herbs nearby to help effect his cures.

One Friday night in the spring of 1869 the fire failed to appear at La Cueva. Antonio Garcia led a posse up the mountain to find the Hermit lying face down on his crucifix with a knife in his back. He was wearing a penitential "metal girdle full of spikes." El Ermitano is buried in the Mesilla cemetery. The stone reads (in Spanish); "John Mary Justiniano, Hermit of the Old and New World. He Died the 17th of April, 1869, at 69 Years and 49 Years a Hermit." The Hermit's murder was one of many unsolved murders in the late 1800's in Dona Ana County.

This interpretive sign was made possible by donations at the A. B. Cox Visitor Center. Please stay on the trail and viewing platform so that fragile cultural deposits are not damaged and do not pick up or remove artifacts from the site.

Plaque in La Cueva.

Chapter 15 | Journey's End

It is winter, 1868, when Agostini returns to La Cueva.[1]

On April 30, 1869, the regular signal fire that Agostini builds each Friday night does not appear.

The next day, in the morning, Antonio García, *"a good friend of the Hermit,"* rides to La Cueva to see if something has happened:

> *"I got to the cave. I found the Hermit's books, his bedding and clothing, etc., but the Hermit was gone. I then was convinced that the good Hermit had been killed. I searched for the body for a while, but failed to find it, and then decided to come and report to Mr. Mariano Barela, the Sheriff of Dona Ana. On my way coming back I met two sheep herders with a flock of sheep going to the mountains. I told them that I thought that the Hermit had been killed, but that I couldn't find the body and I promised to give five dollars if they found the body...."* [2]

On Sunday, one of the sheep herders comes into Mesilla and tells García they have found the body.

> *"I reported to Mr. Barela. We invited a few men to go with us. We took a coffin to bring the body in. It had been reported that the body was intact and in a good state of preservation, [and] so it was when we found it."* [3]

García and the sheriff's party, which includes Pedro Onopa and Rodrigo Ruelas, are led to the body by the sheep herder: [4]

> *"It seems that the murders attacked the Hermit while he was in bed, as he only had his underwear clothes on. It appears that he was taken from the cave to the place where the body was found."*

> *"It also seemed that the Hermit knelt down before he was killed. He had a heavy blow on the back of his head. The body was face down, had a crucifix in his hand, both of his lungs were pierced by a sword or a lance, the body was intact notwithstanding the fact that the weather was quite warm being then about the 20th of April, and that there were lots of coyotes, wildcats, mountain lions and other wild beasts, the body was in no way destroyed, decomposed, or molested by wild beasts."* [5]

The body is taken to María Rafaela Barela's house, where a coroner's jury led by Pablo Gamboa rules the death a homicide.[6]

When Agostini's underwear is removed, it is discovered that he was wearing an iron belt:

> *"...with small spikes welded around his waist which must have been... placed there when the saintly man was quite young, as it was so adhered*

to the waist that they had to leave it as it was. He had another sicilian [cilicium] hanging to his breast and back." [7]

The wearing of cilices such as those found on Agostini is a practice that goes back to the first centuries of Christianity. The most common cilice was a "hair-shirt," which is probably what Agostini was wearing on his "breast and back." The iron belt with the inwardly pointing spikes, which had been in place for so long that Agostini's skin had partially grown over it, had probably been donned before he left Europe. Although wearing hair-shirts was a not uncommon practice for monks in the 1800s, iron cilices were rarer. [8]

The intention of wearing a cilice is to inflict pain or discomfort on one's body as a penance. It is a voluntary payment of pain to remind oneself of the suffering of people in the world, and to impose self-discipline.

Following the coroner's inquest, Agostini's body is laid out in María Rafaela's house so that all who want to can *"pay their last respects to the remains of the martyr...."* [9]

That evening, the body is carried from María Rafaela's house to the village church, San Albino. Father Baca performs the funeral Mass for Agostini, which is attended by almost everyone in town. After the service, a large procession of mourners led by Father Baca accompanies Agostini's body to the Mesilla Cemetery for burial. [10] There, following Catholic ritual, Father Baca blesses the open grave; then, after sprinkling the coffin with holy water, he performs the graveside sacrament, ending with a prayer for Agostini's soul. [11]

The San Albino de Mesilla *Book of Deaths and Burials* records the following:

"On the second of May, one thousand and eighteen hundred and sixty-nine, I the priest Don José de Jesús Baca in charge of the spiritual order of the parish of San Albino of Mesilla did bury ecclesiastically in the holy ground the body of Juan Ma. Agostiniani adult from Italy, hermit of the deserts, who did not receive Sacraments for having been assassinated in the mountains and for this I sign."

"José de Jesús Cabesa de Baca" [12]

The following day, a second trip is made to La Cueva to recover Agostini's possessions. On arriving at La Cueva, Sheriff Mariano Barela, who was *"quite a heavy man,"* sits on Agostini's bed. He immediately jumps up, crying *"I am stung."* When the blankets are lifted, Agostini's bed is found to consist of *"a layer of prickly pear cactus"* covered by a layer of grass. [13]

Death Date

Numerous sources give Agostini's death date as April 17, 1869. This cannot be correct. The interment record by Father Baca establishes indisputably that May 2 is the funeral and burial date. This date is confirmed by the timeline established by the account of events by Colonel Fountain: The signal fire is missed on Friday. The search that fails to locate the body is on Saturday. The next day, Sunday, the body is found and brought to Mesilla; with the funeral held that evening.

On May 8, 1869, the Santa Fe *Daily New Mexican* reports Agostini's death:

"The remains of the Italian recluse, who, for the past five or six years, has lived in the mountains of New Mexico, was brought to Mesilla on the second inst. He was killed by Indians in the Organ mountains, and had apparently been dead six or eight days. His mode of life proclaimed him a zealot. He was known by the Mexicans as the Hermitano." [14]

Four days later, the same paper publishes a second death notice, in Spanish:

"The 'Hermit' has died, or better stated the savage Indians, in Doña Ana County, have killed him. The poor Italian walked alone, as usual, in the Sierra of 'Los Organos,' where the Apaches found him defenseless and they killed him in cold blood, it is assumed on or close to April 25, because when they found the body it laid unburied on the mountain for what was seem to be around six days. They took him to the Mesilla on Sunday the second, and he was buried there." [15]

The newspaper puts the date of death as April 25. The facts of the newspaper account are almost certainly drawn from the coroner's report, which, sadly, has been lost.

The first Friday prior to May 2, is April 30. The one before that is April 23. April 17 is the Friday prior to April 23. If the death occurred on April 17, then presumably there would be no signal fire that Friday, and certainly no signal fire Friday, April 23. And yet it is not until after the missing fire on April 30 that a search is made for Agostini.

So why the false April 17 death date reported by prior researchers and even recorded on his tombstone?

The answer probably lies in the erroneous date given by García for finding the body, *"about the 20th of April,"* recorded in Fountain's account. Working backwards from that guess, one could arrive a death date of April 17. The actual date the body is found is May 2, as established by Father Baca's record and the newspaper account, putting April 17 outside the estimated time of the death *"six or eight days"* earlier and conflicting with the evidence of the signal fires.

Culprits Unknown

Who murdered Agostini?

He is roused from his bed and forced to walk either some distance from the cave or to a relatively hidden spot, as García is unable to find the body. He is stabbed twice in the lungs, i.e., chest, which are wounds inflicted from the front. These wounds – an act of intentional cruelty – are not fatal, but they must have been substantial, as they are described as made by a sword or lance, and not a knife. This deliberate torture could have been inflicted either in the cave where Agostini was first attacked, or while forcing him to the death site.

He is killed by *"a heavy blow on the back of his head,"* driving him to the ground, face-forward. He has his crucifix in his hand – the symbol he loved – and is permitted to prepare himself, however briefly, for his death by kneeling and praying.

It is obvious that the killer or killers intended to kill him, and they didn't want to leave the body in the cave. Not allowing him to dress indicates their goal was not captivity. Nor is he stripped to steal his clothes, as they are found in the cave.

All of the early accounts assume Agostini is killed by Indians, drawing this conclusion from the assumption that the chest wounds are by Indian lance and knowing that the Indian danger was enormous. Essentially, it is open war between the Native Americans – the original area residents – and the settlers. About the time Agostini arrives at La Cueva, the *Daily New Mexican* editorializes:

> *"We have almost daily published instances of robbery, murder, and outrages of all descriptions in different parts of the Territory.... there is scarcely any portion of our country that can be traveled over without danger of meeting the savage foe...."* [16]

The use of lances by Indians in attacks was common.[17]

The band of Indians that kills Agostini, if Indians are the culprits, is almost certainly the same band that makes an attack at San Augustin Pass just 12 days after Agostini's death.

> *"On the 7th instant [May 7] four soldiers in company with Don Perfecto Armijo, while coming through San Augustine Pass, were attacked by a party of fifty Indians. A desperate fight ensued in which Corporal Young was killed, and Don Perfecto and two soldiers wounded. Corporal Young fought bravely to the last and fell with fifteen mortal wounds in his body. The party succeeded in getting back to Shedd's ranch, the Indians pursuing them closely, keeping up a rapid fire for three miles."* [18]

San Augustin Pass, the primary pass through the Organ Mountains, is located 12 miles north of La Cueva.

This may be the same band that attacked the town of Tularosa two weeks earlier:

> *"A gentleman just in from the Tularosa reports that on the 23rd Indians to the number of between two and three hundred attacked their settlement. The Indians were certainly formidable in numbers, inasmuch as they were enabled to resist the concentrated force of the inhabitants, who were driven back and glad to fly to shelter. [Two men] were killed, and two others severely if not fatally wounded."*

> *"They killed twenty or twenty-five head of cattle and drove off one hundred and sixty together with six horses."* [19]

Tularosa is about 70 miles east of San Augustin Pass.

Father Chávez Indicted

Agostini's murder by Indians seemed highly likely to those who recovered his body. But then, to the surprise of many, Father Manuel Felipe de Jesús Chávez, the parish priest of Las Cruces, is indicted for his murder.[20] Unfortunately, the legal documents for the case are lost. The indictment is based on the allegation that Chávez incited Agostini's murder for reasons of religious jealousy.

Father Chávez became a priest late in life, at the age of 34. He was born in north-ern New Mexico and had married young. His wife died in 1854, leaving Chávez to raise their three-year old son. In 1859, he was ordained a priest and assigned to La Iglesia de Saint Genevieve of Las Cruces. After two years, he was moved to a series of parishes near Santa Fe, returning to Saint Genevieve in 1867.[21]

In 1869, Mesilla is the county capital. The indictment against Chávez is handed down at the courthouse in Mesilla, although grand jurors would have been selected from the entire county, including Las Cruces, which is located five miles northeast of Mesilla. That a county grand jury was willing to indict Chávez suggests either the belief that Chávez was involved was widespread or the evidence introduced to the jury was highly suggestive of his complicity.

But the reaction to Chávez's indictment by his parishioners is furious indigna-tion, as expressed in their joint letter to the *Daily New Mexican* (in Spanish):

"Las Cruces, New Mexico, May 6, 1869"

"Editors of the New Mexican:"

"I must comply with the painful duty to announce to you that in my humble opinion it is nothing less than an insult, if not an assault on the Catholic Church, to arrest the respectable and estimable pastor, Curate Don Manuel Chávez, for suspicion of complicity in the recent murder of a hermit, who was found recently in the Organ Mountains, at a place notori-ously frequented by savage Indians at a time when they were assassinating others in the vicinity. No man can consider himself safe for a moment when traveling there."

"The human and evangelical feelings of the inhabitants of these vil-lages can not fail to recognize in Señor Chávez his peaceful intentions and character that are a guarantee that his arrest has been made in order to satisfy personal vendettas against the Catholic community, in the person of this reverent and appreciable pastor. By the fact of not admitting bail so that he could represent his cause in court the following day, but that he was to be humiliated by spending the night in the public jail, this seems apparent."

"In the deplorable state of public morality in the times we live in, it would not be surprising that the evidence in this case against Curate Chávez has been calculated in dollars and cents, with the advance knowl-edge that it would cost the humiliation of this congregation."

"MANY CATHOLICS" [22]

On May 9, 1869, the charges against Chávez are dropped (this is two days after the Indian attack at San Augustin Pass).[23]

So Chávez becomes the second possible suspect in Agostini's murder. Chávez's motivation is assumed to be the belief that Agostini, rather then being a respected teacher and exemplar of devotional life, is a malign and perhaps heretical influence.

El Indio Chacón

Connected to the feeling that Agostini was killed because of religious jealousy is the theory that he was killed by an Indian resident of Mesilla known as Chacón. This explanation has been a part of the local oral history of the story of the Hermit from early times. Chacón is said to have killed Agostini either at his own instigation or at the inducement of Father Chávez.[24]

Chacón was *"neither a bright man nor particularly stable."* He claimed to be an Indian Chief, for which there is no evidence.[25]

This story, or something similar, could well have been the basis for Chávez's indictment.

Robbery

This is the fourth theory – robbers. It is based on the (probably untrue) tale that when Agostini left La Cueva for the Hueco Mountains, he was given 40 gold dollars for his trip by Father Baca.[26] He was assumed to still have this money, or most of it, on his return.

According to this theory, Agostini was killed so he could be robbed. The cruel stabbings in the chest are intended to make it look as if he was killed by Indians.

Assassins

This is the most commonly repeated theory by writers – that Agostini had been in fear of his life since his time at Hermit's Peak, and possibly earlier, from unidentified persons who were scheming to murder him – for reasons never explained. This theory probably has its origins in the account of the confrontation at Sierra de Sapello between Agostini and the two men he described then as assassins.[27] Agostini had a predilection for the description "assassin," having used it in reference to the 18 policemen who arrested him at Mount Orizaba.

Author's Opinion

In the author's opinion, Agostini was killed by Indians. The discovery that there was a large band of invading Indians in the Organ Mountains at the time of death, unknown to other researchers, and the eyewitness description relayed by Fountain of how he was killed are overwhelming evidence for this theory. Whereas Indians living in the mountains around La Cueva might have tolerated Agostini, recognizing him as a religious man, a band from outside the area likely had no feelings for him.

I do not believe that Father Chávez had any connection with Agostini's murder. There is no evidence of antagonism between Chávez and Agostini, or between the churches of Mesilla and Las Cruces. Father Baca of Mesilla was a friend and supporter of Agostini and his respect for Agostini probably produced equal respect for Agostini by Chávez. Chávez created 18 principles, which he called his personal "Rule of Life," that he strove to live by. These included:

> *"Retire at 9 or 10 after rosary and night prayer. Rise at 5."*

> *"Half hour meditation on rising."*

"Daily spiritual reading, examination of conscience with reference to one defect."

"Daily reading at least quarter hour of Sacred Scripture."

"Wear always the cassock, sash, tonsure, conical hat, according to diocesan rules."

"Dress neatly but without luxury. Avoid gambling most carefully, worldly company, suspicious houses, and anything that would lead to disruption." [28]

There is nothing in Chávez's known character or behavior that would suggest any act as despicable as inciting murder.

It is impossible to say absolutely that Chacón did not kill Agostini. Discounting the theory that he was induced to do so by Father Chávez, his motivation may have been his mental instability. That may also have been why he could so easily be accused of it.

Murdered by robbers. Agostini may have had a small amount of money, and any amount, no matter how small, can be a motive for robbery. There is no mention in Fountain's account of his death that his possessions showed signs of being searched, and the sheriff was at the scene and fully able to make that judgment; and his surviving possessions of a large cross, several rosaries, and a number of religious medallions, which had some value, were not taken.

The theory that Agostini was living in fear of his life from unknown assassins is not credible, in spite of the near attack on him at Sierra de Sapello. That experience is explainable as an aborted robbery by two criminals hoping Agostini had property worth taking.

Photo

Chacón, unknown date. Courtesy Archives and Special Collections, New
Mexico State University.

Chapter 16 | Burial

The expenses to bury Agostini in the Mesilla Cemetery are paid by Sheriff Mariano Barela.[1]

His gravestone is quarried from a location near La Cueva by Colonel Fountain.[2] The trip to quarry the stone and bring it to Mesilla takes Fountain two days. The marker has the same color as the outcropping in which La Cueva is located, is similar stone, and lays flat over the grave. Fountain engraved the following words on the stone:

> *"Juan Maria Justiniano"*
> *"Ermitaño del Viejo y Nuevo Mundo"*
> *"Lo Murieron el dia 17 de Abril de 1869 a los 69 anos de edad y los 49 haviendo profesado una vida rara en esta siglo XIX"* [3]

In English:

> *"Juan Maria Justiniano"*
> *"Hermit of the Old and New World"*
> *"He was killed the 17 of April, 1869, at the age of 69 years, having professed 49 years a rare life in this XIX century"*

Note the engraving has both his name and date of his death wrong.

Several years after the burial, Fountain places a *"railing around the grave."* [4] There is no sign of this railing today.

Fountain quarried and engraved numerous similar gravestones, such as the one for John Patton, the oldest grave marker in the Las Cruces Masonic Cemetery.

By 1949, Agostini's gravestone is worn to such an extent that it was almost unreadable. That year, an unknown person pays to put up a cement stone marker. The engraving on the cement marker reads:

> *"DON JUAN MARIA"*
> *"DE JUSTINIANI"*
> *"HERMIT ANO"*
> *"MURIO 17 ABRIL"*
> *"1869 A LOS"*
> *"69 ANOS DE EDAD"*
> *"R. I. P."*
> *"8. 12. 49."*

The date on the marker is the date it is placed over the grave.

Debasing Agostini's Grave

In the fall of 2013, some unknown, self-appointed do-gooder decided to put a new stone on Agostini's grave. To do so, this person broke the historic marker created with such effort and affection by Colonel Fountain. This is a gross violation of the historical imperative to NEVER damage an existing artifact. They had absolutely no right to do this. They have my contempt for this act of gross disrespect and ignorance.[5]

Photos

Agostini's cement gravestone, Mesilla Cemetery.

Agostini's grave showing the original flat marker, the cement marker erected in 1949, and the grossly ugly marker added in the fall of 2013.

One of the pieces broken from Agostini's original marker so the self-appointed do-gooder could add their "own" marker.

Chapter 17 | Agostini's Possessions

Books

Apparently undisturbed, Agostini's possessions are recovered from La Cueva the day following his burial. When his diary is opened, the first entry is:

> *"Whoever reads this will know the piety and innocence of Juan Maria de Augustiniani."* [1]

The diary gives Agostini's thoughts on many of the critical moments of his life – for example, the intense clerical pressure he endures in trying to decide whether to become a priest in 1857; or his feelings on having his lamps, wax, shirts, tools, and money stolen by the 18 policemen, *"armed like so many assassins,"* who arrest him at Mount Orizaba in 1861. [2]

Besides his diary, his possessions include his extraordinary travel documents, 152 items wrapped with a piece of cloth and covered with deerskin. [3]

The first owner of these artifacts is the "Salazar family" in Mesilla (no other details known). It is from the Salazar family that Margarito Romero buys them for $200. [4] The last person known to have seen them is Florio Santini in 1970, as related in the first chapter. The author believes these documents today are most likely somewhere in Italy.

Agostini had other books. The two that are known to still exist are in the Mesilla Gadsden Museum. They contain written devotionals, presumably in Agostini's hand (see photos pages 8 and 159).

Photograph

Also in the Gadsden Museum is a deeply intriguing photo (page 160). It belonged to Agostini and the cryptic markings on it are certainly his.

I believe this photo predates the "Wonder of Our Century" photo taken in Cuba (shown in Chapter 11), for two reasons. The simple reason is that he appears younger looking. The principal reason is that he is wearing traditional garments for a monk – without a T sewn to the cloak as in the Wonder photo. Instead, he has *hand drawn* a T on the photo. (The "T" is Saint Anthony's Cross, as discussed in Chapter 11.) This strongly suggests that the photo predates Agostini's unpleasant experience of being accused of impersonating clergy in Chile in 1857. In response to that dangerous accusation, Agostini *"dropped the habit."* [5] And to ensure he is never again wrongly taken for clergy, he sews a conspicuous (red) T on his cape, as shown in the Wonder photo. To avoid any accusation that in the past he has pretended to be clergy, he draws a T on the older photo, which he carries with his travel documents.

In the upper left corner, he has drawn an insignia containing a cross and what the author believes is an M, for "Maronite," indicating his faithful allegiance to the Maronite Monastery of Saint Anthony Abbot.

There is another hand-drawn insignia in the bottom right corner, its meaning unknown, but probably intended to look like an official seal.

The dots under the T and in the two insignias seem to be artistic enhancements. But the dots on his right hand are a mystery.

The photo clearly shows his left hand is crippled, as reported in the two passports quoted earlier in this book (Chapters 2 and 5). He appears to be wearing crude gloves. In the Wonder photo, he is wearing thick hand wrappings. It is surprising, with all the oral and written histories of Agostini over the years, that no one seems to have known he was handicapped.

It has been proposed that the dots represent wounds that Agostini inflicted on himself as penances, a theory with no credibility in the author's opinion.[6]

Saint Anthony Imagery

Shown on page 161 is a woodcut image of Saint Anthony from a book by Théophile Raynaud published in 1649.[7] Even a brief comparison of this image with the circa 1857 photo of Agostini shows how carefully he has posed himself to imitate what is an archetypal iconic representation of Saint Anthony. The obvious correspondences are the habit and cloak tied at the neck, the staff, and the book. Although not shown in the photo, Agostini also carried a small brass bell and rosary with an attached cross, matching those items in the icon. And Saint Anthony is always portrayed with a long beard, just as Agostini groomed himself.

The icon also shows the T cross on the left shoulder, which Agostini will later stitch to his cloak.

The book carried under the arm in the icon is usually interpreted as representing Saint Anthony's deep learning of Christianity due to his long and intense ascetic experiences, even though he was said to not value books highly. This is the one significant characteristic in which Agostini differs from his model – Agostini always has books, and they are a vital part of his life.

The bell which Saint Anthony carried, as does Agostini, is to announce his presence as he walks, to avoid surprising anyone.[8]

Other Possessions

Also recovered was Agostini's cross, bearing the figure of a crucified Jesus, with a scroll emblem engraved with the letters INRI, an abbreviation for the Latin phrase Iesus Nazarenus Rex Iudeorum, "Jesus the Nazarene King of the Jews" (see photo on page 159).

His other possessions are two rosaries, with attached handmade crosses; a small staff, seemingly hardly strong enough to lean on, but with the traditional crooked neck of Saint Anthony's staff; a bell; and two medals. One of the medals shows Mary comforting Jesus and is attached by chain to a ring with outwardly point spikes. It has been suggested the ring is a cilice, the spikes to be used to inflict pain on one-self.[9] More likely the points are used to tell the Rosary. The second medal appears hand-made and shows a cross within a decorative pattern (page 164).

All of these items are in the Gadsden Museum and were collected by Colonel Fountain. They are the only possessions of Agostini known to be extant, other than his documents (wherever they are).

Photos

Cross and hand-written devotional book belonging to Agostini recovered from La Cueva following his murder. Gadsden Museum. Courtesy Archives and Special Collections, New Mexico State University.

Agostini's photo with his hand-drawings, probably taken circa 1857. Recovered from La Cueva following his murder. Gadsden Museum. Courtesy Palace of the Governors Photo Archives (NMHM/DCA), Negative No. 110777.

Saint Anthony icon from *In Symbolicam S.Antonii Magni Imaginem Commentatio,* by Théophile Raynaud. Note Tau cross, book, rosary with attached cross, staff with attached bell, and cape with hood.

Rosaries and cross belonging to Agostini, Gadsden Museum. The small
crosses attached to the rosaries are hand-made, probably by Agostini.
Courtesy Archives and Special Collections, New Mexico State University.

Medal with attached chain belonging to Agostini, Gadsden Museum. The ring with the spikes is probably used to tell the Rosary. Courtesy Archives and Special Collections, New Mexico State University.

Medal belonging to Agostini, resting on a piece of his original gravestone, Gadsden Museum. Courtesy Archives and Special Collections, New Mexico State University.

Epilogue

Two years after Agostini's death, Mesilla resident Enos Cutler and some friends ride to La Cueva looking for *"evidence of an old hermit who... had made his home among these peaks."*

> *"We found a human skull which no doubt was that of the old hermit but as no other bones were found; it is probable that the wolves had torn the body to pieces and scattered the bones in all directions. After having a good time we started for home, but the thought of the old hermit's desolation and death haunted me for weeks afterward."* [1]

Cutler sees Agostini's murder as ending a life of desolation – emptiness, isolation, and loneliness.

But Agostini lived in a different world. He loved solitude. Alone in a cold, bare cave was not an empty world. It was a vast inner world, enlarged by a lifetime of self-discipline and asceticism, directed toward a lifelong purpose. It was a life of stunning uniqueness.

Search history. Can you find another who combined world travel with hermitic life?

On that fateful night of April 25, lives living in two different worlds, with hugely different intentions, came abruptly together. A man who directed violence only at himself, who made payments in self-denial in the belief that it helped mitigate the suffering of other humans, had his skull crushed by one who thought pitiless murder a glorious deed and a natural right.

Today, among many, there is suspicion of devotional religious life: that it is motivated by self-aggrandizement, self-promotion, control of others; that a hermitic life is probably a sign of imbalance or an inability to accept normal life.

Agostini was educated, charismatic, mentally-balanced, intellectually-engaged in the world, and deeply concerned with others. He believed in Christianity and its promise of a life after death. French mathematician Blaise Pascal, in his famous wager, argued that all humans bet their lives that God and life after death either exists or it does not. If it does, the reward is infinite. If it does not, the cost of living as if it did is only finite. Thus the wager is a finite amount for an infinite return. [2]

Agostini believed in the infinite return promised by Christianity and worked all his life to help others attain that too. He devised a unique method of pursuing that goal, one that was independent of any connection with church or clergy; one that was modeled after the life of Saint Anthony.

If he had not been murdered, his plan was to go next to the Sacramento Mountains. [3] There, once again, he would search for a high place and a source of water – and see what willing followers he could attract.

Timeline

- 1801 – Born in Sizzano, Novara, Kingdom of Piedmont-Sardinia (Italy)
- 1802 – Mother dies
- 1818 – Has vision of Virgin Mary directing him to travel
- 1821 – Leaves Sizzano for Rome
- 1821-1828 – Solitary devotion in Lazio Region of Italy
- October, 1830 – Leaves Italy for Spain
- March 1, 1831 – Abbey of Our Lady of Montserrat, Catalonia, Spain
- April, 1831 – Our Lady of the Pillar, Zaragoza, Spain
- February, 1832 – Santiago de Compostela, Galicia, Spain
- February, 1833 – Novara, Italy
- 1833-1837 – Pilgrim, novitiate in Carthusian and Trappist Orders
- January, 1838 – Takes vows of Saint Anthony the Abbot in Rome
- March-April, 1838 – Boards ship for Venezuela at Nantes, France
- June, 1838 – Arrives at Caracas, Venezuela, South America
- June 5, 1838 – Obtains passport for Bogotá, Colombia
- July 13, 1838 – Pamplona, Colombia
- August 17, 1838 – Bogotá, Colombia
- October 11, 1838 – Quito, Ecuador
- November 20, 1838 – La Paz, Bolivia
- January, 1839 – Mount Illimani, Bolivia (2 months)
- December, 1839 – Mount Illampu, Bolivia (7 months)
- Early 1840 – Motupe, Peru
- October 15, 1840 – Obtains passport for Lima, Peru
- January 3, 1841 – San Buenaventura, Peru
- November 4, 1841 – Lima, Peru
- December 4, 1841 – Obtains letter from Italian Consul in Lima, Peru
- January-February, 1842 – Cerro de Pasco, Peru
- March, 1842 – Moyobamba, Peru
- April, 1842 – Obtains passport at Moyobamba to enter Brazil
- March 6, 1843 – Santa María, Peru
- Mid-March, 1843 – Tabatinga, Brazil
- March-Fall, 1843 – Travels down the Amazon River by canoe
- Fall, 1843 – Santa Maria de Belém, Brazil (mouth of Amazon River)
- Late 1843 – (Recife) Pernambuco, Brazil – has Malaria
- Early 1844 – Natal, Rio Grande do Norte, Brazil
- June 20, 1844 – São José de Mipibu, Rio Grande do Norte, Brazil
- Early August, 1844 – Leaves São José, Brazil
- August 18, 1844 – Rio de Janeiro, Brazil
- Late August, 1844 – Meets with Brazilian Emperor Pedro II
- September-December, 1844 – Living on Pedra da Gávea, Rio de Janeiro

- December 15, 1844 – Leaves Rio de Janeiro for Santos, São Paulo, Brazil
- December 24, 1844 – Sorocaba, São Paulo, Brazil
- December 28, 1844 – Araçoiaba Hill, São Paulo, Brazil
- October, 16, 1845 – Porto Alegre, Brazil
- Late-October-November 1845 – Arrives in Buenos Aires, Argentina
- Late 1845-Early 1846 – Meets with Argentinean Dictator Juan Manuel de Rosas
- Mid-1846 – Leaves Buenos Aires, Argentina
- November 22, 1846 – Uruguaiana, Brazil
- 1846-1847 – Goya, Argentina
- December, 1847 – Porto Alegre, Brazil
- January, 1848 – Campestre Hill, Brazil
- May 17, 1848 – Newspaper reports discovery of água milagros at Campestre
- August, 1848 – Leaves Campestre for Botucaraí Hill
- October 17, 1848 – Arrested at Botucaraí Hill
- November 21, 1848 – Newspaper reports arrest at Botucaraí
- December 9, 1848 – Deported to Desterro, Santa Catarina, Brazil
- December 15, 1848 – Arrives at Desterro, Santa Catarina
- December 27, 1848 – Taken to Grove Island
- February 10, 1849 – Visited by Vicar Oliveira and soldiers at Grove Island
- May 19, 1849 – Granted free passage
- May 20, 1849 – Put on steamboat for Rio de Janeiro, Brazil
- May 23, 1849 – Arrives in Rio de Janeiro, Brazil
- June or July 1849 – Mariana, Minas Gerais, Brazil
- July, 1849 – Living on Mount Itacolumi, Minas Gerais, Brazil
- Late 1849-1850 – Ouro Preto, then Monte Alto, Minas Gerais, Brazil
- Early 1851 – Lapa, Paraná, Brazil
- June 30, 1851 – Rio Negro, Paraná, Brazil
- January 7, 1852 – São Borja, Brazil
- February 10, 1852 – Porto Alegre, Brazil
- February 11, 1852 – Obtains passport at Porto Alegre – must leave Brazil in 30 days
- March, 1852 – Monk's Hill, San Javier, Argentina
- November, 1852 – Signs Community Rules for Monk's Hill
- February 6, 1853 – Has left Monk's Hill
- August 31, 1853 – Buenos Aires, Argentina
- September, 1853 – Rosario, Argentina
- October, 1853 – Mendoza, Argentina
- Late 1853 – June, 1854 – Lives in cave outside Mendoza
- May 1, 1854 – Leaves cave at Mendoza
- September, 1854 – Leaves Mendoza
- October, 1854 – Santiago, Chile
- 1854-1857 – Visits many cities in Chile
- Late 1857 – Talca, Chile
- 1857-1858 – Spends 11 months in Atacama Desert, Chile
- November 25, 1858 – Mount Illimani, Bolivia (again!)
- June, 1859 – La Paz, Bolivia

- June 30, 1859 – Obtains passport for Mexico at El Alto, Bolivia
- November-December, 1859 – Departs to Mexico from Mollendo, Peru
- December 1859 – Panama and Guatemala
- January 1, 1860 – Soconusco, Mexico
- February-September, 1860 – Lives in cave at La Gineta, Mexico
- September 30, 1860 – Leaves cave at La Gineta
- November, 1860 – Living in cave at Mount Orizaba, Mexico
- May 18, 1861 – Newspaper reports his presence at Mount Orizaba
- May 19, 1861 – Newspaper reports false charges and demands arrest
- May 26, 1861 – Imprisoned under arrest in insane asylum at Puebla, Mexico
- May 29, 1861 – U. S. newspaper reports his arrest
- June 2, 1861 – Newspaper reports doctor finds no symptoms of mental loss
- September 14, 1861 – Newspaper reports finding of magistrate – ordered deported from Mexico
- October 26, 1861 – Leaves Puebla for Veracruz, Mexico under guard
- October 30-31, 1861 – Arrives in Havana, Cuba
- November, 1861 – Photographed as "Wonder of Our Century"
- November, 1861 – Arrives in New York, United States
- December, 1861 – Montreal, Canada
- December, 1861-July-August, 1862 – Canada
- July-August, 1862 – Duluth, Minnesota, United States
- August-September, 1862 – Travels down Mississippi by canoe
- September 24, 1862 – St. Louis, Missouri
- Fall, 1862 – Westport, Missouri
- April, 1863 – Leaves Westport
- May 1863 – Council Grove, Kansas
- May 28, 1863 – Leaves Council Grove
- August, 1863 – Las Vegas, New Mexico
- September, 1863 – Hermit's Peak, Las Vegas
- May 31, 1866 – Leaves Hermit's Peak
- July-August, 1866 – La Cueva (Mesilla)
- December 22, 1866 – Hueco Mountains, Texas
- 1867-Summer, 1868 – Ysleta, Socorro, and San Elizario, Texas
- Fall, 1868 – Sierra de Sapello, Mexico
- Winter, 1868 – Returns to La Cueva
- April 25, 1869 – Murdered by unknown person(s)
- April 30, 1869 – Fails to build signal fire
- May 1, 1869 – Search for body
- May 2, 1869 – Body found, funeral, and burial
- May 6, 1869 – Father Manuel Felipe de Jesús Chávez indicted for murder
- May 7, 1869 – Band of 50 Indians kill soldier at San Augustin pass
- May 9, 1869 – Chávez indictment dropped
- Fall, 2013 – Grave debased by self-appointed do-gooder

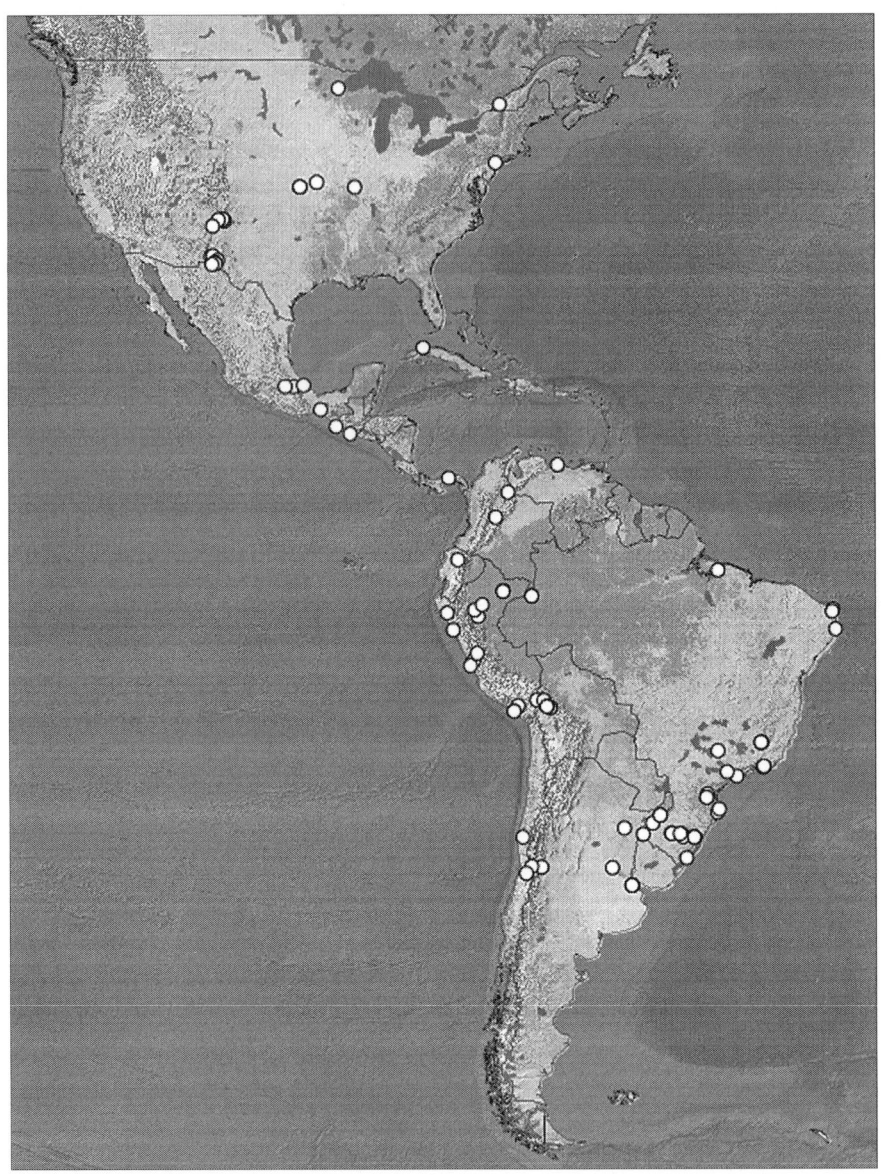

Agostini's travel destinations in South, Central, and North America, 1838 to 1869.

Miracle Water at Campestre

Rio Grande, November 11 [1848]

We have in our power a long list of the healings done by the medicinal water in Santa Maria da Boca do Monte. You will find amazing and incredibly real cases described with the simple colors of the purest of faith, a robust faith when confronted with the eyewitness testimonies of these prodigies of human kindness. Here we deliver this knowledge to humankind, ignoring many cases because they are not as interesting.

List of the sick people that have come into the water and returned safe:

Rofino Teixeira de Andrade, white, living in Santa Bárbara, age 22. Has been suffering from an internal problem on his right side. He arrived on May 13th and by May 16th he was perfectly well.

Nicolao José Manoel, half black/half white, age 26. Had been suffering for over 8 years of asthmatic flux and had a swollen leg that he had broken in three places. He went home completely healed.

José Antonio Maciel, living close to the line in Ponche Verde, age 67. Disease: seven fistulas for around 28 years. In 19 days, he was healed.

Florinda, half black/half white, 80 years old, living in Tia Anna. Disease: asthma for 13 years. Went home with perfect health.

Pedro Padilha, age 112, living in S. Martinho. Complained of his eyesight and legs. He was healed with three baths.

Rita, sister of Rodrigues de Moraes, age 35. Has been suffering from ear pain for 16 years. After six baths, she took some sort of skin shaped like a funnel and with two little legs out of one ear, and from then on she did not feel anything more.

Mrs. María, from the family of Mr. Pomposo, from Santa María, age 35. She had a swelling on the left side of her neck, with the size of an egg that affected her speech very often and also tormented her with cruel pain. The swelling is now reduced to a tenth of its previous size.

Mrs. Delfina, wife of Mr. Leodegario dos Santos Oliveira, living in Cachoeira de S. Sebastião, age 30. Disease: nervous attacks and suffocation. She was healed after ten baths.

José Aguiar, half black/half white, 45 years old, living in Santa Bárbara. Disease: pain in his legs, swelling of the feet and wounds. With five baths, he was well.

Mrs. Francisca Correia, age 30, living in Taquatiá. She was bedridden for eight months after delivering two children. With six baths, she was perfectly healed.

José Lorpa, age 62, from Taquatiá. He had a fistula, suffered from the eyes and had rheumatism. After nine baths, he felt nothing.

Francisco Machado, 44 years of age, from Taquatiá. Disease: tingling in a foot and a shrunken leg ten years ago. With nine baths, he was fully healed.

José Martins dos Santos, age 40, living on the coast of Quaraim. Asthma and chest disease [pulmonary tuberculosis]. With five baths, he was completely healed.

Eloy Samora, age 47 years, from Pamaroty. Nervous laxity, swelling and wounds in the feet and lack of movement for 37 years, he was cured.

José Pompeo do Toledo, age 45, living in the first district of Santa María. Wounds in his legs and hands. He was cured. He was also suffering from pain in his throat that did not allow him to speak, eat or drink for 3 days. After going to the fountain and bathing himself, he returned home, where he threw up blood and other matter. He took a broth, and without any further treatment, he was fine.

Adriana Pompeo do Toledo, from Ramal de S. João. She had a severe wart for 18 years. She is completely well.

Manoel Pompeo do Toledo. Swelling of the body for six months, asthmatic reflux for 25 to 26 years. He was completely healed.

Lieutenant Colonel João Gonçalves Padilha, age 65, living in Boa Vista, district of S. Martinho. Discomfort in the chest, big cough and almost unable to walk because of pain in his back and feet. Does not feel anything anymore.

Old Serpa, from Taquatiá, 70 years old. Lack of eyesight and rheumatism for many years. Went home fully healed.

Maurício dos Santos, 40 years old, from Santa Anna do Livramento. Rheumatism for 12 to 14 years. Recovered his health.

Old Oliveira, from S. Gabriel, age 50. Hernia for eight months. He is perfect.

María, daughter of Domiciano Soares Machado, 25 years old, from Torrinhas. Six years ago, she was stabbed on her left side, underneath her heart, and since then she could not breathe properly. With the holy water, she was cured of her ailments.

Leopoldina, wife of Manoel Francisco do Santos, age 32. The day she arrived, she suffered from cramps. After having three spills [glasses] of water over her head, she was immediately fine.

Anna Clara de Jesus, 27 years old, from Torrinhas. Head and stomach ache, and continuous lack of appetite. With six baths, she was cured.

João Alves Pereira, from Pontes de Irapoá, age 47. Chest pains, and his eyesight would grow dark and he would lose his senses, even falling to the ground. He had been suffering for 36 years. With four baths, he was free of his cruel ailments.

Januário Luiz da Silva. Had been suffering from an inflammation in his belly and dizziness for eleven years. With six baths, he was fine.

Fidencio Alves, 42 years old, from Camaquã. Pain underneath his stomach and pangs on his left side. The evil he was suffering from was so intense that he would be left close to death. With four baths, his ailment was gone.

João, Indian, from Caçapava. Age 13. Had a leg immobilized. With three baths, he was healed.

Thaddéo da Silva Brum, from S. Sepê, age 20. Immobilized of the legs and arms and could not move his neck. With eleven baths, he was fully healed.

Polidor Freire de Andrade, from the municipality of S. Gabriel, age 57. S. Lazaro's disease for 13 years. Took ten baths over the course of four months and with that he was healed.

Floriano José Rodrigues, age 55, living in Campestres. S. Lazaro's disease. For 15 years, he could not move his legs and just two months ago, his body became an open wound. Today his health is fully restored.

Florinda Rodrigues, from Taquatiá, 48 years of age. For 30 years, she had been suffering of a cough. Today she is healed.

Sebastião Soares Lima, son of the captain Aurélio Soares, 22 years old, from the municipality of Cachoeira. Both arms and legs immobilized for 10 years. With a bottle of water, he bathed his sick legs nine times and [unreadable] with fifteen drops because he had no more left. With just that, he was healed.

Antonio Pinto, 40 years old, living in Estado Oriental. Water retention. With four baths, he was well.

Pedro Ribeiro, from Pontes das Lavras, 90 years old. Deafness and an internal fester due to a fall where he had broken two ribs. With five baths, he has no more complaints.

Custódio da Silva Bruno, 60 years old, from Santo Antonio da Patrulha. Sores, swelling of the face and all over his body for 14 years. With his baths, he was perfectly healed.

Manoel José Caetano, born in Porto Alegre, age 17. S. Lazaro's disease with open wounds in his face, hand and feet. With 16 baths, he is almost fully healed.

A person with almost 58 years of age, living near Arroio Grande, 4th district of Piratiny. A fistula in a dangerous place above his anus, since 1818. With three baths, he was healed.

Rosaura Francisco, age 51, wife of Manoel Francisco de Moura, living in [unreadable] farm, district of Piratiny. Stomach inflammation and rheumatic pains. She is perfectly well.

José Cardoso Santiago, 30 years old, from the district of Taquaraí. Pain when urinating. With nine baths, he was healed.

***

The Monk João Maria Agostinho, to whom we owe the discovery of the holy waters, was arrested at the hill of Botucaraí on the 17th of October as ordered by the deputy of that district and sent to the capital of the province.

It seems that the police became aware of a fact that threatened the public peace and in which the Monk was involved.

Source: *Jornal do Commercio,* November 21, 1848 (Also published in *Correio Mercantil,* December 6, 1848).

Note: "S." is an abbreviation for São.

Notes

1 – Tragedy – Agostini's Missing Papers

1. E. Dana Johnson, "Diary of 'El Hermitano' of Hermit's Peak Strange Story," *Santa Fe New Mexican,* May 22, 1933.

2. Johnson, "Diary of 'El Hermitano' of Hermit's Peak Strange Story," May 22, 1933.

3. Johnson, "Diary of 'El Hermitano' of Hermit's Peak Strange Story," May 22, 1933.

4. Eleanor Hinde Powell, "The Brotherhood of the Holy Cross," *The Overland Monthly*, n 6, June, 1911, p 596.

5. *Weekly Champion and Press*, April 18, 1863.

6. Manuel Romero, "Tecolote Mountain and Its Rare Inhabitant," *El Nuevo Mexicano,* July 14, 1866, quoted in Anselmo F. Arrellano and Julian Josue Vigil, *Las Vegas Grandes on the Gallinas 1835-1985* (Editorial Telerana, 1985), pp 38-41.

7. *Times-Picayune*, December 22, 1866.

8. *Las-Cruces-Citizen,* April 30, 1953.

9. *Kansas City Times*, June 22, 1890.

10. *Montgomery Advertiser*, July 12, 1908.

11. Powell, "The Brotherhood of the Holy Cross," pp 593-597.

12. Giuseppe Cuneo, *Vita, Viaggi E Tragica Fine Del Padre Giovanni Maria de Agostino Da Sizzano,* quoted in Frederick G. Bohme, *A History of the Italians in New Mexico,* (Ayer Company Publishers, Inc., 1975), p 112.

13. Cuneo, *Vita, Viaggi E Tragica Fine Del Padre Giovanni Maria de Agostino Da Sizzano,* quoted in Frederick G. Bohme, *A History of the Italians in New Mexico,* p 112.

14. *Las Vegas Daily Optic,* May 2, 1925.

15. Hipolito C. de Baca, letter to Hon. John W. Garrett, August 10, 1931, Fray Angélico Chávez History Library, New Mexico History Museum.

16. John Work Garrett, American Ambassador to Italy, 1929-1933.

17. C. de Baca, letter to Hon. John W. Garrett, August 10, 1931.

18. C. de Baca, letter to Hon. John W. Garrett, August 10, 1931.

19. Writer living in Anthony, New Mexico at the time of the interview.

20. Marie Carter, "Old Timer's Stories: Elizabeth Fountain Armendariz," interview with Elizabeth Fountain Armendariz, Works Progress Administration Federal Writers' Project, May 3, 1937.

21. Arthur L. Campa, *Treasure of the Sangre de Cristos,* (University of Oklahoma Press, 1963), pp 168-169.

22. Campa, *Treasure of the Sangre de Cristos,* pp 168-169.

23. Campa, *Treasure of the Sangre de Cristos,* pp 168-169.

24. Handwritten note, October 3, 1961, Archives of the Archdiocese of Santa Fe, New Mexico. Names withheld for privacy reasons.

25. Handwritten note, October 3, 1961, Archives of the Archdiocese of Santa Fe, New Mexico. Names withheld for privacy reasons.

26. Frederick G. Bohme, *A History of the Italians in New Mexico,* (Ayer Company Publishers, Inc., 1975), p 112. Published version of a dissertation submitted to NMSU, 1958.

27. Florio Santini, "Giovanni Maria de Agostini: Eremita Italiano Sulle Montagne del Nuovo Messico," *Lucca*, November, 1970, year 10, n 11, pp 3-8 and December, 1970, year 10, n 12, pp 9-18.

28. Santini, "Giovanni Maria de Agostini," n 12, p 18. Name withheld for privacy reasons.

29. Charles, Wolfe, "New Mexico's Hermit." Ms. Fray Angélico Chávez History Library, New Mexico History Museum. Some sources spell the name Wolf.

30. Santini, "Giovanni Maria de Agostini."

31. Wolfe, "New Mexico's Hermit."

2 – Europe

1. Santino Tognacca, letter to Ottavio A. Coggiola-Mower, November 30, 1955, Archives of the Archdiocese of Santa Fe, New Mexico. Father Tognacca also gives a baptismal record for John's brother, Joseph Maria de Agostini, born August 29, 1801, father Joseph de Agostini, mother Francesca Comera. Dr. Giuseppe Cuneo appeared to think this later was Agostini's record as he gives this as Agostini's birth date. But again, the parential names do not match Agostini's as given in his quote.

2. E. Dana Johnson, "Diary of 'El Hermitano' of Hermit's Peak Strange Story," *Santa Fe New Mexican*, May 22, 1933, p 4. Johnson had trouble transcribing the Italian: 'Lizzano' is Sizzano and 'Nubara' is Novara ("b" was used commonly in Spanish in the 1800s were today "v" is used). 'Reyno de Piamonte' is Kingdom of Piedmont. 'Funtaneto' is Fontaneto. Johnson's interest in Agostini is long-standing – he published one of the earliest accounts of Agostini's life in *The Great Southwest Magazine,* 1908, p 94-97.

3. *Diário do Rio de Janeiro,* August 19, 1844.

4. *Kansas City Times,* June 22, 1890. The attribution Boccalini led to the author to assert that Agostini was a descendent of Trajano Bocalini, the Italian satirist and author of *Ragguagit di Parnaso,* born in Venice in 1613. This and other articles wrongly give his birth place as Capri.

5. Geoffrey Trease, *The Italian Story, From the Etruscans to Modern Times* (Vanguard Press, 1963) pp 242-244.

6. Charles L. Killinger, *The History of Italy* (Greenwood Press, 2002), pp 83-85.

7. A. J. H. Duganne, *The War in Europe* (Robert M. De Witt, 1859), p 10.

8. Fontaneto D'agogna is named after the nearby stream, Agogna.

9. *Las Vegas Daily Optic,* May 13, 1908.

10. The 1908 *Daily Optic* article published a photo of Agostini, the only printed account to do so until the 1960s. This suggests that the author's primary source is Margarito Romero, founder of the Society of the Hermit, who is known to have owned a copy of this photo. This article is the source of almost all later histories of Agostini.

11. *The Socorro Chieftain,* January 5, 1907.

12. Romero, "Tecolote Mountain and Its Rare Inhabitant." This article is published three years before Agostini's death.

13. E. Dana Johnson, "The Romance of Hermit's Peak," *The Great Southwest Magazine,* vol 1, n 1, January, 1908. (New Southwest Publishing Co., 1908), pp 94-97.

14. Wolfe, "New Mexico's Hermit."

15. *Valparaíso Messenger,* quoted in Romero, "Tecolote Mountain and Its Rare Inhabitant," July 14, 1866.

16. *Las Vegas Daily Optic,* May 13, 1908.

17 Wolfe, "New Mexico's Hermit."

18. *Las Vegas Daily Optic,* May 13, 1908.

19. Santini, "Giovanni Maria de Agostini," n 11, p 3.

20. *Valparaíso Messenger,* quoted in Romero, "Tecolote Mountain and Its Rare Inhabitant."

21. Santini, "Giovanni Maria de Agostini," n 11, p 3.

22. Wolfe, "New Mexico's Hermit."

23. Santini, "Giovanni Maria de Agostini," n 11, p 3.

24. *The Catholic Encyclopedia,* (Robert Appleton Company, 1907), vol 2, p 467.

25. Wolfe, "New Mexico's Hermit."

26. *The Catholic Encyclopedia,* vol 12, p 85.

27. *The Catholic Encyclopedia,* vol 11, p 306.

28. Wolfe, "New Mexico's Hermit."

29. Abadia de Montserrat web site: abadiamontserrat.net.

30. *The Catholic Encyclopedia,* vol 7, p 639.

31. Basilica Our Lady of the Pillar web site: basilicadelpilar.es/inicio.htm.

32. Wolfe, "New Mexico's Hermit."

33. *The Catholic Encyclopedia,* vol 8, p 273.

34. Santiago de Compostela web site: santiago-compostela.net

35. Santini, "Giovanni Maria de Agostini," n 11, p 4.

36. "Presentation of Foreigners," Sheet 18, December 24, 1844, Arquivo Histórico do Rio Grande do Sul, Porto Alegre, quoted in Alexandre de Oliveira Karsburg, "O Eremita do Novo Mundo: A trajetória de um peregrino italiano na América do século XIX (1838-1869)," (PhD dissertation, Universidade Federal do Rio de Janeiro, April, 2012), p 178.

37. Homer Montague, "A Priestly Calling", *Herald Magazine,* February, 2002.

38. Wolfe, "New Mexico's Hermit."

39. *The Catholic Encyclopedia,* vol 3, p 388.

40. *The Catholic Encyclopedia,* vol 14, p 24.

41. Wolfe, "New Mexico's Hermit."

42. Santini, "Giovanni Maria de Agostini," n 11, p 4.

43. Santini, "Giovanni Maria de Agostini," n 11, p 4.

3 – Saint Anthony the Abbot

1. *The Catholic Encyclopedia,* vol 1, p 553.

2. Peter H. Görg, *The Desert Fathers: Anthony and the Beginnings of Monasticism,* trans. Michael J. Miller, (Ignatius Press, 2011) p 7.

3. Jack L. Arnold "Church History: Persecution by the State A.D. 60-313," *RPM Magazine,* vol 1, n 23, 1999, p 44.

4. Keith Hopkins, "Christian Number and its Implications," *Journal of Early Christian Studies,* Vol 6, N. 2, Summer 1998, pp 185-226. The Christian population in 200 AD is estimated by Hopkins at about 217,000.

5. Athanasius of Alexandria, "Life of Anthony," *Selected Writings and Letters of Anthanasius, Bishop of Alexandria,* edited by Archibald Robertson (New York, 1892), vol 4 pp 581-632.

6. Athanasius, "Life of Anthony," pp 582-583.

7. Athanasius, "Life of Anthony," p 583.

8. Athanasius, "Life of Anthony," p 583.

9. Sana Faruq, "The First Christian Monastery," *Arab West Journal* (Watani International, 2009), No 37, p 3. This cemetery was located near the modern town of Deir al-Maymoun, about 80 miles south of Cairo. The church of Anba Antonious in Deir al-Maymoun is built over the cave (which probably was a tomb) in which Anthony is believed to have lived. The cave is about 5 feet long and 2 feet wide. Pictures of the church can be seen here: www.holyfamilyegypt.com/map/upperegypt/Dayrel.htm.

10. Athanasius, "Life of Anthony," p 589.

11. Athanasius, "Life of Anthony," p 590.

12. Athanasius, "Life of Anthony, " p 607. Manichaeism is also banned and persecuted by Diocletian.

13. Arnold, "Church History: Persecution by the State A.D. 60-313."

14. Athanasius, "Life of Anthony," p 607.

15. Athanasius, "Life of Anthony," p 609.

16. Athanasius, "Life of Anthony," p 609.

17. Görg, *The Desert Fathers: Anthony and the Beginnings of Monasticism.*

18. Athanasius, "Life of Anthony," p 630.

19. "The Copts," *The Dublin Review,* 3rd ser, n 21, January, 1884 (M. H. Gill & Sons, 1884), p 114.

20. Official web site of the Monastery of Saint Anthony: stantony.com.au. Accessed January 13, 2014.

21. Web site: stantony.com.au.

22. Web site: stantony.com.au.

23. Web site: stantony.com.au.

24. Web site: stantony.com.au.

25. *The Catholic Encyclopedia,* vol 1, p 555.

26. Wolfe, "New Mexico's Hermit."

27. Santini, "Giovanni Maria de Agostini," n 12, p 10.

28. Santini, "Giovanni Maria de Agostini," n 12, p 9.

29. Aziz Atiya, *History of Eastern Christianity* (Gorgias Press, 2010), p 396. Maron's name is variously spelled Marun, Maroun, Maroon, and Maro.

30. Paul Sfeir and Guita G. Hourani, "The Maronite Hermits: From the Fourth to the Twentieth Century," *Journal of Maronite Studies,* Vol 3, No 4 October 1999. Web site: maroniteinstitute.org.

31. Theodoret, Bishop of Cyrrhus, Historia Religiosa, quoted in Sfeir and Hourani, "The Maronite Hermits: From the Fourth to the Twentieth Century."

32. Sfeir and Hourani, "The Maronite Hermits: From the Fourth to the Twentieth Century."

33. History provided to the author by the Collegio Maronita della Beata Vergine Maria, June, 2014.

34. History provided to the author by the Collegio Maronita della Beata Vergine Maria, June, 2014.

35. Hare is referring to the church of San Pietro in Vincoli, now a Basilica, located opposite the Abbey.

36. Augustus J. C. Hare, *Walks in Rome* (W. Isbister & Co., 1874) London, 1874.

37. Wolfe, "New Mexico's Hermit."

38. Sfeir and Hourani, "The Maronite Hermits: From the Fourth to the Twentieth Century;" Paul Naaman, "The Maronites," *The Origins of an Antiochene Church* (Order of Saint Benedict, 2011), p 70.

39. *The Catholic Encyclopedia,* vol 12, pp 324-327, vol 3, pp 637-639, vol 11, pp 182-184, vol 7, pp 543-544.

40. History provided to the author by the Collegio Maronita della Beata Vergine Maria, June, 2014.

41. Father Tarek, Collegio Maronita della Beata Vergine Maria, email exchange with the author, 2014.

42. History provided to the author by the Collegio Maronita della Beata Vergine Maria, June, 2014.

4 – A New Life Begins

1. David A. Fryxell, "History of Steamships," *Family Tree Magazine,* August, 2009.

2. Wolfe, "New Mexico's Hermit."

3. Wolfe, "New Mexico's Hermit."

4. Santini, "Giovanni Maria de Agostini," n 11 p 4.

7. Web site: www.venezuelatuya.com/biografias/martin_tovar_ponte.htm, retrieved December, 2013.

6. Wolfe, "New Mexico's Hermit."

7. Santini, "Giovanni Maria de Agostini," n 11 p 8.

8. Santini, "Giovanni Maria de Agostini," n 11 p 8.

9. Gilberto Loaiza Cano, *Sociabilidad, religión y política en la definición de la nación: Colombia 1820-1886* (Universidad Externado de Colombia, 2011), p 40.

10. Santini, "Giovanni Maria de Agostini," n 11 p 8.

11. Santini, "Giovanni Maria de Agostini," n 11 p 8.

12. Santini, "Giovanni Maria de Agostini," n 11 p 8.

13. Santini, "Giovanni Maria de Agostini," n 12, p 9.

14. Santini, "Giovanni Maria de Agostini," n 12 p 9.

15. Santini, "Giovanni Maria de Agostini," n 12 p 9.

16. Santini, "Giovanni Maria de Agostini," n 12 p 9.

17. Paul Marcoy (Laurent Saint Cricq), *Travels in South America* (Scribner Armstrong & Co. 1875), Vol II, p 2. Note photo in Alex.

18. Santini, "Giovanni Maria de Agostini," n 12 p 9.

19. Santini, "Giovanni Maria de Agostini," n 12 p 9.

20. Santini, "Giovanni Maria de Agostini," n 12 p 10.

21. Wolfe, "New Mexico's Hermit."

22. Santini, "Giovanni Maria de Agostini," n 12 p 10.

23. Wolfe, "New Mexico's Hermit."

24. Santini, "Giovanni Maria de Agostini," n 12 p 10.

25. Wolfe, "New Mexico's Hermit."

26. Santini, "Giovanni Maria de Agostini," n 12 p 10.

27. Wolfe, "New Mexico's Hermit." The correct altitude is 14,200 feet.

28. Wolfe, "New Mexico's Hermit."

29. Santini, "Giovanni Maria de Agostini," n 12 p 10.

30. Santini, "Giovanni Maria de Agostini," n 12 p 10.

31. Santini, "Giovanni Maria de Agostini," n 12 p 10.

32. Santini, "Giovanni Maria de Agostini," n 12 p 10.

33. Marcoy, *Travels in South America,* vol 2, p 298. Tabatinga is located at the three-corner junction of Peru, Columbia, and Brazil.

34. Marcoy, *Travels in South America,* vol 2, p 315.

35. Marcoy, *Travels in South America,* vol 2, pp 315-316.

36. Wolfe, "New Mexico's Hermit."

5 – Brazil

1. Paul Marcoy (Laurent Saint Cricq), *Travels in South America,* vol 2, p 332. The Ticuna are the indigenous people of this portion of the Amazon rainforest.

2. Wolfe, "New Mexico's Hermit."

3. William Scully, Brazil, *Its Provinces and Chief Cities* (Murray & Co., 1866), London, p 275.

4. Marcoy, *Travels in South America,* vol 2, p 484.

5. Marcoy, *Travels in South America,* vol 2, pp 489.

6. Santini, "Giovanni Maria de Agostini," n 12 p 11.

7. Santini, "Giovanni Maria de Agostini," n 12 p 11.

8. Wolfe, "New Mexico's Hermit."

9. Josiah Conder, *The Modern Traveller, Brazil and Buenos Ayres,* vol 2, (W. Clowes, 1830), p 263.

10. Santini, "Giovanni Maria de Agostini," n 12 p 11.

11. Santini, "Giovanni Maria de Agostini," n 12 p 11.

12. *Diário do Rio de Janeiro,* August 19, 1844. "Ma" with or without a diacritical above the "a" is an abbreviation for Maria.

13. *Diário do Rio de Janeiro,* August 19, 1844.

14. Alexandre de Oliveira Karsburg, "O Eremita do Novo Mundo: A trajetória de um peregrino italiano na América do século XIX (1838-1869)," dissertation in Social History at the Federal University of Rio de Janeiro, April, 2012, p 165.

15. Wolfe, "New Mexico's Hermit." He did return, in 1849.

16. E. Bradford Burns, *A History of Brazil,* third edition (Columbia University Press, 1993), pp. 130-148.

17. *New International Encyclopedia,* vol 18, second edition (Dodd, Mead and Company, 1916), p. 250.

18. G. R. B. Horner, *Medical Topography of Brazil and Uruguay,* (Lindsay & Blakiston, 1845), p. 114.

19. William Scully, *Brazil, Its Provinces and Chief Cities* (Murray & Co., 1866), p 173.

20. Série Justiça, IJ1-558. Documento de 3 de abril de 1849, do Inspetor do 9 Quarteirão, Sr. José Francisco Ferreira (Statement of Inspector José Francisco Ferreira about Agostini's actions in 1844), quoted in Karsburg, "O Eremita do Novo Mundo," p 172.

21. Série Justiça, IJ1-558, quoted in Karsburg, "O Eremita do Novo Mundo," p 172.

22. Karsburg, "O Eremita do Novo Mundo," p 171.

23. *Diário do Rio de Janeiro,* December 16, 1844.

24. Livro de Registros de Estrangeiros, folha 18, 1842-1865, Apresentação de Estrangeiros – Delegacia, Sorocaba, SP (Registration Book of Foreign Visitors of the Town Hall of the City of Sorocaba), quoted in Karsburg, "O Eremita do Novo Mundo," p 178.

25. Livro de Registros de Estrangeiros, quoted in Karsburg, "O Eremita do Novo Mundo," p 178.

26. E. & F. N. Spon, *The Journal of the Iron and Steel Institute,* vol 29, (E. & F. N, 1886), p. 900.

27. *Extending the Diaspora: New Histories of the Black People,* edited by Dawne Y. Curry, Eric D. Duke, and Marshanda A. Smith (University of Illinois, 2009), p 34.

28. Daniel Parish Kidder, *Sketches of Residence and Travels in Brazil,* vol 1 (Sorin & Ball, 1845), p 280

29. Helio José Magnani, "Fatos Da História," aracoiaba.sp.gov.br/v1/arquivos/fatos.pdf, retrieved December, 2013.

30. Oswaldo R. Cabral, *João Maria: Interpretação da Campanha do Contestado* (Companhia Editora Nacional, 1960), p. 109.

31. Cabral, *João Maria: Interpretação da Campanha do Contestado,* p. 120.

32. Cabral, *João Maria: Interpretação da Campanha do Contestado,* p. 120.

33. José Fraga Fachel, *Monge João Maria: Recusa Dos Excluídos,* (Editora da UFRGS, 1995), quoted in Karsburg, "O Eremita do Novo Mundo," p 196.

34. Santini, "Giovanni Maria de Agostini," n 12 p 12.

6 – Argentina

1. "Documento de 10 de Fevereiro de 1849, do Secretário Bernardo Joaquim de Matos ao Chefe de Polícia da Província do RS João Negreiros de Sayão Lobato," Códice A-5.45, 1848-1851, quoted in Karsburg, "O Eremita do Novo Mundo," p 213.

2. "Documento de 10 de Fevereiro de 1849, do Secretário Bernardo Joaquim de Matos ao Chefe de Polícia da Província do RS João Negreiros de Sayão Lobato," quoted in quoted in Karsburg, "O Eremita do Novo Mundo," p 214.

3. John Lynch, *Argentine Caudillo: Juan Manuel de Rosas,* second edition (SR Books, 2001), p 81.

4. Lynch, *Argentine Caudillo: Juan Manuel de Rosas,* pp. 99-102.

5. Lynch, *Argentine Caudillo: Juan Manuel de Rosas,* p 160.

6. Wolfe, "New Mexico's Hermit."

7. Wolfe, "New Mexico's Hermit."

8. Santini, "Giovanni Maria de Agostini," n 12 p 12.

9. Santini, "Giovanni Maria de Agostini," n 12 p 12.

10. Lauchian Bellingham MacKinnon, *Steam Warfare in the Parana,* vol 1 (Charles Ollier, 1848), p 263.

11. MacKinnon, *Steam Warfare in the Parana,* p 96.

7 – Return to Brazil – Success and Troubles

1. *Correio do Povo,* January 27, 1898.

2. *Correio do Povo,* January 27, 1898.

3. *A Federação,* March 15, 1895.

4. Wolfe, "New Mexico's Hermit."

5. *Correio do Povo,* January 27, 1898.

6. *A Federação,* March 15, 1895.

7. *Correio do Povo,* January 27, 1898.

8. *A Federação,* March 15, 1895.

9. *O Porto Alegrense,* May 17, 1848. Quoted in Karsburg, "O Eremita do Novo Mundo," pp 30-31.

10. *O Porto Alegrense,* June 8, 1849. Quoted in Karsburg, "O Eremita do Novo Mundo," p 84.

11. The "Jesuit Missions" area of Brazil, Argentina, and Paraguay. See Chapter 8 for a discussion.

12. *Correio do Povo,* January 27, 1898.

13. *Correio do Povo,* January 27, 1898.

14. *Correio do Povo,* January 27, 1898.

15. *Correio do Povo,* January 28, 1898.

16. *A Federação,* March 15, 1895.

17. *Correio do Povo,* January 28, 1898.

18. *A Federação,* March 18, 1895.

19. *A Federação,* March 18, 1895.

20. *Diário do Rio Grande,* October 16, 1848.

21. *Jornal do Commércio,* November 21, 1848.

22. *Jornal do Commércio,* November 21, 1848.

23. *Diário do Rio Grande,* June 25, 1849.

24. *Diário do Rio Grande,* June 25, 1849.

25. *Diário do Rio Grande,* June 25, 1849.

26. *Diário do Rio Grande,* June 25, 1849.

27. Wolfe, "New Mexico's Hermit."

28. *Correio do Povo,* January 28, 1898.

29. *A Federação,* March 18, 1895.

30. Anais do Senado, 1874, Sessão em 15 de Junho, p. 261, Setor de Periódicos, Biblioteca Nacional, Rio de Janeiro, quoted in Quoted in Karsburg, "O Eremita do Novo Mundo," p 69.

31. Anais do Senado, p. 261, quoted in Quoted in Karsburg, "O Eremita do Novo Mundo," p 69.

32. *A Federação,* March 18, 1895.

33. *Correio do Povo,* January 28, 1898.

34. Códice A-5.53 (1848-1856), Palácio do Governo em Porto Alegre ao Delegado de Polícia Serafim dos Anjos França Junior, 21 de Outubro de 1848, Arquivo Histórico do Rio Grande do Sul, Porto Alegre, quoted in Quoted in Karsburg, "O Eremita do Novo Mundo," p 58.

35. *Jornal do Commércio,* November 21, 1848.

36. Códice A-5.90 (1848-1849), Palácio do Governo da Cidade de Rio Pardo, Carta Particular de 26 de Novembro de 1848 Ao Presidente de Santa Catarina, Marechal Antero Ferreira de Brito, Arquivo Histórico do Rio Grande do Sul, Porto Alegre, quoted in Quoted in Karsburg, "O Eremita do Novo Mundo," p 139.

37. Fundo Autoridades Militares, Maço 149, 02, Documentos n. 385 e 386, Quartel do Comando do 5 Batalhão de Caçadores e Guarnição da Capital, do ten. Cel. Martins Batista Ferreira Tamarindo Ao Gen. Francisco José de Souza Soares de Andrea, 8 de Dezembro de 1848, Arquivo Histórico do Rio Grande do Sul, Porto Alegre, quoted in Quoted in Karsburg, "O Eremita do Novo Mundo," p 62.

38. Códice A-5.92 (1848-1850), Secretaria do Governo em Porto Alegre, do Secretário Bernardo Joaquim de Matos Ao 1 Tenente Manoel Luis Pereira da Cunha, 9 de Dezembro de 1848, Arquivo Histórico do Rio Grande do Sul, Porto Alegre, quoted in Quoted in Karsburg, "O Eremita do Novo Mundo," p 62.

39. Karsburg, "O Eremita do Novo Mundo," pp 141-142.

40. G. H. Von Langsdorff, *Voyages and Travels in Various Parts of the World* (George Philips, 1817), p 42.

41. Josiah Conder, editor, *The Modern Traveller, Brazil and Buenos Ayres,* vol 1 (Clowes, 1830), p 268.

42. Anais do Senado, 1874, Sessão em 15 de junho, p. 262, Biblioteca Nacional, Rio de Janeiro, quoted in Karsburg, "O Eremita do Novo Mundo," p 143.

43. Karsburg, "O Eremita do Novo Mundo," p 143.

44. Karsburg, "O Eremita do Novo Mundo," p 143.

45. Karsburg, "O Eremita do Novo Mundo," p 146.

46. Karsburg, "O Eremita do Novo Mundo," p 146.

47. *A Republica,* October 15, 1012.

48. Karsburg, "O Eremita do Novo Mundo," p 168.

49. Série Justiça, IJ1-558, Documento de 23 de Fevereiro de 1849, do Padre Joaquim Gomes de Oliveira e Paiva Ao Vice-Presidente de Santa Catarina Severo Amorim do Vale, Arquivo Nacional, Rio de Janeiro, quoted in Karsburg, "O Eremita do Novo Mundo," pp 200-201.

50. Série Justiça, IJ1-558, Documento de 23 de Fevereiro de 1849, quoted in Karsburg, "O Eremita do Novo Mundo," p 201.

51. Série Justiça, IJ1-558, Documento de 23 de Fevereiro de 1849, quoted in Karsburg, "O Eremita do Novo Mundo," p 201.

52. Série Justiça, IJ1-558, Documento de 23 de Fevereiro de 1849, quoted in Karsburg, "O Eremita do Novo Mundo," p 201.

53. Série Justiça, IJ1-558, Documento de 23 de Fevereiro de 1849, quoted in Karsburg, "O Eremita do Novo Mundo," p 201.

54. Série Justiça, IJ1-558, Documento de 23 de Fevereiro de 1849, quoted in Karsburg, "O Eremita do Novo Mundo," p 167.

55. *O Conciliador Catarinense,* May 26, 1849.

56. Série Justiça, IJ1-558. O Registro Deste Ofício Está Em: APSC, Registro Min. J. Pres. P. 1846-1851, f. 87v e 88, Aviso n. 31, Avisos Do Presidente Da Província de Santa Catarina ao Ministro da Justiça, quoted in Karsburg, "O Eremita do Novo Mundo," p 266.

57. *O Conciliador Catarinense,* June 23, 1849.

58. *O Conciliador Catarinense,* June 27, 1849.

59. *O Conciliador Catarinense,* May 23, 1849.

60. *Diário do Rio de Janeiro,* May 25, 1849.

61. Santini, "Giovanni Maria de Agostini," n 12 p 12.

62. George Gardner, *Travels in the Interior of Brazil* (Reeve Brothers, 1846), p 508.

63. J. B. Von Spix and C. F. P. Von Martius, *Travels in Brazil,* vol 1, (Longman, Hurst, Rees, Orme, Brown, and Green, 1824), p 208.

64. Santini, "Giovanni Maria de Agostini," n 12 p 12.

65. J. B. Von Spix and C. F. P. Von Martius, *Travels in Brazil,* vol 1, p 207.

66. Santini, "Giovanni Maria de Agostini," n 12 p 12.

67. Santini, "Giovanni Maria de Agostini," n 12 p 12.

68. Santini, "Giovanni Maria de Agostini," n 12 p 12.

69. Santini, "Giovanni Maria de Agostini," n 12 p 12.

70. Karsburg, "O Eremita do Novo Mundo," p 318.

71. Livro Tombo N. 2, 1882-1884, Folha 84. Paróquia de Santo Antônio da Lapa, Paraná, quoted in Karsburg, "O Eremita do Novo Mundo," p 317.

72. Livro Tombo N. 4, 1895, Folha 92, Padre Brito. Paróquia de Santo Antônio da Lapa, Paraná, quoted in Karsburg, "O Eremita do Novo Mundo," p 317.

73. Oswaldo R. Cabral, *João Maria: Interpretação da Campanha do Contestado* (Companhia Editora Nacional, 1960), p 137.

74. Oswaldo R. Cabral, *João Maria: Interpretação da Campanha do Contestado,* p 137.

75. Oswaldo R. Cabral, *João Maria: Interpretação da Campanha do Contestado,* p 137.

76. *O Combatente,* January 17, 1901, quoted in *Annuario da Provencia do Rio Grande do Sul Para O Anno de 1904,* editors Krahe & Cia (Graciano A. De Azambuja, 1904), pp 209-210.

77. Cláudia Priebe, "Romaria Leva 7 Mil ao Botucaraí," Folha de Candelária, Edition N. 1633, April 6, 2010. Web site: folhadecandelaria.com.br/?6055, access March, 2014.

78. Iuri Azeredo, "Botucaraí: Um Local Muito Especial," Other Cositas Y Más. Web Site: iuriaz.blogspot.com/2008/10/porta-na-muralha-sobre-uma-viglia.html. Accessed March, 2014.

79. Iuri Azeredo, "Botucaraí: Um Local Muito Especial."

80. Iuri Azeredo, "Botucaraí: Um Local Muito Especial."

81. Paraná, Governo do Estado, Informações Gerais da Unidade de Conservação, "Secretaria Do Meio Ambiente E Recursos Hídricos," Web Site: iap.pr.gov.br/arquivos/File/Plano_de_Manejo/Parque_Estadual_Monge. Accessed March, 2014.

82. Paraná, Governo do Estado, Agência de Notícias, "Beto Richa Anuncia Retomada das Obras do Parque do Monge, na Lapa," February 7, 2013. Web Site: aen.pr.gov.br/modules/noticias/article.php?storyid=75382. Accessed March, 2014.

8 – Argentina Again

1. João Pedro Gay, letter to Barão de Caxias, President of the state of Rio Grande do Sul, January 7, 1852, Fundo Assuntos Religiosos, Maço 24 Cx 12. Documentos entre 1852 e 1857, Arquivo Histórico do Rio Grande do Sul. Copy provided to author by Dr. Alexandre de Oliveira Karsburg.

2. Bernard Moses, *The Spanish Dependencies in South America,* vol 2 (Harper & Brothers, 1914), pp 144-147.

3. Moses, *The Spanish Dependencies in South America,* pp 145-146.

4. José María Rosa, *Historia Argentina: Unitarios y Federales (1826-1841),* Tomo IV, (Editorial Oriente S. A., 1841), p. 78.

5. Moses, *The Spanish Dependencies in South America,* p 170.

6. Gay, letter to Barão de Caxias, January 7, 1852.

7. *Diário do Rio de Janeiro,* May 25, 1849.

8. J. Power, *History of the Argentine Republic* (Fraenkel & Bremer, 1891), pp 61-62.

9. Karsburg, "O Eremita do Novo Mundo," p 60.

10. Karsburg, "O Eremita do Novo Mundo," p 339.

11. Ladislau de Figueiredo Rocha, letter to Luis Alves de Oliveira Bello, February 10, 1852, Palácio do Governo em Porto Alegre, Códice A-5.46, 1851-1855, Arquivo Histórico do Rio Grande do Sul, quoted in Karsburg, "O Eremita do Novo Mundo," pp 339-340.

12. Passport No. 73, February 11, 1852, Arquivo Histórico do Rio Grande do Sul, Fundo Polícia, Códice P-143. Copy provided to author by Dr. Alexandre de Oliveira Karsburg.

13. Luis Alves de Oliveira Bello, February 11, 1852, Arquivo Histórico do Rio Grande do Sul, Fundo Polícia, Códice P-231, quoted in Karsburg, "O Eremita do Novo Mundo," p 342.

14. Gay, letter to Barão de Caxias, January 7, 1852.

15. Luis Alves de Oliveira Bello, letter to João Pedro Gay, March 8, 1852, Arquivo Histórico do Rio Grande do Sul, Codex A- 5100 , 1852-1853, quoted in Karsburg, "O Eremita do Novo Mundo," p 354.

16. Juan Queirel, *Misiones* (Typographic Workshop Of The National Prison, 1897), p 422.

17. Queirel, *Misiones,* p 421.

18. Juan B. Ambrosetti, *Supersticiones y Leyendas* (La Cultura Argentina, 1917), p 121.

19. Ambrosetti, *Supersticiones y Leyendas,* p 122.

20. Queirel, *Misiones,* p 422.

21. Queirel, *Misiones,* p 422.

22. Ambrosetti, *Supersticiones y Leyendas,* p 120.

23. Ambrosetti, *Supersticiones y Leyendas,* p 121.

24. Ambrosetti, *Supersticiones y Leyendas,* p 121.

25. *A República,* December 14, 1912.

26. *A República,* December 14, 1912.

27. Francisco José de Souza Soares de Andréa, letter to Antero Ferreira de Brito, November 26, 1848, Arquivo Histórico do Rio Grande do Sul, Códice A-5.90 (1848-1849), quoted in Karsburg, "O Eremita do Novo Mundo," p 139.

28. Ambrosetti, *Supersticiones y Leyendas,* p 121.

29. Queirel, *Misiones,* p 421.

30. Ambrosetti, *Supersticiones y Leyendas,* p 122.

31. "Miles de personas se acercaron al Cerro Monje en San Javier," Noticias De La Calle, Edición Web, April 24, 2011: noticiasdelacalle.com.ar/ampliar.php?id=34531. Accessed February, 2014.

32. "Más de 15.000 peregrinos acudieron al Cerro Monje en San Javier," Misiones Online, March 29, 2013: misionesonline.net/noticias/29/03/2013/m-s-de-15-000-peregrinos-acudieron-al-cerro-monje-en-san-javier. Accessed February, 2014.

33. João Pedro Gay, letter to João Lins Vieira Cansanção de Sinimbú, President of the state of Rio Grande do Sul, February 6, 1853, Assuntos Religiosos, Maço 24, Cx 12, Arquivo Histórico do Rio Grande do Sul. Copy provided to author by Dr. Alexandre de Oliveira Karsburg.

34. Wolfe, "New Mexico's Hermit."

9 – Chile and Bolivia – Crisis and Trouble

1. Wolfe, "New Mexico's Hermit."

2. Thomas Jefferson Page, *La Plata, the Argentine Confederation, and Paraguay* (Trubner & Co., 1859), p 72.

3. Wolfe, "New Mexico's Hermit."

4. Page, *La Plata, The Argentine Confederation, and Paraguay,* p 72.

5. Wolfe, "New Mexico's Hermit."

6. Robert Elwes, *A Sketcher's Tour Round the World* (London, Hurst and Blackett, 1854), p 140.

7. Gordon Ross, *Argentina and Uruguay* (The MacMillan Company, 1916), p 87.

8. *New International Encyclopedia,* Second Edition, vol 15 (Dodd, Mead and Company, 1916), p 396.

9. Wolfe, "New Mexico's Hermit."

10. Wolfe, "New Mexico's Hermit."

11. Wolfe, "New Mexico's Hermit."

12. Elwes, *A Sketcher's Tour Round the World,* p 142.

13. Elwes, *A Sketcher's Tour Round the World,* p 148.

14. Elwes, *A Sketcher's Tour Round the World,* p 148.

15. Elwes, *A Sketcher's Tour Round the World,* p 148.

16. Santini, "Giovanni Maria de Agostini."

17. Wolfe, "New Mexico's Hermit."

18. Charles Darwin, *The Voyage of the Beagle,* vol 29 (P. F. Collier & Son Company, 1909), p 355.

19. Wolfe, "New Mexico's Hermit."

20. Wolfe, "New Mexico's Hermit."

21. "Justo Donoso Vivanco," Reseña Biográfica Parlamentaria, web site: historiapolitica.bcn.cl/resenas_parlamentarias/wiki/Justo_Donoso_Vivanco. Accessed February, 2014.

22. Wolfe, "New Mexico's Hermit."

23. Wolfe, "New Mexico's Hermit."

24. Wolfe, "New Mexico's Hermit."

25. Wolfe, "New Mexico's Hermit."

26. Santini, "Giovanni Maria de Agostini," n 12 p 13.

27. Wolfe, "New Mexico's Hermit."

28. Wolfe, "New Mexico's Hermit."

29. Wolfe, "New Mexico's Hermit."

10 – Leaving South America

1. Santini, "Giovanni Maria de Agostini," n 12 p 13.

2. Santini, "Giovanni Maria de Agostini," n 12 p 13.

3. *Commercial Reports Received at The Foreign Office from Her Majesty's Consuls,* Vol I (Harrison and Sons, 1862), p 295.

4. Wolfe, "New Mexico's Hermit."

11 – Mexico and Cuba

1. John Kennedy, *The History of Steam Navigation* (Charles Birchall, Limited, 1903), pp 58-62.

2. Santini, "Giovanni Maria de Agostini."

3. *Monograph on Mexico* (Government Printing Office, 1914), p 54.

4. Santini, "Giovanni Maria de Agostini."

5. William Davis Robinson, *Memoirs of the Mexican Revolution* (Lydia R. Bailey Printer, 1820), p 353.

6. Wolfe, "New Mexico's Hermit."

7. Mount McKinley (20,237 feet) and Mount Logan (19,550 feet) are higher.

8. Brantz Mayer, *Mexico: Aztec, Spanish and Republican,* Vol II (Hartford, S. Drake and Company, 1853), p 188.

9. "Old Irish Travel," Blackwood's Magazine, vol 186, July-December, 1909 (Leonard Scott Publication Co., 909), p 344.

10. Brantz Mayer, *Mexico: Aztec, Spanish and Republican,* p 191.

11. Wolfe, "New Mexico's Hermit."

12. *La Independencia,* May 18, 1861.

13. *La Independencia,* May 18, 1861.

14. *New American Cyclopaedia,* vol 5, Edited by George Ripley and Charles A. Dana (D. Appleton and Company, 1864), pp 556-557.

15. *El Constitucional,* May 19, 1861.

16. *El Siglo Diez y Nueve,* May 26, 1861.

17. Wolfe, "New Mexico's Hermit."

18. Wolfe, "New Mexico's Hermit."

19. *San Francisco Bulletin,* July 22, 1861.

20. Martin Joseph Kerney, *The Metropolitan,* vol 4 (John Murphy & Co, 1856), p 327.

21. *El Siglo Diez y Nueve,* June 2, 1861.

22. Wolfe, "New Mexico's Hermit."

23. *San Francisco Bulletin,* July 22, 1861.

24. *San Francisco Bulletin,* July 22, 1861.

25. Wolfe, "New Mexico's Hermit."

26. *El Siglo Diez y Nueve,* September 14, 1861.

27. *El Siglo Diez y Nueve,* September 14, 1861.

28. *El Siglo Diez y Nueve,* September 14, 1861.

29. *El Siglo Diez y Nueve,* September 14, 1861.

30. Wolfe, "New Mexico's Hermit."

31. *La Orquesta,* October 26, 1861.

32. Wolfe, "New Mexico's Hermit."

33. *Disturnell's Railway and Steamship Guide* (J. Disturnell, 1857), p 208.

34. Wolfe, "New Mexico's Hermit."

35. *El Siglo Diez y Nueve,* May 26, 1861.

36. *Catholic Encyclopedia,* p 521, vol 4, p 521.

37. *Catholic Encyclopedia,* p 521, vol 4, p 521.

12 – North America

1. Santini, "Giovanni Maria de Agostini," n 12 p 14.

2. Karlyn Kohrs Campbell and Kathleen Hall Jamieson, *Presidents: Creating the Presidency* (University of Chicago Press, 2008), p 236.

3. John Disturnell, *Disturnell's American and European Railway and Steamship Guide,* (J. Disturnell, 1865), p 85.

4. Santini, "Giovanni Maria de Agostini," n 12 p 14.

5. Santini, "Giovanni Maria de Agostini," n 12 p 14.

6. *Las Vegas Daily Optic,* May 13, 1908.

7. Wolfe, "New Mexico's Hermit."

8. Wolfe, "New Mexico's Hermit."

9. *Las Vegas Daily Optic,* May 13, 1908.

10. Santini, "Giovanni Maria de Agostini," n 12 p 14.

11. E. Dana Johnson, "The Romance of Hermit's Peak," *The Great Southwest,* January, 1908 (New Southwest Publishing Co, 1908), p 95.

12. Santini, "Giovanni Maria de Agostini," n 12 p 14.

13. Santini, "Giovanni Maria de Agostini," n 12 p 14. Westport, Missouri is now incorporated into Kansas City, Missouri.

14. M. C. Gottschalk, "Pioneer Merchants of the Las Vegas Plaza: The Booming Trail Days," *Wagon Tracks,* vol 16, February, 2002, p 8. In 1862, New Mexico is a territory of the United States. It will not become a state until 1912.

15. James F. Meline, *Two Thousand Miles on Horseback. Santa Fe and Back* (Hurd and Houghton, 1868), p 3.

16. *Weekly Champion and Press,* April 18, 1863.

17. *Weekly Champion and Press,* April 18, 1863.

18. *Weekly Champion and Press,* April 18, 1863.

19. Johnson, "The Romance of Hermit's Peak," p 95.

20. Suzan Jezak Ford, "Thomas J. Goforth, Westport Mayor 1805-1882," manuscript, Kansas City Public Library, 1999.

21. Deborah Barker, Joab Bernard, Santa Fe Trader, Town Founder and Franklin County Pioneer, Franklin County Historical Society, 2012.

22. Ed Blair, *History of Johnson County, Kansas* (Standard Publishing Co., 1915), pp 23-24.

23. Santini, "Giovanni Maria de Agostini," n 12 p 15.

24. Web site: councilgrove.com/24-historic-sites-of-council-g. Accessed February, 2014.

25. *Humeston New Era,* May 29, 1901.

26. Alice Strieby Smith, "Through the Eyes of My Father," *Collections of the Kansas State Historical Society,* 1926-1928, Vol XVII, edited by William Elsey Connelley (Kansas State Printing Plant, 1928), pp 715-716.

27. *Kansas City Times,* June 22, 1890.

28. *Council Grove Press,* April 27, 1863.

29. Santini, "Giovanni Maria de Agostini," n 12 p 15.

30. Santini, "Giovanni Maria de Agostini," n 12 p 15.

31. Gottschalk, "Pioneer Merchants of the Las Vegas Plaza: The Booming Trail Days," p 9.

32. James M. McPherson, *The Atlas of the Civil War* (Courage Books, 2005), p 58.

33. David G. Thomas, *La Posta: From the Founding of Mesilla, to Corn Exchange Hotel, to Billy the Kid Museum, to Famous Landmark* (Doc45 Publishing, 2013), p 72.

13 – Las Vegas, New Mexico

1. *Las Vegas Daily Optic,* May 13, 1908.

2. *Kansas City Times,* June 22, 1890.

3. Eleanor Hinde Powell, "The Brotherhood of the Holy Cross," *The Overland Monthly,* vol 57, n 6, Second Series, January-June 1911, (The Overland Monthly Co., 1911), p 594.

4. *Las Vegas Daily Optic,* May 13, 1908.

5. Powell, "The Brotherhood of the Holy Cross," p 594.

6. *Las Vegas Daily Optic,* May 13, 1908.

7. *Las Vegas Daily Optic,* May 13, 1908.

8. Powell, "The Brotherhood of the Holy Cross," p 594.

9. S. Omar Barker, "The Hermit of Owl's Peak," *Rocky Mountain Empire Magazine,* March 26, 1950, pp 4-5.

10. *Las Cruces Citizen,* April 30, 1953.

11. Rozier Paul Hughes, The Hermit of the Peak, *Santa Fe Magazine,* April, 1935, p 28.

12. Manuel Romero, "Tecolote Mountain and Its Rare Inhabitant," p 39.

13. William H. Strickfaden, "Hermit's Peak and the Crosses," *New Mexico Sun Trails,* vol 10, n 3, August, 1952, p 16.

14. *Montgomery Advertiser,* July 12, 1908.

15. Benigno Romero, Porfirio Gonzalez, Placido Sandoval, *Sociedad del Ermitano,* Dec 31, 1898, p 3.

16. Manuel Romero, "Tecolote Mountain and Its Rare Inhabitant," p 39.

17. Barker, "The Hermit of Owl's Peak," p 5.

18. *Salt Lake Tribune,* November 5, 1891.

19 Manuel Romero, "Tecolote Mountain and Its Rare Inhabitant," p 39.

20. *Salt Lake Tribune,* November 5, 1891.

21. Hughes, The Hermit of the Peak, p 30.

22 Campa, *Treasure of the Sangre de Cristos,* pp 188-189.

23. Powell, "The Brotherhood of the Holy Cross," p 594.

24. Hughes, The Hermit of the Peak, p 28.

25. *Las Vegas Daily Optic,* May 13, 1908.

26. *Salt Lake Tribune,* November 5, 1891.

27. *Boston Daily Advertiser,* June 5, 1896.

28. *Boston Daily Advertiser,* June 5, 1896.

29. Benigno Romero, Porfirio Gonzalez, Placido Sandoval, *Sociedad del Ermitano,* p 5.

30. Benigno Romero, Porfirio Gonzalez, Placido Sandoval, *Sociedad del Ermitano,* p 6.

31. Benigno Romero, Porfirio Gonzalez, Placido Sandoval, *Sociedad del Ermitano,* p 7.

32. Benigno Romero, Porfirio Gonzalez, Placido Sandoval, *Sociedad del Ermitano,* p 8.

33. Benigno Romero, Porfirio Gonzalez, Placido Sandoval, *Sociedad del Ermitano,* p 2.

34. Helen Haines, *History of New Mexico* (New Mexico Historical Publishing Co, 1891), p 333.

35. M. C. Gottschalk, "Pioneer Merchants of the Las Vegas Plaza," p 8.

36. Haines, *History of New Mexico,* p 428.

37. *Las Vegas Daily Optic,* October 26, 1896.

38. *Las Vegas Daily Optic,* October 26, 1896.

39. *Annual Reports of the Department of the Interior, Miscellaneous Reports,* Part III (Government Printing Office, 1901), p 518.

40. *Daily Examiner,* August 30, 1895.

41. *Las Vegas Daily Optic,* October 26, 1896.

42. Benigno Romero, Porfirio Gonzalez, Placido Sandoval, *Sociedad del Ermitano,* p 3.

43. William deBuys, *Enchantment and Exploitation* (UNM Press, 1985), pp 9-10.

44. *Las Vegas Daily Optic,* April 30, 1908.

45. *Las Vegas Daily Optic,* September 3, 1908.

46. *Las Vegas Daily Optic,* April 30, 1908.

47. *Las Vegas Daily Optic,* September 3, 1908.

48. *Las Vegas Daily Optic,* September 4, 1908.

49. *Las Vegas Daily Optic,* March 16, 1917.

50. *The Catholic Encyclopedia,* vol 11, p 635.

51. Leo C. de Baca, quoted in Milton W. Callon, *Las Vegas New Mexico: The Town That Wouldn't Gamble* (The Las Vegas Publishing Company, 1962), p 320.

14 – New Mexico, Texas, Mexico

1. *Las Vegas Daily Optic,* May 13, 1908. Numerous printed sources give 1867 as the year Agostini left Hermit's Peak. This is incorrect.

2. Santini, "Giovanni Maria de Agostini," n 12 p 17.

3. Albert J. Fountain, Sr., "The Hermit," undated manuscript, MS 162, bx 28, fd 3, Archives and Special Collections, NMSU.

4. Stoes, "El Ermitano Searched Three Continents for Peace, Found Brutal Death in Organ Mountains," *Las Cruces Citizen,* April 30, 1953.

5. Fountain, "The Hermit," p 1.

6. Thomas, *La Posta: From the Founding of Mesilla, to Corn Exchange Hotel, to Billy the Kid Museum, to Famous Landmark*, p 57.

7. *Enos and Jennie Culver, Memoir, Travel Diary, and Correspondence, 1869-1871,* edited by Joy Poole and Mike Olsen, Santa Fe Trail Association, p 30.

8. *Rio Grande Republican,* Feb 18, 1882. Today this spring is barely discernible.

9. Fountain, "The Hermit," p 1.

10. Stoes, "El Ermitano Searched Three Continents for Peace, Found Brutal Death in Organ Mountains," *Las Cruces Citizen,* April 30, 1953.

11. Fountain, "The Hermit," p 1.

12. *Times-Picayune,* December 22, 1866.

13. *El Paso Herald,* December 15, 1926.

14. Fountain, "The Hermit," p 2.

15. Fountain, "The Hermit," p 2.

16. Fountain, "The Hermit," p 2.

17. Fountain, "The Hermit," p 2.

18. Fountain, "The Hermit," p 2.

19. S. Omar and Elsa Barker, "Hermit of the Mountain," *New Mexico Quarterly,* vol 31, n 4, Winter 1961-62, p 354.

15 – Journey's End

1. Fountain, "The Hermit," p 2.

2. Fountain, "The Hermit," p 3. Antonio García is Colonel Fountain's father-in-law.

3. Fountain, "The Hermit," p 3.

4. Daniel , "A Reflection on the Enigmatic Hermit," *Southern New Mexico Historical Review,* vol 14, January, 2007, Dona Ana County Historical Society, p 82.

5. Fountain, "The Hermit," p 3.

6. Fountain, "The Hermit," p 4.

7. Fountain, "The Hermit," p 4.

8. *The Catholic Encyclopedia,* vol 7, pp 113-114.

9. Fountain, "The Hermit," p 4.

10. Fountain, "The Hermit," p 4.

11. Richard Challoner, *The Catholic Christian Instructed in the Sacraments, Sacrifice, Ceremonies, and Observances of the Church* (John Murphy & Co, 1878), pp 147-148.

12. Book of Deaths and Burials, January 1852 to April 1873, San Albino Church Records, p 93.

13. Fountain, "The Hermit," p 4.

14. *Daily New Mexican,* May 8, 1869.

15. *Daily New Mexican,* May 11, 1869.

16. *Daily New Mexican,* August 26, 1868.

17. *Daily New Mexican,* July 17, 1868.

18. *Daily New Mexican,* May 18, 1869.

19. *Daily New Mexican,* May 3, 1869.

20. *Daily New Mexican,* May 13, 1869.

21. Christopher Williams, "The Catholic Church in the City of Las Cruces from 1848 to 1910," n.d. ms.

22. *Daily New Mexican,* May 13, 1869.

23. *Daily New Mexican,* May 17, 1869.

24. Aranda, "A Reflection on the Enigmatic Hermit," p 82.

25. Aranda, "A Reflection on the Enigmatic Hermit," p 82.

26. Santini, "Giovanni Maria de Agostini," n 12 p 17.

27. Fountain, "The Hermit," p 4.

28. Williams, "The Catholic Church in the City of Las Cruces from 1848 to 1910."

16 – Burial

1. Fountain, "The Hermit," p 4.

2. *Las Cruces Citizen,* April 30, 1953.

3. Fountain, "The Hermit," p 4. The last line of the inscription is often mistakenly rendered as "El murio dia del 17 de Abril, ano de 1869 a los 69 anos de edad y los 49 de Hermitano" ("He died the 17th of April, 1869 at 69 years of age and 49 years a hermit").

4. Fountain, "The Hermit," p 4.

5. This action is self-glorification in the guise of pretending to benefit Agostini.

17 – Agostini's Possessions

1. *Santa Fe New Mexican,* May 22, 1933.

2. Wolfe, "New Mexico's Hermit."

3. Santini, "Giovanni Maria de Agostini," n 12 p 17.

4. *Santa Fe New Mexican,* May 22, 1933.

5. Wolfe, "New Mexico's Hermit."

6. *El Paso Herald,* December 1, 1962.

7. Théophile Raynaud, *In Symbolicam S.Antonii Magni Imaginem Commentatio,* 1659, frontispiece.

8. *Las Cruces Citizen,* April 30, 1953.

9. Armendariz, interview by Marie Carter.

18 – Epilogue

1. Culver, *Memoir, Travel Diary, and Correspondence, 1869-1871,* p 30. Archeological excavations in La Cueva shows human occupation of the cave goes back to at least 5,000 BC. The skull found by Culver is not Agostini's, obviously.

2. William James, *The Will To Believe* (Longmans Green and Co, 1907), p 5.

3. Fountain, "The Hermit,' p 4. The Sacramento Mountains are about 70 miles east of the Organ Mountains. The range's highest peak, Sierra Blanca, is 11,980 feet above sea level, exactly the kind of high place that Agostini loved.

Bibliography

This bibliography is limited to sources referencing Agostini.

Books and Periodicals

Ackerman, Marian Baca. "The Legend of El Ermitaño." *La Herencia del Norte.* 9. Spring 1996: 22-23.

Ambrosetti, Juan B. *Supersticiones y Leyendas* (Superstitions and Legends). Buenos Aires: La Cultura Argentina, 1917. 119-123.

Aranda, Daniel. "A Reflection on the Enigmatic Hermit." *Southern New Mexico Historical Review.* 14.1 (2007): 78-83.

---. "Western Lore." *Wild West.* Oct 2006: 61-62.

Barker, Elsa. "Hermit of the Mountains." In *Legends and Tales of the Old West.* Ed. S. Omar Barker. New York: Doubleday and Co, 1962. 199-206.

Barker, Omar and Elsa. "Hermit of the Mountains." *New Mexico Quarterly.* 31.4 (Winter 1961-62): 349-355.

Barker, S. Omar. "The Hermit of Owl's Peak." *Rocky Mountain Empire Magazine.* Mar 1950: 4-5.

Bohme, Frederick G. *A History of the Italians in New Mexico.* North Stratford: Ayer Co, 1975. Published dissertation submitted to NMSU, 1958. 111-115.

C. de Baca, Elba. *Legends of a Hermit.* NMSU, 1980.

Cabeza de Baca, Fabiola. *We Fed Them Cactus.* Albuquerque: UNM Press, 1954. 86-88.

Cabral, Oswaldo R. *João Maria: Interpretação da Campanha do Contestado.* Brasiliana 310. São Paulo: Companhia Editora Nacional, 1960. 107-143.

Callon, Milton W. *Las Vegas New Mexico: The Town That Wouldn't Gamble.* Las Vegas: Las Vegas Publishing Co, 1962. 316-321.

Campa, Arthur L. *Treasure of the Sangre de Cristos.* Norman:University of Oklahoma Press, 1963. 161-196.

Culver, Enos and Jennie. "Culver Memoir, Travel Diary, and Correspondence, 1869-1871." Ed. Joy Poole and Mike Olsen. Sante Fe Trail Association. 30. Accessed Mar 2014. www.nps.gov/safe/historyculture/trailwide.htm.

Dary, David. *True Tales of the Old-Time Plains.* New York: Crown Publishers, 1979. 194-198.

deBuys, William. *Enchantment and Exploitation.* Albuquerque, UNM Press 1985. 135-145.

Hughes, Rozier Paul. "Yesterdays Along the Santa Fe." *The Santa Fe Magazine.* Aug 1935: 27-30.

Inman, Henry. *Tales of the Trail.* Topeka: Crane and Company, 1898. 24-44.

Johnson, E. Dana. "The Romance of Hermit's Peak," *Great Southwest Magazine.* Jan 1908: 94-96.

Jones, F. Meredith. "Hermit's Peak." *The Santa Fe Magazine.* Jul 1916: 49-50.

Krahe & Cia, Eds. *Annuario da Provencia do Rio Grande do Sul Para O Anno de 1904.* Porto Alegre: Graciano A. De Azambuja, 1902. 209-210.

Lenoir, Phil. "The Hermit of Las Vegas." *Publications of the Texas Folklore Society.* 10. Austin: Texas Folklore Society, 1932. 124-126.

Maloy, John. "The Hermit Priest." In *Collections of the Kansas State Historical Society.* Ed. William E. Connelley. 16. Topeka: Kansas State Historical Society, 1923. 538-542.

Mondrall, Constance C. *The Centennial of the Hermit in New Mexico.* Las Cruces: NMSU, 1969.

Perrigo, Lynn. *Gateway to Glorieta.* Boulder: Pruett Publishing Co, 1982. 162-164.

Powell, Eleanor Hinde. "The Brotherhood of the Holy Cross." *The Overland Monthly.* 57.6 (Jun 1911). San Francisco: Overland Monthly Co, 1911. 593-597.

Queirel, Juan. *Misiones* (Missions). Buenos Aires: Typographic Workshop Of The National Prison, 1897. 421-423.

Santini, Florio. "Giovanni Maria de Agostini: Eremita Italiano Sulle Montagne del Nuovo Messico." *Lucca.* 10.11 (Nov 1970). 3-8; 10.12 (Dec 1970). 9-18.

Simpson, Audrey. "Hermit's Peak Legend." *Old West Magazine,* Spring 1988: 48.

Smith, Alice Strieby. "Through the Eyes of my Father." In *Collections of the Kansas State Historical Society.* Ed. William Elsey Connelley. 17. Topeka: Kansas State Historical Society, 1928. 708-718.

Stanley, F. *The Grant that Maxwell Bought.* Sante Fe: Sunstone Press, 2008. 79.

Strickfaden, William H. "Hermit's Peak and the Crosses." *New Mexico Sun Trails.* Aug 1952: 15.

Van Loan, H. H. "The Hermit of Las Vegas." *Motion Picture Classic.* Dec, 1915. 62-65.

Vigil, Julian Josue and Anselmo F. Arrellano. *Las Vegas Grandes on the Gallinas.* Las Vegas: Editorial Telerana, 1985. 38-41.

Whistler, R. M. "How Hermit's Peak Gained Its Name." *The Overland Monthly.* 74.2 (Aug 1919). San Francisco: Overland Monthly Co, 1919. 174-175.

Unpublished Sources

Alves, Robinson Fernando. "Alves Romeiros E Peregrinos Na Romaria De Santo Antão: O Povo Da Cruz Rumo A Salvação Latino-Americana." MA thesis. Universidade Federal De Santa Maria Centro De Ciências Sociais E Humanas Programa De Pós-Graduação Mestrado Em Integração Latino-Americana, Santa Maria, RS, Brasil, 2008.

Book of Deaths and Burials, January 1852 to April 1873, San Albino Church Records.

C. de Baca, Hipolito. Letter to Hon. John W. Garrett, August 10, 1931, Fray Angélico Chávez History Library, New Mexico History Museum.

Carter, Marie. "Old Timers Stories: Elizabeth Fountain Armendariz." May 3, 1937. NMFWP, WPA #197, NMSRC.

Fountain, Sr., Albert J. "The Hermit," ms. nd. MS 162, Bx 28, Fd 3. Archives and Special Collections, NMSU.

Goes, Cesar Hamilton Brito. "Nos Caminhos Do Santo Monge: Religião, Sociabilidade E Lutas Sociais No Sul Do Brasil." Diss. Universidade Federal Do Rio Grande Do Sul Instituto De Filosofia E Ciências Humanas Programa De Pós-Graduação Em Sociologia, Porto Alegre, RS, Brasil, 2007.

Karsburg, Alexandre de Oliveira. "O Eremita do Novo Mundo: A Trajetória De Um Peregrino Italiano Na América Do Século XIX (1838-1869)." Diss. Universidade Federal Do Rio De Janeiro Instituto De Filosofia E Ciências Sociais Programa De Pós-Graduação Em História Social, Rio de Janeiro, RJ, Brasil, 2012.

Romero, Benigno, and Porfirio Gonzalez, Placido Sandoval. Sociedad del Ermitano. Dec 31, 1898. Mss 742 BC, Bx 4, Fd 30. Center for Southwest Research, UNM.

Tognacca, Santino. Letter to Ottavio A. Coggiola-Mower, November 30, 1955, Archives of the Archdiocese of Santa Fe, New Mexico.

Wolfe, Charles. "New Mexico's Hermit." Ts. Fray Angélico Chávez History Library, New Mexico History Museum.

Newspapers - Brazil

A Federação, March 15, 1895; March 18, 1895; April 25, 1906; September 25, 1912; September 26, 1912; October 15, 1912; December 14, 1912.

Correio Mercantil, November 23, 1848; December 6, 1848.

Correio do Povo, January 27, 1898; January 28, 1898.

Diário do Rio de Janeiro, August 19, 1844; December 16, 1844; July 6, 1848; October 16, 1848; May 25, 1849; June 25, 1849.

Jornal do Comércio, November 21, 1848.

O Conciliador Catarinense, May 23, 1849; May 26, 1849; June 23, 1849; June 27, 1849.

S Pedro do Sul, December 6, 1848.

Newspapers - Mexico

El Constitucional, May 18, 1861; May 19, 1861; May 22, 1861; May 25, 1861.

El Monitor Republicano, May 27, 1861.

El Siglo Diez y Nueve, May 19, 1861; May 21, 1861; May 26, 1861; June 2, 1861; July 3, 1861; September 14, 1861.

La Orquesta, October 26, 1861.

La Trait d Union, May 27, 1861.

Newspapers - United States

Albuquerque Tribune, November 24, 1955.

Attica Daily Tribune, May 2, 1916.

Bloomington Evening World, April 21, 1916.

Boston Daily Advertiser, August 28, 1861; June 5, 1896.

Butte Weekly Miner, June 23, 1898.

Chicago Record, July 22, 1899.

Clovis News Journal, November 30, 1944.

Council Grove Press, April 27, 1863.

Daily Illinois State Journal, January 27, 1867.

Daily New Mexican, May 8, 1869; May 12, 1869; May 13, 1869; May 17, 1869; May 18, 1869; July 22, 1899; August 16, 1923; May 22, 1933; March 13, 1977.

El Nuevo Mexicano, July 14, 1866.

El Paso Herald, January 23, 1903; July 15, 1908; December 15, 1926; December 1, 1962; February 23, 1963.

Evening Post, August 23, 1861.

Evening Star, June 18, 1898.

Flake's Bulletin, March 20, 1867.

Kansas City Star, August 2, 1925.

Kansas City Times, June 22, 1890.

Las Cruces Citizen, April 30, 1953.

Las Cruces Sun News, October 9, 1949; September 26, 1982.

Las Vegas Daily Optic, April 30, 1908; May 13, 1908; September 2, 1908; September 3, 1908; September 4, 1908; May 2, 1925; May 25, 1926; May 27, 1933; June 3, 1939; November 28, 1944; August 1, 1957; August 4, 1960; July 18, 1962; August 5, 1965; October 8, 1965.

Massachusetts Spy, September 4, 1861.

Montgomery Advertiser, July 12, 1908.

New Albany Evening Tribune, August 3, 1908.

Omaha World Herald, July 21, 1896.

Oregonian, June 19, 1898.

Patriot Ledger, May 11, 1916.

Pittston Gazette, December 15, 1902.

Plain Dealer, September 3,1861.

Providence Evening Press, Jaunuary 7, 1867.

Rio Grande Republican, February 18, 1882; June 16, 1883.

Rockport Weekly Umpire, January 24, 1867.

Rocky Mountain News, May 17, 1869.

Salt Lake Tribune, November 5, 1891.

San Francisco Bulletin, July 22, 1861.

San Francisco Chronicle, July 5, 1896.

Sausalito News, May 13, 1916.

Tampa Tribune, July 11, 1909; July 11, 1914; July 24, 1921.

The Emporia News, April 18, 1863.

The Inter Ocean, June 19, 1898.

The Socorro Chieftain, January 5, 1907.

Times-Picayune, December 22, 1866.

Van Nuys News, June 2, 1916.

Weekly Champion and Press, April 18, 1863.

Weekly New Mexican, November 22, 1879.

Index

Doc45 Publications

La Posta – From the Founding of Mesilla, to Corn Exchange Hotel, to Billy the Kid Museum, to Famous Landmark, David G. Thomas, paperback, 118 pages, 59 photos, e-book available.

"For someone who grew up in the area of Mesilla, it's nice to have a well-researched book about the area – and the giant photographs don't hurt either.... And the thing I was most excited to see is a photo of the hotel registry where the name of "William Bonney" is scrawled on the page.... There is some debate as to whether or not Billy the Kid really signed the book, which the author goes into, but what would Billy the Kid history be without a little controversy?" –Billy the Kid Outlaw Gang Newsletter, Winter, 2013.

Torpedo Squadron Four – A Cockpit View of World War II, Gerald W. Thomas, paperback, 280 pages, 209 photos, e-book available.

"This book contains more first-person accounts than I have seen in several years. ...we can feel the emotion... tempered by the daily losses that characterized this final stage of the war in the Pacific. All in all, one of the best books on the Pacific War I have seen lately." – Naval Aviation News, Fall 2011.

Made in the USA
San Bernardino, CA
09 July 2014